SOVIET WARSHIPS

Overleaf: Kirov, *1980; the propeller guards are positioned exceptionally well forward and, in view of the ship's beam, unusually far outboard. (MoD)*

SOVIET WARSHIPS

The Soviet Surface Fleet
1960 to the present

John Jordan

Naval Institute Press
Annapolis, Maryland

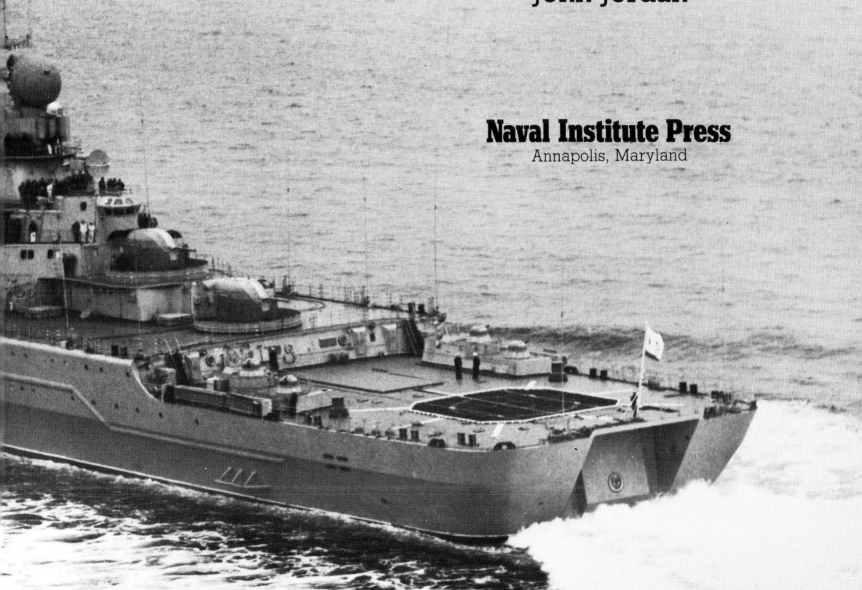

To my late father,
John Alfred Jordan.

Contents

Published and distributed in the
United States of America by the
Naval Institute Press, Annapolis,
Maryland 21402

First published in 1983
Reprinted 1989

Library of Congress Catalogue
Card No. 83-80385

ISBN 0-87021-878-6

Edited by Tessa Rose.
Layout by Anthony A. Evans.
First printed and bound in Great Britain
by Robert Hartnoll Limited,
Bodmin Cornwall.
Reprinted in Great Britain at
The Bath Press, Avon

Below: *Kirov heels over under full
helm while on sea trials, 1980. The
twin SS-N-14 launcher, which is
elevated, is visible immediately aft
of the forecastle. (US Navy)*

Preface

The idea for this book came out of a series on major Soviet surface warships that I wrote for the magazine *Defence*. The series was undertaken with a view to building up a complete picture of Soviet naval developments since the late 1950s, while at the same time presenting a fundamental reappraisal of the earlier ship-types of the period in the light of current knowledge about those developments. This reappraisal was necessary because of the inaccuracies and dubious assertions prevalent in Western sources, some of which had been repeated so often as to be regarded as 'authoritative'.

There is but one 'authority' on the Soviet Navy, and that is the Soviet Navy itself. Whereas Soviet-built tanks and Soviet-built aircraft have been widely employed in conflicts around the globe, and have been engaged, captured and examined by armed forces belonging to pro-Western regimes, no major Soviet-built surface ship has seen action since the Second World War. The details given in Western reference books regarding the dimensions, displacement and propulsion of Soviet ships and the size and performance of their weapons are based largely on a combination of visual evidence and theory. It will therefore be readily apparent that figures expressed as 'fact' are frequently little better than crude assessments or educated guesswork. A single new photograph of a pop-up launcher in the raised position or a glimpse inside a missile tube can change our perception of the capability, the modus operandi, or the purpose of a particular system; on at least one occasion it has led to a fundamental reappraisal of the mission of the ships themselves.

The figures published in this book — complete as I have endeavoured to make them — should not be taken as fact, but should be examined as critically as I have tried to examine the figures given by other sources (for which see Bibliography). The purpose of this book is to investigate and to compare; in the course of my investigations I have tried not to evade technical issues, which are all too often ignored altogether or, alternatively, are brushed over with a wash of broad and essentially meaningless statements.

A number of people have assisted in the preparation of this book. I am particularly indebted to Mike Gething of *Defence* for allowing me unrestricted access to the photographic resources of that magazine, and also for his help in checking through the passages and tables that deal with Soviet naval aviation. Norman Polmar was good enough to read through sections of the text and made a number of helpful suggestions which I have tried to incorporate. Documentation on the development of VTOL aircraft was kindly provided by John Fozard of British Aerospace. I would also like to thank Hugh Lucas, Patty Maddocks of *USNI Proceedings*, Sadie Alford of Novosti, Clive and Sue Taylor, Jean Labayle Couhat, and Ray Bonds of Salamander Books for their assistance in providing additional photographs. Finally, my sincerest thanks go to my wife, Sue, for her infinite patience and tolerance; and to Antony Preston, who searched on my behalf for additional photographic material, and without whose help and encouragement this book would not have been possible.

John Jordan, 1983

Left: Admiral Oktyabrsky in the English Channel in 1974. The Kresta II class is generally regarded as one of the most successful and seaworthy Soviet designs. (Skyfotos)

Introduction

The Soviet Union is essentially a continental land power, both in terms of its geography and its history. Many of its major ports are icebound for several months of the year and in three out of the four fleet areas access to open waters is severely restricted. The two major shipbuilding and repair complexes, at Leningrad and Kaliningrad in the Baltic and at Nikolayev in the Black Sea, are separated from the open seas by narrow straits that could be sealed off with relative ease by hostile powers.

The Soviet Union has never needed to exercise control over large areas of ocean in order to provide for the security of its merchant shipping. It is virtually self-sufficient in resources, and its vital communications are internal. Maritime strategy since the Revolution has therefore been primarily concerned with the defence of the territorial integrity of the Soviet Union and not with control of the seas. The purpose of the Soviet Navy has been two-fold: the denial of the waters adjacent to the Soviet land mass to hostile maritime forces, and support of the Soviet land forces on the flanks.

The 'sea denial' role imposed on the Soviet Navy by geography and by its political masters has resulted in a pattern of development that is essentially 'reactive'. This means that, rather than creating a 'battle-fleet' capable of independent operations on the high seas, the Soviets have chosen to counter whatever maritime threat is posed by the particular hostile powers it is facing. The composition of the Soviet naval forces has changed, therefore, as the nature of the threat has changed. In contrast, the Western navies — which because of their own strategic position have traditionally been concerned with establishing control over those seas crucial to their own commercial or political interests — have developed along similar lines to one another. They have undergone a steady, consistent and logical evolution, without the dramatic reversals of policies and strategies commonplace in the Soviet Navy.

One consequence of this is the essentially innovatory nature of Soviet ship construction, especially in the post-war period. This innovatory approach is not, as some analysts have implied, a quality which is admirable in itself; nor, for that matter, is it an undesirable one. The essential point is that innovation is *necessary*, given the frequent changes in the nature of the threat that the Soviet Navy has had to counter as a result of technological developments in the West.

A major problem with this 'reactive' maritime strategy is that the reaction has not always been immediate, appropriate or successful. This, too, is inevitable, given that the immediacy of the reaction is dependent on how accurate is the perception of the nature of the threat, and that the success of the reaction depends on the 'correctness' of the response (in purely theoretical terms) and on the ability to provide the technological advances that may be implicit in that chosen response. The rapidity of Soviet technological progress in some areas — again seen by many analysts as a virtue in itself — has frequently been the result of a dramatic change in policy and strategy requiring the immediate build-up of capabilities that did not previously exist. In some cases these rapid advances have given the Soviet Navy a technological edge over their opponents in a particular area of weapon or sensor development; in others, they have merely compensated for years of neglect. In all cases these advances have been seen as a necessary response to a real, or perceived threat, and not as an attempt to achieve superiority per se.

The advanced nature of Soviet maritime electronic countermeasures provision in the late 1960s, for example, was necessary given that Soviet warships operating outside their own waters did not have carrier-borne fighters to defend them against missile attack. Similarly, the rapid advances made in sonar development during the late 1960s were necessary because anti-submarine warfare in the immediate post-war period had been given such a low priority that the Soviet Navy was still fitting small high-frequency sonars, which hardly constituted an advance on the early models obtained from the West during the Second World War.

It is important, therefore, to see recent Soviet naval developments in their true light; not as an attempt to win control of the sea, but as a persistent drive to counter — and if possible short-circuit by the introduction of new technology — Western sea-power as a force capable of threatening Soviet territory. The dramatic increase in Soviet ocean-going capabilities over the past two decades has been sanctioned by the land-minded Soviet High Command only because changes in Western strategy have involved greater reliance on the use of the seas to support the land battle in Europe and to threaten Soviet territory. The key factors in these changes have been: the large-scale withdrawal of North American troops from Germany since the 1950s, and the consequent importance of the North Atlantic as a 'bridge' for transporting vital military equipment and supplies to Western Europe in the event of hostilities between NATO and the Warsaw Pact; the shift in the strategic nuclear threat to Soviet territory from the land to the sea; and the need to protect a growing force of Soviet strategic missile submarines made necessary by the threat posed to land-based systems of fixed location by increasingly accurate Western missiles.

List of Abbreviations

AA	Anti-aircraft
AAW	Anti-air warfare
AEW	Airborne early warning
A/S	Anti-submarine
ASAT	Anti-satellite
ASM	Anti-ship missile
ASROC	Anti-submarine rocket
ASuW	Anti-surface warfare
ASW	Anti-submarine warfare
AV-MF	Aviatsiya Voenno-Morskovo Flota (Naval Air Force)
bhp	Brake horsepower
BPK	Bol'shoy Protivolodochny Korabl', Large Anti-Submarine Ship (see Appendix 1, p. 125)
BRK	Bol'shoy Raketny Korabl', Large Rocket Ship (see Appendix 1)
CAP	Combat air patrol
CG	Missile cruiser
CGN	Cruiser, guided missile (nuclear powered)
CIWS	Close-in weapon system
CODAG	Combined diesel and gas
CODOG	Combined diesel or gas
COGAG	Combined gas and gas
COGOG	Combined gas or gas
CONAS	Combined nuclear and steam
COSAG	Combined steam and gas
CVA	Aircraft carrier, attack
DD	Destroyer
DDG	Destroyer, guided missile
DLG	Frigate, guided missile
ECM	Electronic countermeasures
ESM	Electronic support measures
ft	Feet
FPB	Fast patrol boat
FRESCAN	Frequency scanning
GIUK	Greenland/Iceland/UK
HE	High explosive
HF	High frequency
HF/DF	High-frequency direction finder
ICBM	Inter-continental ballistic missile
in	Inches
IVDS	Independent variable depth sonar
JATO	Jet-assisted take-off
kg	Kilogramme(s)
km	Kilometre(s)
km/hr	Kilometres per hour
kt	Kilotonne
LAMPS	Light airborne multi-purpose system
lb	Pound(s)
LF	Low frequency
LLTV	Low Light television
m	Metre(s)
'mack'	Combined mast and stack
MAD	Magnetic anomaly detector
MCLWG	Major calibre lightweight gun
MF	Medium frequency
mm	Millimetres
mph	Miles per hour
MPK	Maly Protivolodochny Korabl', Small Anti-Submarine Ship
MRK	Maly Raketny Korabl', Small Rocket Ship
MTB	Motor torpedo-boat
NATO	North Atlantic Treaty Organization
NBC	Nuclear, biological, chemical
nm	Nautical miles (1,852m = 1nm)
NTDS	Naval tactical data system
PKR	Protivolodochny Kreyser, Anti-Submarine Cruiser (see Appendix 1)
RKR	Raketny Kreyser, Rocket Cruiser (see Appendix 1)
SAG	Surface action group
SAM	Surface-to-air missile
sec	Second
SFC	Specific fuel consumption
shp	Shaft horsepower
SKR	Storozhevoy Korabl', Patrol Ship (see Appendix 1)
SLBM	Submarine-launched ballistic missile
SOSUS	Sound surveillance system
SS	Attack submarine (diesel-electric)
SSBN	Ballistic missile submarine (nuclear)
SSGN	Submarine, cruise missile (nuclear-powered)
SSM	Surface-to-surface missile
SSN	Attack submarine (nuclear)
SUBROC	Submarine-launched rocket
SUW	Surface-to-underwater
TACAN	Tactical air navigation
TAKR	Taktychesky Avionosny Kreyser, Tactical Aircraft-Carrying Cruiser (see Appendix 1)
TT	Torpedo tubes
TVM	Track-via-missile
UHF	Ultra high frequency
VDS	Variable depth sonar
VERTREP	Vertical replenishment
VHF	Very high frequency
VIFF	Vectoring in forward flight
VLS	Vertical launch system
VTOL	Vertical take-off and landing

Right: *Kiev as photographed by an RAF Nimrod aircraft during her transit from the Black Sea to the Arctic in 1976. Four Ka-25 Hormones are lined up on the flight deck, and there is a single Yak-36 Forger on the deck park aft.*

Kynda Class

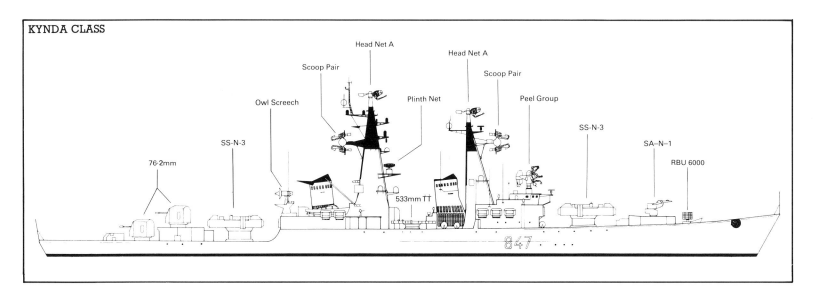

KYNDA CLASS — Head Net A, Scoop Pair, Owl Screech, Plinth Net, Head Net A, Scoop Pair, Peel Group, SS-N-3, SA–N–1, RBU 6000, 76·2mm, SS-N-3, 533mm TT, 847

KYNDA CLASS
Soviet designation: Raketny Kreyser (RKR — Rocket Cruiser)

Construction

Ship	Builder	Laid down	Launched	In service
Grozny	Zhdanov Yard,	June 1959	April 1962	June 1962
Admiral Fokin	Leningrad	1960	Nov 1961	Aug 1963
Admiral Golovko	(all units)	1961	1963	July 1964
Varyag		1962	1964	Feb 1965

Displacement
Standard: 4,400 tons. Full load: 5,600 tons.

Dimensions
Length: 142m (466ft), overall.
Beam: 15.8m (52ft).
Draught: 5.3m (17ft).

Armament
ASuW: 2 quadruple SS-N-3 launchers (16 missiles).
AAW: 1 twin SA-N-1 launcher (22 Goa missiles); 2 twin 76.2mm (3in) guns; 4 30mm Gatlings in *Varyag* since 1981.
ASW: 2 12-barrelled RBU 6000 rocket launchers; 2 triple banks of 533mm (21in) torpedo tubes.

Electronic equipment
Surveillance radar(s): 2 Head Net A (see text for later modifications); 2 Don-2.
Fire control radar(s): 2 Scoop Pair (SS-N-3), 2 Plinth Net (see Modifications in text); 1 Peel Group (SA-N-1); 1 Owl Screech (76.2mm guns); 2 Bass Tilt (30mm Gatlings) in *Varyag* since 1981.
Sonar(s): 1 keel-mounted high-frequency sonar.
ECM: 1 Bell Clout, 1 Bell Slam, 1 Bell Tap; 4 Top Hat.

Machinery
2-shaft geared steam turbines; 100,000shp = 34 knots maximum.

Complement
375.

A Pre-History
The end of the Great Patriotic War in 1945 found the Soviet Union in possession of the largest army in the world, and a navy that had been all but eliminated by a combination of pre-war neglect and wartime attrition. Yet the new system of politico-military alliances already being etched out placed the Soviet Union in the opposite camp to the world's two foremost ocean-going fleets, the British Royal Navy and the US Navy. The Soviets had looked on as interested observers for the previous two years while first the Japanese Empire and then the Japanese homeland itself was being battered into submission by American carrier task forces, with the specialized assault forces of the US Marines never far behind. These powerful, wide-ranging fleets, able to direct their concentrated power against any point on the face of the globe, now threatened the peripheries of the Soviet land mass. The US Navy had more carriers than the Soviet Union had cruisers and destroyers. Stalin himself felt that a large ocean-going fleet was needed as a counter to Western sea-power and, when funds became available in the early 1950s, the Soviet Navy embarked on a massive programme of new construction under the energetic Admiral Kuznetsov.

The outstanding feature of the new programme was its conservatism. Although the need for a dramatic expansion of the Navy appears to have been predicated on the need to counter the naval forces of the NATO allies, the basic components of the new programme were little different from those envisaged under the Soviet naval programmes of the late 1930s, when Hitler's Germany had been the potential enemy. The surface ships in particular were the embodiment of a Baltic/Black Sea mentality. The cruisers of the Sverdlov class, with their rapid-firing 152mm guns and their heavy AA battery, were well-suited to operations in an enclosed sea, and could provide useful fire support for the flanks of the Army. The new destroyers of the Skory and Kotlin classes were fast and had a heavy torpedo armament, and were therefore admirably designed for hit-and-run attacks on enemy shipping. A large force of submarines, closely modelled on the latest German types, was planned. However, the geo-strategic position of the Soviet Navy was very different from that of Hitler's navy which, at the height of the Atlantic shipping offensive, was operating from Norway and the west coast of France. The Soviet Whiskey class, of which some 200 were eventually built, were medium-range boats hardly suited to the lengthy transits necessary if they were to threaten the shipping lanes of the North Atlantic. The much larger Zulu class could fulfil this role, but they were built in small numbers. These factors, taken together with the need to distribute the smaller boats between the four Soviet fleets — two of which had virtually no access to open waters — strongly suggest that the submarines, like the surface units, were not built for an open-ocean anti-shipping role but were part of a defensive strategy designed to protect the Soviet Union from seaborne assault.

The Soviet counter to the maritime threat from the West did not, therefore, result in a navy that was a mirror image of the Western navies. Soviet maritime strategy continued to envisage a layered defence system, with concentric rings drawn around each of the four fleet areas to prevent incursions from hostile forces. The inner ring — regarded as Soviet sea-space — would be defended by MTBs backed up by larger torpedo-boats, small submarines and mines. The outer ring would be contested by Whiskey-class submarines backed up by conventional cruisers and destroyers. Reconnaissance and attack at longer ranges would be performed by the larger Zulu-class submarines, which would be the only Soviet units operating in the ocean areas controlled by the enemy.

By the mid-1950s however, when most of the hulls belonging to this first post-war programme were still fitting out, the strategic and tactical thinking on which the programme had been based had already been seriously undermined, and a fundamental reappraisal of Soviet defence policy, prompted by the death of Stalin in 1953, was well under way. The threat posed by the American carriers was no longer simply one of conventional air strikes in support of amphibious landings. The new 'super-carriers' under construction were designed to operate squadrons of long-range nuclear bombers, and the devastation of Soviet territory that could be wrought by airborne nuclear strikes would obviate the need for a follow-up by conventional amphibious assault forces. In consequence, the amphibious threat was down-graded and that of the American strike carriers (CVAs) assumed top priority. It was also becoming clear that a navy whose primary weapons were the gun and the torpedo would be of limited use in a modern conflict. Nuclear weapons and the advent of guided missiles were changing the rules of maritime warfare, and the Soviet post-war programme was based on 1930s technology and tactics.

Kruschev, who assumed power in 1955, appointed the youthful Admiral Gorshkov to implement the new strategy. The naval programme initiated by Stalin was cut and, where possible, halted altogether. A number of hulls of the Sverdlov

Top: A destroyer of the Kotlin class in the North Sea, July 1976. The Kotlins were designed to complement the cruisers of the Sverdlov class, and were given a heavy torpedo armament and mine-rails. They were the last conventional destroyers built by the Soviet Navy. (MoD)
Bottom: Oktyabrskaya Revolutsiya (October Revolution), one of the Sverdlov-class cruisers that were to form the backbone of the Soviet Navy's post-war fleet. The TASS caption is revealing; it states: 'The . . . cruiser's complement is ready to defend the sea frontiers of the USSR [author's roman] against any aggression attempt'. These large, powerful conventional cruisers were the first victims of Kruschev's shake-up of the Navy. (TASS)

class were towed away for scrap or dismantled on the slipways; only those surface ships whose construction was well advanced were completed. Even the submarine construction programme, which had now reached a peak of 70–80 boats per year, was drastically curtailed. Kruschev had a particularly low opinion of the 152mm gun cruisers, which in his view were fit 'only for hauling around admirals'.

The surface ships of the future would have to be capable of operating in a nuclear environment, and would have to adopt the new missile technology if they were to survive. Long-range cruise missiles would make the large-calibre gun obsolete, and surface-to-air missiles would replace the small-calibre AA guns to defend the ships against attack from the air. A rather primitive derivative of the German V1 'buzz-bomb', the SS-N-1 Scrubber, was fitted on four modified Kotlin class hulls in place of the after guns (these vessels were subsequently designated the Kildin class by NATO). Eight hulls of the larger Kruplin class (the projected successor to the Kotlin class) were then taken in hand and fitted with launchers and magazines for the SS-N-1 at either end. A smaller and more successful derivative, the SS-N-2 Styx, was hurriedly fitted to large numbers of crudely modified P-6 torpedo-boats to provide a horizon-range anti-ship capability within the inner ring of the Soviet maritime defences. These, however, were only interim measures. Under Admiral Gorshkov plans were drawn up for new classes of purpose-built missile cruisers, destroyers and submarines, the design of which marked a radical departure from previous types in every respect.

The concept of zonal defence remained unaltered, but the outer ring of the Soviet defences would now be contested by a combination of cruisers, submarines, and land-based bombers, all armed with long-range cruise missiles, whose efforts would be coordinated from a command post ashore. Long-range reconnaissance would be provided by submarines — some of which would be nuclear-powered — and specially fitted aircraft. The function of the new destroyers would be to support the cruisers, for which they would provide additional protection against hostile aircraft and submarines. The first cruiser in the new programme — classified 'Raketny Kreyser' (Rocket Cruiser) — was completed in 1962 and received the NATO designation 'Kynda'.

Left: *In order to provide aerial reconnaissance for the Soviet fleet, a long-range strategic bomber, the Bear, was modified for maritime operations. Besides being fitted for the detection of hostile surface units, the Bear D depicted here is equipped with a video data link to transmit radar pictures back to Soviet Rocket Cruisers such as the Kynda class, and can also transmit mid-course correction signals to ship-launched missiles such as the SS-N-3. (MoD)*

Below: *The forecastle of the Rocket Cruiser Grozny, dominated by the massive quadruple launcher for SS-N-3 anti-ship missiles. Forward of it are the twin-arm SA-N-1 launcher for surface-to-air missiles, seen in the reloading position, and RBU 6000 twelve-barrelled anti-submarine rocket launchers. (C-in-C Fleet)*

The New Cruiser

The Kynda class were the first truly 'modern' Soviet surface ships. Although only four metres longer than the Krupny-class Rocket Ships ('Raketny Korabl'), they are far more imposing in appearance. The hull-form is that of a cruiser with a long forecastle and a low quarterdeck. The superstructure is organized into two neat blocks topped by enclosed tower masts with the funnel uptakes rising behind them. The first block contains the bridge and command spaces; the second carries the ship's boats, for which twin derricks are provided. Immediately forward of the bridge and aft of the forecastle break are the two massive quadruple anti-ship missile launchers that comprise the main armament of the Kynda class, with the defensive weapons located at the ship's extremities. The masts and superstructures bristle with a variety of surveillance and missile guidance antennae. Virtually the entire weapon and sensor outfit made its first appearance on this class. Considerable ingenuity was employed to accommodate the necessary weapon systems which, with the solitary exception of the torpedo tubes, are disposed fore and aft of the superstructures. The funnel uptakes are of a transverse rectangular configuration when viewed from above, and occupy less centre-line space than conventional funnels.

Anti-Ship Missiles

The SS-N-3 Shaddock missile, which is thought to have been designed initially for the strategic attack role and was first fitted in Whiskey-class submarines in the late 1950s, represents a major advance over the SS-N-1 Scrubber fitted in the converted Rocket Ships of the Kildin and Krupny classes. It has a length of approximately 11m compared with only 7.6m for its predecessor, and much longer range. It has an aeroplane-type configuration, like the SS-N-1, with two solid fuel boosters mounted beneath the wings and a ramjet sustainer motor. The launcher arrangements are far superior, however. The SS-N-1 launcher comprised a bulky open ramp on which the missile, once it had been rolled out of its handling room, would be exposed to the elements, possibly in freezing conditions, before firing. The SS-N-3 missiles are housed in cylindrical missile containers, with their swept wings folded upwards for stowage. On the Kynda class, each launcher comprises four missile containers, and the quadruple launchers elevate and train to fire.

In addition to the eight missiles contained in the launchers, a complete set of reloads is carried. Reloads for the forward launcher are housed inside the bridge structure. The reload tubes are in line with the launcher cylinders and are covered by hinged flaps. The missiles are apparently moved across on rollers — by all accounts a difficult and lengthy operation. Reloads for the after launcher tubes are housed inside the after superstructure beneath the boat deck.

Guidance radars for the missiles are mounted on the forward face of the foremast and the after side of the main-mast respectively. Designated 'Scoop Pair', each antenna is stabilized and comprises two elliptical lattice scanners mounted above and below a spherical housing. The guidance radars, which are carried high, have excellent coverage of the radar horizon at the expense of considerable topweight. The flights pattern of the missile involves a steep climb after launch. It then cruises at high altitude, enabling tracking to be carried out from the ship to well beyond horizon range. In order to attain its extreme range of an estimated 300km (170nm), however, the missile would need mid-course guidance from an external source. The Kynda class is heavily dependent, therefore, on land-based aircraft for reconnaissance and targeting, and to provide mid-course correction for its anti-ship missiles. This dependence on external sources of target data would have severely restricted the operational effectiveness of the ship outside Soviet waters at the time of completion, and illustrates the essentially defensive nature of the Rocket Cruiser concept, at least in its origins. Simultaneously with the construction of the Kyndas, long-range bombers initially designed for the Soviet Air Force were being modified for deployment with the Naval Air Force (known as the AV-MF). Tu-20 Bears would provide the necessary reconnaissance and missile targeting capabilities, while the Tu-16 Badgers would have a primary anti-ship strike role.

The active radar homing employed on a missile the size of the SS-N-3 would allow for a fairly large range gate to compensate in part for target movement during flight. But this would not solve the basic targeting problem in anti-carrier operations — that of selecting the carrier from the centre of a task force. It is reported that the SS-N-3 incorporates a link that transmits the radar picture to the launch ship. The latter then selects the target and transmits the appropriate commands to the missile. Such a system is by no means infallible, as it is vulnerable to ECM measures, such as jamming, chaff and 'blip enhancement', by smaller vessels in the group.

These observations on the targeting limitations inherent in the Rocket Cruiser concept are, however, only partially valid. They do not take into account the potentially devastating effect of a massed combined strike by air, surface and submarine-launched missiles on the composition of the task force; nor do they take into account the possibility of a nuclear solution to the over-the-horizon targeting problem. It must be remembered that the early days of the guided missile were also the early days of the small nuclear warhead. Even surface-to-air missiles such as the American Talos and Terrier could employ nuclear warheads in combination with command guidance to achieve a high number of kills against squadrons of hostile aircraft operating in close formation. The large numbers of photographs emanating from the Soviet press agencies depicting Soviet sailors in full NBC clothing suggest that Soviet tactical training in the 1960s and 1970s laid far greater stress on nuclear operations than was the case in the Western navies over the same period.

The employment of a nuclear warhead on the SS-N-3 would resolve many of the targeting problems discussed. Provided that the Rocket Cruiser received accurate target data regarding the position and formation of the enemy task force from reconnaissance aircraft or submarines, missiles could be fired from beyond horizon range without the need for mid-course correction. The explosive force of a nuclear warhead is such that there would be no need to discriminate between individual ships in the enemy force. Evasive manoeuvres by the enemy could be countered by bracketing the predicted target position with three or four missiles. An airburst would effectively disable any carrier aircraft from a considerable distance, and the effect of electro-magnetic disturbance on radar and radio transmission would effectively 'blind' the task force. It appears likely, therefore, that at least some of the SS-N-3 missile rounds carried by the Kyndas — perhaps four out of a total of sixteen — have nuclear warheads.

The ability of the Rocket Cruisers to make nuclear or conventional strikes on land targets should also be mentioned, as it perpetuates a traditional function of Soviet cruisers in support of the Soviet Army. The SS-N-3 missiles could be used to strike at targets on the seaward flanks of the enemy land forces, and to soften up coastal defences in conjunction with an amphibious landing. Against targets of fixed location there would be few problems in employing the missile out to the limits of its effective range.

Air Defence

The missile chosen for the defence of the new generation of Soviet warships against air attack was a derivative of a land-based weapon. The SA-N-1 is a naval version of the land-mobile SA-3, which was to see considerable service in the Middle East War of 1973. Powered by a booster and sustainer, the missile is slim and tapered with large cruciform wings at the rear and small cropped-delta control surfaces on the nose. The booster is short and of greater diameter, and has rectangular fins indexed in line with the other control surfaces. Some modifications were necessary to improve the suitability of the missile for shipborne installation, notably the hinging of the booster fins for more compact stowage.

The twin-arm launcher is sited well forward, and has excellent all-round arcs at the cost of constant exposure to seas taken over the bow. The forecastle position was selected in preference to the alternative position on the quarterdeck because of the lack of sufficient depth of hull aft to accommodate the missile magazine. Some 22 missiles are stowed vertically beneath the launcher in a twin-ring or continuous belt feed system. The twin hatches beneath the launcher are offset to starboard and the launcher reloads while trained to that side — a feature without parallel in Western construction. The launcher is stabilized, suggesting that the missile may have proved difficult to gather when fired from a rolling ship.

The SA-N-1 employs command guidance, as does its land-based counterpart. Initial detection is made by the twin Head Net A air search antennae mounted atop the tower masts. Head Net A comprises an elliptical lattice reflector with the feed horn slung beneath, and distinctive counter-balancing vanes that may be an essential component of a stabilizing system. The radar operates in the S-Band. Its effective range is therefore in the region of 130km (70nm), as compared to the 280km (150nm) plus for contemporary Western air search radars, which generally operate in the L-Band.

The elaborate Peel Group guidance radar is located immediately above the bridge. Peel Group comprises two pairs of solid reflectors, one pair in the vertical and the other pair in the horizontal plane, grouped around a prominent conical lattice antenna. The disposition of the reflectors suggests that they provide tracking in three coordinates; a function generally performed by a separate height-finder in contemporary US Navy ships, and one taken over by the massive Top Sail aerial on later Soviet vessels equipped with Goblet, Goa's successor. The two larger reflectors — one in each plane — may therefore be for long-range target acquisition and 'coarse' tracking, with the smaller pair for precision tracking at closer ranges. The central conical antenna is thought to be a radiator for command guidance signals. In command guidance the tracking radar tracks both the missile and the target, hence the importance of early acquisition of the missile. The angle of error is measured and correction signals are transmitted to the missile via a command link.

Although the degree of control exercised by the launch ship has the advantage of making the system more resistant to countermeasures, one of the problems associated with command guidance is that the angle of error becomes more difficult to assess as the range increases. Taken together with the limited range of the air-search radars of the Kynda class, this would tend to suggest a relatively short effective range for the Goa missile in its naval application, probably in the region of 15–20km (8–11nm). Moreover, the configuration of the Peel Group guidance suggests that only one target per launcher could be engaged simultaneously, a salvo of two missiles per target being standard practice. (Contemporary Western SAM installations employing semi-active guidance could generally handle two targets per launcher.)

Guns

The SA-N-1 missiles are supported in the anti-aircraft role by two twin 76.2mm/60cal mountings, which made their first appearance on this class. The stabilized mountings are grouped together on the low quarterdeck in order to cover the blind after arcs of the SA-N-1 missiles. The gun is almost certainly an army-derived weapon, but is credited with a much higher rate of fire than its land-based counterparts. If this is so, the gun must have a relatively complex reloading mechanism, with some sacrifice of the robust qualities and reliability that have become the hallmark of Soviet artillery pieces. The success of the naval mounting is, however, evidenced by its subsequent acceptance as the standard Soviet medium-calibre gun on all major construction until the end of the 1970s.

The director for the twin 76.2mm is the 'Tellerform' Owl Screech, a larger version of the Hawk Screech director that had appeared in the mid-1950s in association with smaller AA weapons. It can be distinguished from Hawk Screech by the number of separate 'boxes' that comprise the bulky electronics housing behind the solid dish scanner. The director can be rotated and elevated on its pedestal. The Owl Screech installation on the Kynda class is mounted on the end of the after superstructure.

Below: *Goa surface-to-air missiles on the twin arms of an SA-N-1 launcher aboard a Kynda-class vessel. The launcher itself is stabilized to facilitate gathering of the missile into the beam of the guidance radar. (TASS)*

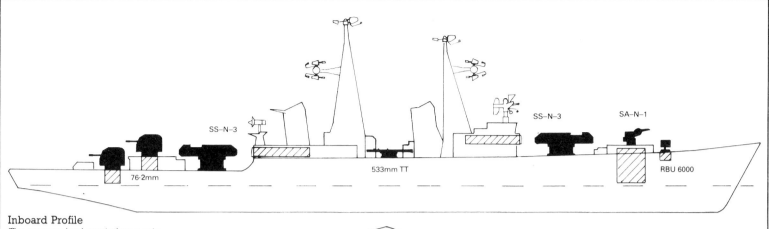

Inboard Profile

The weapon load carried on a relatively small hull is quite remarkable and is achieved only at the expense of considerable top-weight. Note in particular the massive SS-N-3 launchers and their above-decks reload magazines.

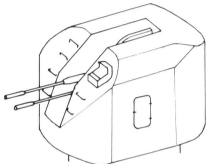

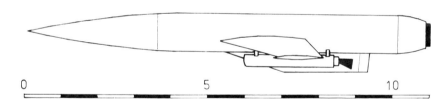

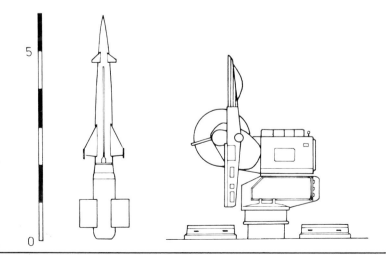

Main Armament

76.2mm gun (twin)

In service: 1962.
Barrel length: 60cal.
Angle of elevation: +80°.
Rate of fire: 45rpm per barrel.
Projectile weight: 6kg (13lb).
Muzzle velocity: 900m/sec (2,955ft/sec).
Range: 12km (6.5nm) max.; 6–7km (3–4nm) effective AA.
Fire control: Owl Screech/local.

SS-N-3 Shaddock

In service: 1962.
Length: 11m (36ft).
Diameter: 1m (3ft 3in).
Span: 2.6m (8ft 6in).
Weight: 4,500kg (9,900lb).
Warhead: 800kg (1,760lb) HE or 350kt nuclear.
Propulsion: 2 solid-fuel boosters for launch/
    acceleration phase; liquid-fuel turbojet sustainer
    motor for cruise phase.
Speed: Mach 0.85.
Range: 320–400km (170–220nm) with mid-course
    guidance.
Guidance: Autopilot and radio altimeter with radar/
    command; active radar terminal homing.
Fire control: Scoop Pair.

SA-N-1 Goa

In service: 1962.
Length: 5.9m (19ft).
Diameter: 0.45m (1ft 6in), missile; 0.60m (2ft), booster.
Span: 1.2m (4ft).
Weight: 600kg (1,320lb).
Warhead: 50kg (110lb) HE.
Propulsion: Solid-propellant booster; solid-propellant
    sustainer.
Speed: Mach 2.
Range: 15–20km (8–11nm).
Ceiling: 12,000m (40,000ft).
Guidance: Radar/command.
Fire Control: Peel Group.

ECM

The Kyndas were completed with a number of empty platforms projecting from the sides of the foremast tower and from the forward face of the mainmast. From the late 1960s, however, the ships were fitted with a variety of ECM antennae, the exact outfit varying from ship to ship. This suggests a development programme hastily embarked upon to provide the new cruisers with some protection against air-launched anti-ship missiles.

ASW

ASW provision on the Kyndas is minimal, as it appears to have been the intention to concentrate anti-submarine — and air defence — capabilities in the Kashin-class destroyers built to accompany them. The state of Soviet ASW was, in any case, rather primitive at the time the two classes were designed, as the threat from Western submarines was rated as a low priority compared with the striking power of the NATO carriers. The Kyndas are, therefore, fitted with a short-range high frequency (HF) sonar, designated 'Hercules', which entered service in about 1957, and two twelve-barrelled anti-submarine rocket launchers. The RBU 6000 rocket launcher (formerly designated MBU 2500A) was an improvement on the earlier sixteen-barrelled RBU 2500 (formerly MBU 2500), both in terms of range and ease of operation. Automatic reloading was provided, which eliminated the need to have men closed up in freezing conditions and allowed the rocket launcher to be located in an exposed position close to the bow. The RBU 6000 reloads from beneath with the barrels fully elevated, and fires anti-submarine rockets out to a maximum range of 6km (3nm). It lays down a 'blanket' pattern, designed to compensate for the limited accuracy of the underwater detection systems available to Soviet warships during this period.

Torpedo Tubes

Amidships there are two triple banks of 533mm torpedo tubes of a model that first saw service in the late 1950s on the Kildin and Krupny classes. The tubes are of the conventional 'long' type. Western navies also continued to show an interest in the 'long' torpedo tube throughout the 1950s, and several attempts were made to marry fixed tubes with anti-submarine homing torpedoes originally designed to be fired by submarines. Indeed, one US Navy design for a fast task force escort envisaged a trainable quintuple mount capable of firing both anti-ship and anti-submarine torpedoes. The trainable triple, quadruple and quintuple mountings installed in Soviet warships of this period may well be designed with a similar function in mind. If so, the Soviets appear to have been more successful in bringing this concept to fruition, as Western attempts to produce a viable ship-launched long-range anti-submarine torpedo generally foundered, leaving the 'short' Mk. 43/44/46 torpedo as the standard model.

Command and Control

Command and control spaces on the Kynda class are minimal. Although the bridge structure is quite large, much of its internal volume is occupied by the reload tubes for the forward SS-N-3 launcher. Western surface ships of the same period are far better equipped in this respect. At the time of the first Kynda's completion, the first naval tactical data systems (NTDS) were already undergoing evaluation aboard missile frigates (DLGs) of the US Navy.

Opposite page: Grozny *serving with the Black Sea Fleet in 1977. In the late 1960s, six Guard Dog ECM radomes were installed on the lower platforms of the foremast and mainmast. Two of these were replaced in 1973 by Plinth Net target designation radars. (Novosti)*
Right: Admiral Fokin *serving with the Pacific Fleet in 1979. She has received a number of modifications, including the replacement of the second Head Net A radar by a back-to-back Head Net C, the fitting of Plinth Net target designation radars, and the replacement of the old-style life-rafts by the modern cocooned variety. (TASS)*

The absence of such spaces aboard the Kyndas and their immediate successors is due to the different tactical philosophies obtaining in the Soviet Navy. Coordinated missile strikes by surface units, submarines and aircraft required that command and control should be exercised by a shore-based commander. The commanding officer of a Kynda-class vessel would be directed to an interception point, supplied with all relevant target data, and instructed when to fire his missiles. He would need to monitor only his own position, and would be responsible only for those surface vessels in his own force. Aircraft and submarines assigned to the same mission would be controlled by the shore commander, eliminating the need for coordination of the battle to be exercised from command spaces located in the cruiser. The NATO carrier task force, on the other hand, would be responsible for every aspect of its operations, including air reconnaissance, air strike, and the defence of the entire group against air and underwater attacks. Extensive command and control facilities, therefore, had to be provided within the surface ships themselves in order to coordinate effectively their various missions.

Propulsion

The broad twin funnels, with their distinctive air vents, and the absence of any major weapon systems amidships, indicate that the entire centre part of the Kynda is taken up with the machinery installation. The unit system of alternating boiler rooms and engine rooms common to all post-war Soviet cruiser and destroyer construction is retained on the Kynda class, thereby reducing the likelihood of crippling action damage. The ships are credited with a total horsepower of 100,000shp, which is not far short of the figure for the 15,000-ton *Sverdlov*. This would give high speed — estimated at well over 30 knots — for the rapid manoeuvres necessary to protect the ship from pre-emptive or retaliatory strikes by carrier aircraft. Range, however, must be limited, as it is difficult to see how adequate bunkerage could be provided in such a cramped design.

The space available for the ship's complement is also clearly very limited indeed, and living conditions on prolonged deployments would be unacceptable by Western standards. There are scuttles at two deck levels directly beneath the bridge and on a single deck beneath one of the 76.2mm mountings aft, suggesting that these are the two major accommodation areas occupied by the crew. There is some officer accommodation in the bridge structure, but this too is cramped owing to the provision of reload tubes for the SS-N-3.

Construction and Service Life

The shipyard chosen for construction of the new cruisers was the Zhdanov Yard, Leningrad. The first ship, *Grozny*, was completed in 1962, and the others followed at yearly intervals. It is thought that no less than twelve ships of the class were projected, but there are indications that stability problems were experienced with the first units completed. The design was ambitious; a lot was attempted on a relatively small hull. The novelty of an all-missile main armament brought with it topweight problems that the Soviet designers do not appear to have fully anticipated. Besides the bulky quadruple launchers for the anti-ship missiles, the reload magazines were also above upper-deck level. Little attention was paid to the design of air search and guidance antennae, which were complex, heavy and — for the most part —

duplicated. Duplication of radar antennae, together with the adoption of the unit machinery layout, also brought with it the requirement for two massive tower masts.

Some modifications may have been worked into the later ships while under construction as a result of experience with *Grozny*, which itself may have been taken in hand for similar modifications in the mid-1960s. As no significant alterations were made above the upper deck, it can be assumed that these modifications involved the addition of ballast and possibly the installation of a fuel compensation system. Measures such as these would have mitigated the effects of the stability problem without tackling its basic causes. Only complete redesign would resolve the problem. Soviet acceptance of this fact is reflected in the curtailment of the original Kynda programme in favour of the Kresta class, the first of which was laid down some two years after completion of the first Kynda. It is perhaps significant that, with the appearance of the first units of the new class of Rocket Cruisers, the Kyndas were allocated to the two 'fair-weather' fleets in the Black Sea and the Pacific. *Grozny* and *Admiral Golovko* were assigned to the Black Sea Fleet, where they have seen considerable service, frequently operating at the centre of anti-carrier groups in the Mediterranean, tasked with shadowing units of the American Sixth Fleet. *Varyag* and *Admiral Fokin* serve in the Pacific, where they were for some ten years the major surface units. While the opportunity for shadowing American carrier battle groups is more restricted in the north-west Pacific than in the Mediterranean, the availability of large numbers of land-based aircraft in the Far East should enable them to operate effectively in the Sea of Japan, especially against the lightly-equipped Japanese Maritime Self-Defence Forces. Their ability to deliver concentrated fire support on the seaward flanks of the Army would be of considerable value in the event of hostilities with China.

Modifications

The drastic half-life modernization of warships, which is common in NATO navies, is a concept that is foreign to the Soviet Navy. Although some units built in the 1950s — notably the Kotlin, Krupny and Kildin classes — have been rebuilt in order to provide a rapid boost to numbers for new tactical concepts, and also because the original main armament was obsolescent when fitted, half-life modernization has not been applied to any of the major warships completed since the early 1960s. Two reasons can be postulated for this: first, Soviet ships are designed around a particular fit of weapon systems, and the 'tightness' of the design means that any modification to the original armament necessarily involves major reconstruction; and, secondly, because of the rapid advance of technology, the Soviet Navy prefers to allocate to new construction funds and shipyard labour resources that would otherwise be taken up by the updating of obsolescent units. A ship is regarded in much the same way as a tank, as a total weapon system; there is not the distinction between 'platform' and 'payload' that is commonly made in the West.

In spite of the early problems experienced with the Kyndas, over their twenty-year lifespan they have received only minor modifications to their weapon and sensor outfits; ironically, these have actually increased topweight! In 1973, *Grozny* had two Plinth Net target designation radars added to the large platforms projecting from the mainmast. This modification was extended to the two Pacific-based ships, *Varyag* and *Admiral Fokin*, in the late 1970s. In addition, *Admiral Fokin* had her second Head Net A radar replaced by the 'V'-beam Head Net C (see p. 30). *Varyag*, which received an even more extensive modernization, emerged in 1981 with two Head Net C antennae and a close-in anti-missile system comprising four 30mm Gatlings and two Bass Tilt fire control radars (see p. 56).

Kashin Class

KASHIN CLASS
Soviet designation: Bol'shoy Protivolodochny Korabl' (BPK — Large Anti-Submarine Ship)

Construction

Ship	Builder	In service
Obraztsovy,* Odarenny,* Ognevoy, Slavny, Steregushchy	Zhdanov Yard, Leningrad	1963–66
Komsomolets Ukrainy*, Krasny Kavkaz,* Krasny Krim, Otvazhny,*[1] Provorny,* Reshitelny, Sderzhanny, Skory, Smely, Smetlivy, Smyshlenny, Soobrazitelny,* Sposobny, Strogy, Stroyny	61 Kommuna Yard, Nikolayev	1963–73

Displacement
Standard: 3,750 tons. Full load: 4,750 tons.

Dimensions
Length: 144m (472ft), overall.
Beam: 15.8m (52ft).
Draught: 4.8m (16ft).

Armament
AAW: 2 twin SA-N-1 launchers (44 Goa missiles); 2 twin 76.2mm (3in) guns.
ASW: 2 12-barrelled RBU 6000 rocket launchers; 2 6-barrelled RBU 1000 rocket launchers; 1 quintuple bank of 533mm (21in) torpedo tubes.

Electronic equipment
Surveillance radar(s): 2 Head Net A*/1 Head Net C, 1 Big Net; 2 Don-2/2 Don-Kay.
Fire control radar(s): 2 Peel Group (SA-N-1); 2 Owl Screech (76.2mm guns).
Sonar(s): 1 keel-mounted high-frequency sonar.
ECM: 1 Bell Clout, 2–6 Bell/Top Hat series (4 Guard Dog in Obraztsovy and Soobrazitelny).

Machinery
2-shaft COGAG; 4 gas-turbines, each 24,000bhp; 96,000bhp = 35 knots maximum.

Complement
280.

[1] Lost, 31 August 1974.

The first Kashin was completed in 1963. In appearance and conception she was as radically different from her conventional predecessors as was the Kynda-class cruiser she was designed to accompany. Her overall length and beam are, in fact, virtually identical to those of the Kynda class, but the low, racy flush-decked hull-form and the lighter masts and superstructures are clear testimony to destroyer origins. The weapons and sensors belong to the same new generation as those of the Kynda class, the major omission being the long-range SS-N-3 anti-ship missile with its bulky launchers and guidance radars.

Propulsion

The most innovative feature of the Kashins was the all-gas-turbine propulsion plant. At the time of the completion of the first Kashin, a number of other countries were experimenting with the installation of gas-turbines on warships. Fast patrol boats (FPBs) powered by gas-turbines were becoming relatively common, but the application of this propulsion system to larger warships was in its infancy. The Royal Navy was bringing into service two major classes employing gas-turbines — County-class destroyers and Tribal-class frigates — and the Federal German Navy was completing the first of the Köln-class frigates. Hybrid propulsion plants were adopted in both cases; the British combined small Metrovick G.6 gas-turbines rated at 7,500bhp with conventional steam propulsion machinery (COSAG, Combined Steam And Gas) while the Germans combined two larger Brown-Boveri 12,000bhp units with smaller diesels (CODAG, Combined Diesel And Gas). In all these installations the gas-turbines were used only for 'cold-starting' or for boost. Complex gearing had to be adopted in order to link the diverse components of the machinery.

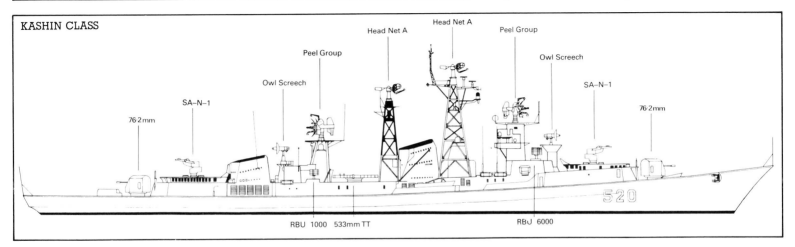

KASHIN CLASS

Opposite page, top: *Obraztsovy*
in the English Channel in 1967. In
common with other early units, she
is fitted with two Head Net A air
surveillance antennae. She can
be distinguished from other
ships of the class by her ECM
array, which includes six Guard
Dog radomes. Two of these
were later removed. (Skyfotos)
Opposite page, bottom:
Soobrazitelny in 1967. The twin
canted funnels give these ships
a distinctive appearance.
(Novosti)
Below right: *A Kashin of the*
Pacific Fleet investigates
wreckage thought to belong to
an American plane shot down
by the North Koreans in 1969.
The guns immediately aft of the
SA-N-1 launcher are for saluting.
Three Tee Plinth electro-optical
sensors are fitted around the
lattice foremast. (Novosti)

The Kashin class was remarkable in that it employed a totally homogeneous all-gas-turbine (COGAG, Combined Gas And Gas) propulsion plant, comprising four large industrial turbines with an estimated individual rating of 24,000bhp for a total installed horsepower of 96,000bhp; the four G.6 turbines of the British County class together produce only 30,000bhp! This figure was necessary if the Kashin class was to keep pace with the Kynda class, which has been credited with a theoretical — if unlikely — speed of 35 knots. It was, nevertheless, unsurpassed in the West until the commissioning of the Royal Navy's HMS *Invincible* nearly twenty years later.

The adoption of an all-gas-turbine plant had a considerable effect on the design and layout of the Kashin class, especially topsides. While gas-turbines are generally lighter and more compact than conventional machinery, they require large air intakes and exhaust uptakes. The striking appearance of the Kashin class is largely attributable to the four broad funnels, arranged in pairs amidships and aft. The air intakes are around the base of the funnels, which are canted outwards in order to keep the hot exhaust gases clear of the delicate electronics. In the first Kashin completed, the forward pair of funnels was similar in height to the after pair, but problems were experienced with hot gases drifting across the decks and they were subsequently heightened by about 1.5m.

The propulsion machinery, together with the extensive trunking involved in providing intakes and uptakes, clearly occupies considerable hull-space in the Kashin, which has the same acute lack of internal volume as the Kynda class. The homogeneous all-gas-turbine installation appears to have been regarded as a success; not only did the Kashin class

continue in production for some ten years, but similar installations using more modern gas-turbines have been adopted by the Krivak, Kara and Udaloy classes. The appeal to the Soviets lies partly in the relative simplicity of the COGAG system. The hybrid plants installed in Western warships of the same generation as the Kashin class frequently proved to be a maintenance nightmare, and the complex linkage of different types of machinery was generally abandoned in the next generation of warships in favour of COGOG (Combined Gas Or Gas) and CODOG (Combined Diesel Or Gas) installations.

There is, however, the inevitable price to pay for the simplicity of a COGAG system such as that installed in the Kashin class. Gas-turbines are notoriously heavy consumers of fuel at lower power ratings, hence the adoption of hybrid plants by other navies. In the West, gas-turbines were considered suitable only for full-power operations; steam and diesel machinery was provided for sustained operations at cruise speed, giving improved fuel economy and, consequently, range. A ship the size of the Kashin class would require 10–12,000shp for a cruising speed of eighteen knots. Two-shaft operation at cruise speed would, therefore, be very costly in terms of fuel consumption; it is reported that the Kashins (and other later Soviet COGAG ships) generally operate on a single engine with one shaft trailing. The fuel thus saved compensates for the additional drag imposed by the trailing shaft. Nevertheless, the poor specific fuel consumption (SFC) rate with which Soviet gas-turbines are generally credited must result in significant range limitations. The priority given to high-speed performance at the expense of endurance in the Kashin class is further evidence of the

Three views of Obraztsovy on her arrival in Portsmouth in 1976, which was the first Soviet visit to a port in the UK since that of the cruiser Sverdlov in 1953. The close-up of the centre section (top left) gives an excellent illustration of the electronics outfit, and, in particular, the ECM/ESM suite, which is more extensive and varied than that of other ships of the class. The close-up of the forward radar tower (top right), which incorporates the navigation bridge, reveals how little space was allocated to command and control facilities in the design. Note the old-style life-rafts, recently replaced on most ships of the class by the modern cocooned variety. (C. and S. Taylor)

different missions for which Soviet and NATO ships of this period were designed.

The quietness of gas-turbines in anti-submarine operations is a feature that has led to their widespread adoption by the Western navies. Gas-turbines are not, however, inherently quiet. It is simply that, by housing them within modules, adopting flexible machinery mountings and installing silencing baffles inside the air intakes, noise emission can be reduced to a level below that of other types of machinery. There is no indication that these considerations were a factor in the selection of gas-turbines for the Kashin class. When *Obraztsovy* visited Portsmouth (UK) in 1976, it was noticeable that her engines emitted a loud high-pitched whine, which suggested that few silencing measures had been undertaken to reduce noise signature. Considerable underwater noise would also result from the fuel-saving practice of trailing one shaft, especially since the propeller blades cannot be 'feathered' in the same way as Western controllable-pitch propellers.

Weapon and Sensor Layout

The Kashin class has a symmetrical, 'double-ended' layout. There is a single superstructure deck running some three-quarters of the length of the ship, interrupted only by the funnel uptakes. At the forward and after ends of this deck are twin SA-N-1 launchers for Goa surface-to-air missiles. Beneath them, at upper-deck level, are twin 76.2mm mountings. There are two tall lattice masts amidships carrying identical Head Net A antennae (later ships of the class have a different air search outfit). The foremast, which is higher and broader at its base, also carries the surface search antennae and has platforms for ECM antennae. To either side of the lattice masts are small radar towers, each with a Peel Group missile guidance radar, an Owl Screech gun fire control radar and a pair of anti-submarine rocket launchers. The forward tower, which is the larger of the two, also contains the bridge and navigation spaces. Finally, there is a quintuple mounting for long 533mm torpedoes amidships.

Anti-Air Defence

The dominant position given to the two SA-N-1 launchers identifies them as the main armament of the Kashins. The extra launcher, as compared with the Kynda class, gives the Kashin class double the rate of fire, the ability to engage simultaneously twice the number of targets, and excellent all-round arcs. The need to locate the launchers atop a super-structure deck was dictated by the lack of hull depth, but this arrangement proved so successful that it was adopted by a number of later cruiser designs.

The launchers reload, as on the Kynda class, while trained on the beam; the forward launcher reloads to starboard and the after launcher to port. This arrangement suggests that the SA-N-1 launcher and magazine form a module for ship instal-lation; a practice well-suited to the mass-production tech-niques favoured by the Soviet Union, but one which offers no possibility of the flexible magazine capacities favoured by some Western navies.

The double-ended layout of the Kashin class has also resulted in superior fire control arrangements for the 76.2mm guns as compared to the Kynda, which has both mountings grouped together close to the stern. Not only can the two mountings of the Kashin class cover all arcs, but each is

Opposite page, top: *A close-up of a Kashin of the Black Sea Fleet, taken in 1979. Note the complex construction of the Peel Group missile guidance radar, with its multiple 'orange peel' reflectors. (TASS)*

Opposite page, bottom: *Goa surface-to-air missiles on the forward SA-N-1 launcher of a Kashin. (TASS)*

Top right: *Two Kashins with Big Net radar, seen here in the Black Sea. The unit in the foreground is Skory. (TASS)*

Bottom right: *Major differences exist in the electronics outfit carried by individual units of the Kashin class, and these differences are particularly evident in this 1980 view of two ships of the Baltic Fleet. Obraztsovy, the older of the two, has two Head Net A air surveillance radars and two Don-2 navigation radars, while the vessel inboard of her has Head Net C and Big Net air surveillance radars, and two Don-Kay surface search radars. The two ships also carry completely different ECM/ESM arrays. (TASS)*

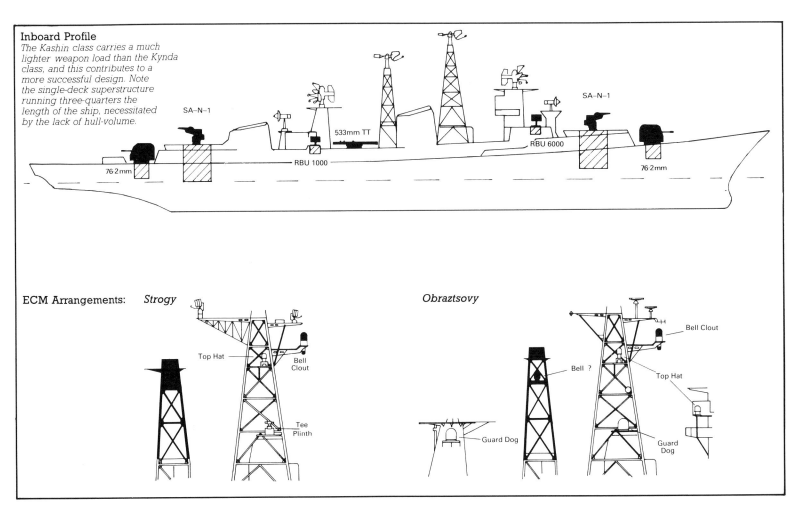

Inboard Profile

The Kashin class carries a much lighter weapon load than the Kynda class, and this contributes to a more successful design. Note the single-deck superstructure running three-quarters the length of the ship, necessitated by the lack of hull-volume.

SA–N–1

SA–N–1

76·2mm

533mm TT

RBU 6000

RBU 1000

76·2mm

ECM Arrangements:

Strogy

Top Hat

Bell Clout

Tee Plinth

Obraztsovy

Bell Clout

Bell ?

Top Hat

Guard Dog

Guard Dog

Opposite page, centre: *The names allocated to the various ECM radomes on these and other Soviet ships should be treated with some caution, as the information given in reference books is conflicting and frequently contradictory. Obraztsovy has a more extensive and varied ECM outfit than any other ship of the class, and may have been used as a trials ship for some of the equipment. Only she and Soobrazitelny have the distinctive Guard Dog radomes. The installation of Strogy is more typical of the unmodified ships. Some ships of the unmodified group have Bell Clout and a third Tee Plinth electro-optical sensor on the platform projecting from the top of the foremast, and some have ECM radomes on the forward radar tower and on platforms projecting from the mainmast (see Obraztsovy).*
Opposite page, left: *An unusual view of four Kashins in line ahead, operating with Ka-25 Hormone anti-submarine helicopters. Such operations could take place only in relative proximity to shore bases, as the Kashin class has no hangar or maintenance facilities. All four vessels in this photograph are fitted with Head Net C and Big Net. (Novosti)*
Opposite page, right: *One of the two RBU 1000 anti-submarine rocket launchers carried on each Kashin-class ship. The RBU 1000 has only six tubes as compared with twelve for the RBU 6000, but fires a larger rocket. It is fully automatic and reloads from beneath with the tubes in the vertical position. (US Navy)*
Right: *The Pacific Fleet ship Strogy at Massawa, Ethiopia, in 1972. Head Net C and Big Net air surveillance radars distinguish her from the early Kashins. (MoD)*

provided with its own radar, enabling two targets to be engaged simultaneously.

Anti-Submarine Weapons

In addition to the twin forward-firing RBU 6000 rocket launchers carried by the Kynda class, the Kashin class is fitted with two RBU 1000 rocket launchers, located abreast the after radar tower. The RBU 1000 (formerly the MBU 4500A) is a six-barrelled rocket launcher that fires a heavier rocket over shorter distances than its twelve-barrelled counterpart. An earlier version of the rocket launcher installed on Kotlin-class destroyers in the early 1960s was hand-loaded, but the model on the Kashin class has automatic reloading on the same pattern as the RBU 6000.

The sonar fitted in the Kashin class is almost certainly the same model installed in the Kynda. It is generally accepted that it is hull-mounted, although some commentators have suggested that it is a bow sonar. Evidence for the latter theory rests largely with the configuration of the ship's stem, which has rather more overhang than either the Kynda or the Kresta I classes. The position of the anchors on the Kashin class is conventional, however, whereas subsequent Soviet practice when fitting a bow sonar is to place the anchors well forward of the sonar dome.

Minelaying

Traditional Soviet naval concerns are reflected in the provision of mine rails, which run from immediately aft the second pair of funnels to the stern. An estimated 30 mines could be accommodated. Fast destroyers such as these would be employed in offensive minelaying operations aimed at disrupting the enemy's sea lines of communication, especially in shallow areas such as the Baltic and the Black Sea.

Construction

Construction of the Kashin class was initially divided between the Zhdanov Yard (Leningrad) in the Baltic and the 61 Kommuna Yard (Nikolayev) in the Black Sea, in itself an indication that large numbers were planned. After completing some five units the Zhdanov Yard was left to concentrate on cruiser construction, and production continued only in the Black Sea. It is even possible that modifications to the Kyndas necessitated the abandonment of the Kashin programme at this yard.

The Soviets clearly regard the Kashins as successful ships, as construction continued well beyond that of the Kynda class they were apparently designed to support. When the Rocket Cruiser concept lost favour in the mid-1960s, because of the shift in Soviet naval priorities from anti-carrier to anti-submarine warfare, the Kashins were redesignated Large Anti-Submarine Ships (Bol'shoy Protivolodochny Korabl'). That they were not designed as such is evident from their weapon fit. The emphasis, as we have seen, was on air defence with only a subsidiary ASW capability, and they lack the important features — anti-submarine missiles, ASW helicopters, and bow and variable-depth sonars — common to major Soviet warships belonging to the anti-submarine programme of the mid-1960s. While it is not clear exactly what classification the Soviet Navy gave to the earliest Kashins on their completion, it may well have been the same 'destroyer' classification (Eskadrenny Minonosets) given to the earlier Skory and Kotlin classes. (The term 'Raketny' — literally 'Rocket', but sometimes translated as 'Missile' — was applied only to vessels armed with anti-ship missiles.)

The first Kashins completed were divided fairly evenly between the four Soviet fleets, but later units were generally allocated to the Black Sea and Pacific. Their lack of freeboard amidships is less of a problem in these two areas.

Modifications

The earliest Kashins, like the Kyndas, were completed with empty platforms designed to accommodate ECM antennae projecting from the sides of the foremast and the after radar tower. These antennae were fitted as they became available in the late 1960s and, consequently, ECM fit varies from ship to ship. Some units have electro-optical sensors at the head of the foremast and on the platforms projecting from its sides, while others have ECM radomes identical to those fitted on the lower mainmast platforms of the Kynda-class cruiser *Grozny*. Surface search radars also vary; early units have the Don-2 antenna while others have Don-Kay, which has a solid elliptical reflector with the feed-horn beneath.

A more significant variation is to be found in the air search radars. From the mid-1960s, Kashins were completed with a Big Net aerial atop the mainmast, and the forward Head Net A antenna was replaced by a new back-to-back version, designated 'Head Net C'. Big Net was not a new radar, but one that had first appeared in 1959 on Chuchotka-class missile-range ships and had subsequently been fitted to two ships of the Sverdlov class, including the missile conversion *Dzerzhinsky*. It is, however, a much larger aerial than Head Net A and even the Soviet designers must have baulked at the idea of locating it atop the missile towers of the Kynda class. Installing Big Net on the Kashin class, with its smaller lattice mainmast, clearly presented fewer problems. Big Net is an L-Band radar and, therefore, operates at a lower frequency than the S-Band Head Net A; its detection range is estimated at 180km (100nm).

Head Net C is a 'V'-beam radar. Two Head Net A aerials are mounted back-to-back with the second tilted at an angle of 30° to the horizontal. This effectively doubles scanning rate, and dispenses with the need for the counterbalancing vanes that are a distinctive feature of the Head Net A antenna. More significantly, tilting the second scanner has the effect of displacing the fan-shaped elevation beam from the vertical, giving Head Net C a height-finding capability previously lacking in Soviet air search radars. The vertical beam performs a conventional search function, and the operator measures altitude on a selected target by marking it and setting range gates on the tilted beam. The technique is simple, although by no means as effective as the frequency scanning (FRESCAN) techniques employed by US Navy 3-D radars from the early 1960s. The combination of Big Net and Head Net C on the later Kashins has brought with it a number of improvements over the original radar capabilities. Aerial detection ranges are improved by about 50 per cent by the installation of Big Net, while the 'V'-beam Head Net C gives a 3-D capability between the air search and the missile guidance radars, with consequent improvements in tracking and target selection.

Below: Smetlivy *at anchor in the Mediterranean. The symmetrical layout of weapons and sensors is an important feature of this class.* (Defence)

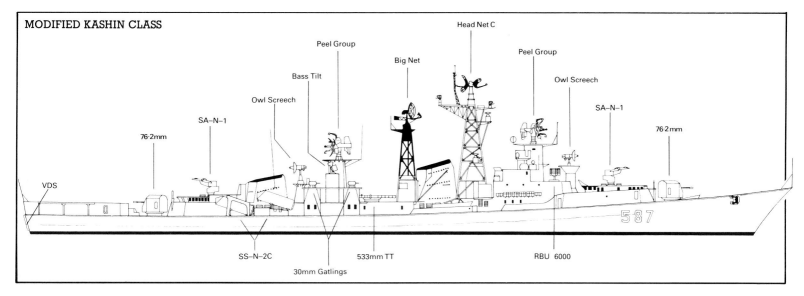

MODIFIED KASHIN CLASS

Labels (left to right): 76·2mm — SA–N–1 — Owl Screech — Bass Tilt — Peel Group — Big Net — Head Net C — Peel Group — Owl Screech — SA–N–1 — 76·2mm

VDS — SS–N–2C — 30mm Gatlings — 533mm TT — RBU 6000

587

Modified Kashin Class

In 1973, a more significant modification of the Kashin class appeared. It is reported that the first ship, *Sderzhanny*, was modified while under construction at the Kommuna 61 shipyard in Nikolayev. Five further units of the class underwent an identical conversion and followed in rapid succession during the mid-1970s, the last being completed in 1980. They were not necessarily the oldest nor the most recent ships, but appear to have been selected for modification on a random basis, and were probably taken in hand as they became due for a refit. The new variation received the NATO designation 'Kashin-Mod'. The Soviet Navy reclassified these units as Large Rocket Ships (Bol'shoy Raketny Korabl').

The principal feature of the modification was the addition of four single SS-N-2C anti-ship missile launchers abreast the after pair of funnels. The SS-N-2C is an updated version of the Styx horizon-range missile fitted to some 300 missile patrol boats of the Komar and Osa classes during the 1960s. The missile was initially intended, therefore, for area defence inside Soviet waters; hostile task forces outside these waters would be engaged by 'stand-off' missiles such as the SS-N-3, the long range of which offered the fast-manoeuvring launch ship some protection against the Western carrier attack squadrons. The installation of the SS-N-2C on the Kashin class and, simultaneously, on three of the older Kildin-class destroyers marked the inauguration of a new tactical concept.

Since the late 1960s the Soviet Navy had regularly deployed to the Mediterranean squadron small anti-carrier groups, each comprising two or three surface ships or submarines armed with cruise missiles. In times of crisis — a notable example being the Middle East War of 1973 — these groups were tasked with shadowing the carrier battle groups of the US Sixth Fleet. Frequently, these groups included the oversized missile patrol boats of the Nanuchka class, which were 'low-value' units with limited ability to defend themselves and whose SS-N-9 missiles have only half the effective range of the SS-N-3. The Kashin and Kildin modifications took this tactic a stage further and, in the process, helped to

MODIFIED KASHIN CLASS
Soviet designation: Bol'shoy Raketny Korabl' (BRK — Large Rocket Ship)

Construction

Ship	Converted
Ognevoy, Sderzhanny, Smyshlenny, Slavny, Smely, Stroyny	1973–80

Displacement
Standard: 3,950 tons. Full load: 4,950 tons.

Dimensions
Length: 146m (480ft), overall.
Beam: as built.
Draught: as built.

Armament
ASuW: 4 single SS-N-2C launchers (4 missiles).
AAW: 2 twin SA-N-1 launchers (44 Goa missiles); 2 twin 76.2mm (3in) guns; 4 30mm Gatling guns.
ASW: 2 12-barrelled RBU 6000 rocket launchers; 1 quintuple bank of 533mm (21in) torpedo tubes.

Electronic equipment
Surveillance radar(s): 1 Head Net C, 1 Big Net (except *Ognevoy* — 2 Head Net A); 2 Don-Kay.
Fire control radar(s): 2 Peel Group (SA-N-1); 2 Owl Screech (76.2mm guns); 2 Bass Tilt (30mm Gatling guns).
Sonar(s): 1 keel-mounted medium high-frequency sonar; 1 medium-frequency VDS.
ECM: 2 Bell Squat, 2 Bell Shroud.

Machinery
as built.

Complement
320.

SS-N-2C
In service: 1973.
Length: 6.25m (21ft).
Diameter: 0.75m (2ft 6in).
Span: 2.75m (9ft).
Weight: 2,300kg (5,070lb).
Warhead: 400kg (880lb) HE.
Propulsion: Solid-fuel booster for launch/acceleration phase; liquid-fuel turbojet sustainer motor for cruise phase.
Speed: Mach 0.8.
Range: 80km (45nm).
Guidance: Active radar/infra-red homing.

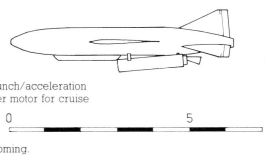

0   5

resolve the targeting problem in a theatre where large-scale supporting operations by the Soviet Naval Air Force are difficult — if not impossible — to sustain. The modified destroyers are intended to operate within visual range of the carrier and to monitor her position. In the event of hostilities the destroyer would 'call down fire' from other anti-carrier units shadowing the task force, and would try to get off a pre-emptive strike of her own before making her escape. The quick response of the gas-turbines of the Kashins makes them well-suited to the rapid evasive manoeuvres that would be required, and the missiles themselves — contrary to normal Soviet practice — are aft-firing.

Most of the modified Kashins and two of the three modified Kildins serve in the Black Sea Fleet. Since the mid-1970s they have frequently been seen in company with Sixth Fleet carriers during NATO exercises in the Mediterranean.

Other Items of New Equipment

In addition to the installation of SS-N-2 missile launchers, the modified Kashins display a number of other important items of new equipment. Abreast the after radar tower a new structure two decks high has been built out to the sides of the ship. Atop the deckhouse are two pairs of 30mm Gatlings (see p. 56 for details) with Bass Tilt fire control radars mounted on pedestals, added at the expense of the two RBU 1000 rocket launchers, which have been removed. These provide the ships with a much-improved close-in defence capability against enemy missiles.

A variable depth sonar, enclosed in a large deckhouse similar to that of the Krivak and Kara classes, has been installed in a remodelled stern, increasing overall length by about 3m. Atop the deckhouse is a helicopter platform, which replaces the rarely-used landing pad marked out on the stern of the earlier units. The variable depth sonar (VDS) installation is puzzling, as it is accompanied by no new anti-submarine weapons; indeed, removal of the two RBU 1000 rocket launchers means that the already inadequate ASW armament has been effectively halved. In part, these anomalies reflect the piecemeal approach the Soviets have adopted towards ship modernization; new items of equipment that have recently become available are simply added on, without any thorough reconsideration of the ship as a total weapon system. This is totally contrary to Western practice. It reflects also the tactical — and political — philosophy of the Soviets, in which the sum of the constituent parts is regarded as more important than the individual contributions. Several ships operating together with variable depth sonars will achieve a significantly higher detection rate against submarines than a single unit, and the long-range stand-off capability of the anti-submarine missiles and helicopters of the specialist ASW ships enables them to attack over a broad area.

The final structural alteration made to the original design in the Kashin-Mod conversion is the extension of the forward superstructure on two decks between the Peel Group radar tower and the foremast. Significantly, the basic electronics array remains largely unchanged. One ship, *Ognevoy*, has retained even her original Head Net A air search antennae.

A Limited Programme

It was thought at first that the entire class of twenty ships would undergo the extensive modernization outlined above. After the first group of conversions, however, the programme

The ECM apparatus on Stroyny represents the outfit of the ships refitted with the SS-N-2C. (See also line drawings of ECM outfits of unmodified Kashins on page 28).

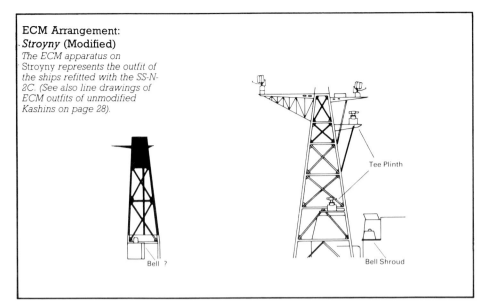

Tee Plinth

Bell ?

Bell Shroud

was abandoned. It is possible that the conversion programme was, in any case, limited in its aims, the intention being simply to fit out a small number of vessels to provide a specific capability in the Mediterranean. However, some aspects of the conversion suggest that it may not have proved entirely successful. Soviet ships of this period were designed to very tight specifications, with little or no weight and space available for later additions of equipment. Western practice in this respect is very strict; in a ship with no weight reserves every new item installed must be compensated for by the removal of an equivalent weight of older equipment. The Kashin modification, however, involves the addition of four missile launchers, together with bed-plates, ramps and blast shields, a variable depth sonar, a two-deck magazine amidships and a two-deck extension to the forward superstructure — all at or above upper-deck level. The only items of equipment removed were the two small anti-submarine rocket launchers. It is possible therefore that the converted ships may have experienced stability problems. This factor may have been responsible for the premature curtailment of the programme, and may explain Soviet reluctance to deploy the modified ships outside the relatively tranquil waters of the Black Sea and Mediterranean.

Opposite page, top: *The replenishment oiler* Boris Chilikin *refuels two ships of the Kashin class east of Sardinia in 1975. Number 173 is a modified Kashin; number 191 is unmodified. (MoD)*

Opposite page, centre: *A modified Kashin of the Black Sea Fleet. A considerable increase in topweight has been accepted in the process of the conversion. The four major modifications – the extended bridge structure, the 30mm Gatlings, the SS-N-2 missile launchers, and the raised helicopter platform – are particularly prominent from this angle. (TASS)*

Opposite page, bottom: Provorny *in late 1981, extensively modified as a result of her conversion as a trials ship for the SA-N-7 surface-to-air missile. (French Navy)*

Right: *A modified Kashin, seen here in 1976. The aft-firing SS-N-2 launchers present a striking contrast with those fitted in the modified Kashins recently completed for India, in which they are abreast the bridge structure. The Soviet choice of position reflects important tactical considerations. (MoD)*

516

Right: *The modified Kashin Sderzhanny in close company with the carrier Nimitz in the eastern Mediterranean. Shadowing the big American carriers of the Sixth Fleet may have provided the rationale for the SS-N-2 conversions. (US Navy)*

Provorny

In the late 1970s one of the Black Sea Kashins, *Provorny*, was reconstructed as a trials ship to test the SA-N-7 surface-to-air system intended for the new destroyers of the Sovremenny class. The ship emerged from the Black Sea only in late 1981, revealing a number of interesting modifications.

Both SA-N-1 launchers and their associated Peel Group radars have been removed and major structural alterations made to the superstructures and masts. The former lattice mainmast has been removed altogether and a new tower mast constructed just forward of the second pair of funnels. Atop the new mast is a large Top Steer 3-D air search and tracking radar. The original Head Net A air surveillance radar has been removed from the foremast, and, instead, there is a Head Net C 'V'-beam antenna atop a remodelled bridge structure. The after SA-N-1 launcher has been replaced by a new single-arm launcher. Two pairs of hatches forward of the bridge may conceivably constitute the feed system of further launchers yet to be installed, but could also be used for vertical-launch testing of the missile.

It is evident that some sort of launch system forward of the bridge either has been or will be installed from the number and position of the Front Dome tracker/illuminators associated with the semi-active guidance system. No less than eight are fitted. Four are forward-facing, being paired atop the remodelled bridge structure and on platforms projecting from the sides of the foremast respectively. The other four face aft; one pair is on platforms projecting from the sides of the tower mast and the other is at the level of the first superstructure deck abreast the after funnel uptakes.

Interestingly, the Soviets appear to have been anxious to preserve the operational capabilities of the ship. Both sets of anti-submarine rocket launchers have been retained, in spite of their proximity to new installations. The torpedo tubes and the 76.2mm guns, together with their Owl Screech fire control radars, also remain in place. Although the original ECM outfit has been removed, there are platforms for Bell Shroud antennae at the after end of the bridge structure. Although the SA-N-7 system appears to be a replacement for the SA-N-1, it is unlikely that the new surface-to-air missile will see service on other units of the Kashin class, in view of their age.

PROVORNY

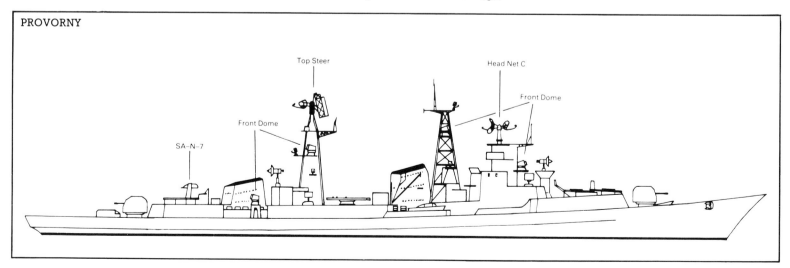

Top Steer   Head Net C   Front Dome   Front Dome   SA-N-7

Kresta I Class

The first of the Kresta-class cruisers is reported to have been laid down in 1964. The date is significant, as it marks a two-year gap between the completion of the first Kynda and the laying down of the new class, allowing an adequate period of time — by Soviet standards — for a complete redesign of a type of ship which, by all accounts, had more than its fair share of teething troubles. The Kresta I, when completed, presented a striking contrast in appearance and general layout to the Kynda class, in spite of overall similarities in the basic weapon systems carried. Closer comparisons are revealing, because they tell us which features the Soviet designers persisted with, and which ones were 'selected out' as a result of experience with Kynda.

The hull-form is basically that of the Kynda class, although length, significantly, was increased by some thirteen metres, and the forecastle deck was extended aft, thereby increasing internal volume. Steam propulsion machinery similar to that of the Kynda class was adopted, but the unit machinery layout was abandoned in favour of a more compact installation in which the boiler rooms and engine rooms appear to be located side by side, the twin uptakes being led up into a single broad funnel. This is generally considered by Western designers to be unsatisfactory in a ship of this size, as an unlucky hit amidships could disable the ship and leave her dead in the water. Nevertheless, it restricts vulnerability to machinery damage to a single, relatively small area of the ship. It is also very economical on centre-line space both below-decks and topsides, allowing more room for weapons and magazines fore and aft. In place of the twin radar towers of the Kynda class, there is a single tower amidships, almost as broad at its base as the ship itself. The tower carries a

Scoop Pair missile guidance radar on its forward face and a Head Net C air search radar at its summit; the second air search radar common to major Soviet ships of the period — in this case Big Net — is located on a platform between the twin funnel uptakes.

Whereas the weapons layout of the Kynda class was dominated by the two quadruple launchers for SS-N-3 anti-ship missiles, the Kresta I class has a layout similar to that of the Kashin class, with the key centre-line positions fore and aft occupied by twin SA-N-1 launchers for Goa surface-to-air missiles. The influence of the Kashin class can also be seen in the resulting superstructure layout. The Kynda superstructures comprised two neat, isolated blocks with the weapons fore and aft of them. The Kresta class, on the other hand, has a long rambling superstructure deck running from the forecastle to the quarterdeck and weaving in and out to accommodate a variety of weapons and magazines. This deck extends to the sides of the ship at its forward end, thereby protecting from heavy seas the side-mounted weapons mounted farther aft. The Peel Group guidance radars for Goa are located, as on the Kashin class, on small towers fore and aft of the tall central structure. The first of these extends forward to accommodate the bridge, and beneath the cantilevered bridge wings there are paired SS-N-3 launchers port and starboard. The launchers can be elevated to about 18° in this position, but cannot train.

The anti-submarine rocket launchers and torpedo mountings show the influence of both the Kashin and Kynda classes. Twin RBU 6000 anti-submarine rocket launchers are located close to the bow as on the Kynda class, but there are also RBU 1000 rocket launchers on either side of the

Below: *The Rocket Cruiser* Vladivostok *being shadowed by a US Navy Knox-class frigate off the coast of Hawaii in September 1971. The close attention given to air defence in this class is evidenced by the dominant positions occupied by the two surface-to-air missile launchers and their associated tracking and guidance radars. Also of note are the large Side Globe ECM radomes, which made their first appearance on this class. (US Navy)*

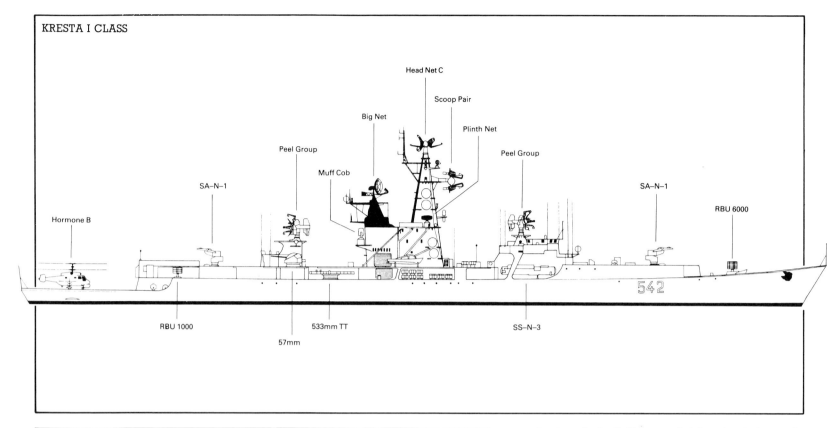

KRESTA I CLASS

KRESTA I CLASS
Soviet designation: Raketny Kreyser (RKR — Rocket Cruiser)

Construction

Ship	Builder	Laid down	Launched	In service
Admiral Zozulya	Zhdanov Yard,	1964	1966	1967
Vladivostok	Leningrad	1965	1967	1968
Vitse Admiral Drozd	(all units)	1965	1967	1968
Sevastopol		1966	1968	1969

Displacement
Standard: 6,000 tons. Full load: 7,500 tons.

Dimensions
Length: 155m (508ft), overall.
Beam: 17m (56ft).
Draught: 5.5m (18ft).

Armament
ASuW: 2 twin SS-N-3 launchers (4 missiles).
AAW: 2 twin SA-N-1 launchers (44 Goa missiles); 2 twin 57mm guns, 4 30mm Gatlings in *Drozd* since 1975.
ASW: 2 12-barrelled RBU 6000 rocket launchers; 2 6-barrelled RBU 1000 rocket launchers; 2 quintuple banks of 533mm (21in) torpedo tubes; 1 Ka-25 Hormone B missile targeting helicopter.

Electronic equipment
Surveillance radar(s): 1 Head Net C, 1 Big Net; as built, 1 Don-Kay, 1 Don-2 — now, Palm Frond fitted.
Fire control radar(s): 1 Scoop Pair (SS-N-3); 2 Peel Group (SA-N-1); 2 Muff Cob (57mm guns); 2 Bass Tilt (30mm Gatlings) in *Drozd* since 1975.
Sonar(s): 1 keel-mounted high-frequency sonar.
ECM: 8 Side Globe; 1 Bell Clout, 2 Bell Slam, 2 Bell Tap.

Machinery
2-shaft geared steam turbines; 100,000shp = 34 knots maximum.

Complement
380.

superstructure deck aft. The torpedo tubes, located as on the Kyndas at upper-deck level, are quintuple mountings with no reloads.

The Helicopter
A new departure was the provision of a helicopter hangar aft for a Hormone B, which is a missile targeting variant of the basic Ka-25 helicopter. Beneath the chin of the Hormone B is a radome, reportedly designated 'Puff Ball', which contains a surface search radar. There is a smaller protrusion for electronics beneath the rear of the fuselage, which may transmit correction signals to the missiles for which the Hormone B provides mid-course guidance.

The Ka-25 has coaxial rotors, which provide excellent lift characteristics but impose serious limitations on shipboard operation owing to the additional hangar clearance required. The height of the hangar needed to accommodate the Ka-25 brings with it problems both of topweight and of location; specifically, where it can be located without obstructing the arcs of other weapon systems. The Ka-25, therefore, requires a large ship from which to operate. The solution adopted in the Kresta I design was to operate the helicopter from the low quarterdeck and to locate the hangar immediately forward of the landing pad. In this way, the hangar, which is approximately 11.5m long, 5.5m wide and 5.5m high, rises only slightly above the level of the first superstructure deck, leaving clear arcs for the after SA-N-1 launcher. The disadvantage implicit in this solution is that operating the helicopter from the low quarterdeck must be particularly hazardous in rough weather, thereby limiting the operational

effectiveness and availability of the Ka-25. This appears to have proved a serious enough problem to merit the adoption of revised helicopter handling arrangements on the Kresta II and later vessels.

Anti-Aircraft Guns

The helicopter hangar effectively displaced the twin 76.2mm mountings of the Kyndas, so lighter AA guns mounted at a higher level amidships were adopted for the Kresta I. The weapon chosen was the twin 57mm/80cal mounting, which had first seen service on the Ugra-class submarine support ships and the Poti-class corvettes some years previously. A development of earlier Soviet twin and quadruple 57mm mountings, the mounting on the Kresta class is fully automatic and radar-controlled with a rate of fire estimated at 100–120rpm. The fire control radar is Muff Cob, one of a series of Soviet fire control radars with a 'searchlight' configuration. It can be distinguished from the Drum Tilt and Bass Tilt radars that accompany smaller weapons by the trunnion yoke, which enables it to elevate as well as train. Muff Cob also has what appears to be an on-mounted TV or optical tracking sensor. On the Kresta class there is a Muff Cob director for each of the twin 57mm mountings; the directors are mounted on platforms projecting from the after sides of the funnel uptakes.

New Sensors

The Soviet predilection for duplicating weapon and sensor systems is thought by some to reflect Soviet concern about the effect of action damage on operational capabilities. By others it is seen as an indication of high break-down rates in Soviet equipment and the difficulty of adequately maintaining sensitive modern electronics with a predominantly conscript force. Available evidence suggests that both these theories may well be correct.

Given the Soviet operational concept of small anti-carrier surface groups, a Soviet unit with action damage would be more vulnerable and more difficult to protect from air attack than, say, a NATO destroyer or cruiser forming part of the screen of a large carrier task force. Moreover, since it is intended that all Soviet units present — cruisers, submarines, bombers — would launch their missiles in a single co-ordinated attack, it is vital that all necessary guidance radars should function at the exact moment that the command to fire is received. The Soviet Navy of this period was very much a 'one-shot' force and could not, therefore, be satisfied with even 80–90 per cent availability of its electronic equipment. In the NATO carrier task force, on the other hand, 80–90 per cent availability would still enable a carrier to launch most of her aircraft, with the damaged destroyer in the screen being only one of a number contributing to overall air search and defence capabilities. In addition, the new emphasis on data transfer links in the NATO navies would further diminish the impact of the breakdown of a single air search radar in a single unit of the task force. Western and Soviet radar developments over the past two decades have moved in opposite directions. The West has moved towards a lesser number of multi-function radars and has placed considerable emphasis on the coordination of data both within the individual ship and within the task force as a whole. The

Soviet Navy has persisted with single-function radars linked to a single missile or gun installation; the layout of their ships throughout the period suggests that transmitters, receivers, and even control consoles are often located close to the individual items of equipment, thereby minimizing the vulnerability of the ship's total weapons capability to a single unlucky hit or a single systems failure.

The philosophy of systems redundancy is taken a stage further in the Kresta class which, in addition to the fire control radars previously seen on the Kyndas and early Kashins, is fitted with new 'back-up' systems. On either side of the central radar tower are Plinth Net tracking radars, which are probably used for target designation. Plinth Net has been retro-fitted to three of the Kyndas since about 1973, but it is not clear whether this was the original intention, as *Grozny* — the first ship to receive this modification — had ECM radomes installed in this position only a few years previously.

The other new sensor to appear on the Kresta class was Tee Plinth, an electro-optical device fitted in the bridge wings above the anti-ship missile launchers. The fitting of electro-optical devices in Soviet ships has mushroomed since their first appearance on the Kresta class, and they have been retro-fitted to a number of earlier major units, including the Kashins and the Kyndas. They provide an important back-up capability to the ships' guidance radars in hostile ECM conditions.

ECM

The Kyndas had brought into service a variety of small ECM radomes, which were fitted around the mainmast top in the mid-1960s. The radomes were of conventional cylindrical configuration with rounded tops, and some were double-ended with a smaller protrusion projecting beneath the platform on which they were mounted. These became the NATO 'Bell' series, some examples being Bell Clout, Bell Slam and Bell Tap. The 'Bell' half of the designation is clearly a reference to the radome shape, but the other half probably derives from the frequency of the signal emitted. It appears that these ECM antennae, which range from medium size to very small, are intended to jam hostile radar emissions over a defined part of the frequency spectrum.

On the Kresta class, these smaller antennae are supplemented by eight large ECM radomes, four on either side of the central radar tower, mounted one above the other. They are, in spite of their size, not dissimilar in shape to the smaller radomes, but because they project horizontally from the side of the tower — not vertically from side-mounted platforms — they have a spherical appearance when viewed from a distance and have received the NATO designation 'Side Globe'. Side Globe radomes, which are always installed as a set of four pairs, have been fitted to every Soviet cruiser-sized vessel from the Kresta class to *Kirov*. They clearly represent a powerful ECM capability and probably function as broadband jammers, creating a high level of noise throughout the frequency spectrum.

One disadvantage to confront the Soviet Navy in operating against ships of the NATO alliance is the variety of frequencies they would face in attempting to counter radar emissions from aircraft and anti-ship missiles. (This is the one great benefit conferred on NATO by the inability, or unwillingness, of the member nations to standardize equipment.) The Western navies are in a better position to concentrate their own ECM measures against the particular

frequencies that they know to be used by the Soviets. Broad-band jamming on a large scale makes far more sense for the Soviet Navy than it does for NATO.

The massive ECM provision on Soviet surface units from the Kresta class onwards should, therefore, be seen in context; it is not so much a matter of Soviet *superiority* in this particular field as of *necessity*. Greater ECM provision as compared to Western vessels is necessary, both because of the diversity of the threat and because of the different operational context envisaged for the Soviet ships. Soviet cruisers have no combat air patrol to protect them from attack from the air, but rely entirely on their own weapons and sensors for self-defence. Surface-to-air missiles might take their toll of enemy aircraft, but jamming and deception seemed to provide the only effective counter to small air-launched anti-ship missiles in the late 1960s.

An unusual feature of the Side Globe installation on the Kresta class is that the waveguides for the antennae are run down in conduits on the outside of the radar tower. As the latter is not a true 'mack' — the boiler uptakes are led up aft of the main structure — it is somewhat surprising that the waveguides were not located inside the tower mast, which would have given added protection against splinters in the event of a missile attack on the ship. One reason for placing them outside the tower may be that the lower section of the latter is used for accommodation.

The waveguide conduits all converge at the base of the tower mast immediately forward of the boiler uptakes. This would tend to suggest that there is some sort of operations room amidships, probably just below the level of the upper deck. Further evidence for this is provided by the location of the other electronic antennae carried by the ship. Both air search radars, the Scoop Pair missile guidance radar, the Plinth Net target designation radars, the Muff Cob gun fire control radars, and all ECM antennae — everything, in fact, except the Peel Group SAM radars and the Tee Plinth electro-optical sensors — are mounted on the central mast/funnel structure. A centralized operations room directly below the tower itself would, therefore, bring with it improvements in the coordination of search, tracking and counter-measures, and would also minimize horizontal cable runs. The only disadvantage of this central position is the considerable distance from the bridge. Surface combatants of the NATO navies generally have their operations room either immediately behind or directly beneath the bridge, which is usual in the US Navy and European navies respectively.

A Classification Problem

When first completed, the ships of the Kresta class were referred to as Large Anti-Submarine Ships (Bol'shoy Protivolodochny Korabl') by the Soviet Navy. It would, however, be a mistake to take this designation too seriously. The first Krestas were constructed at a time when the Soviet High Command was displaying great concern over the new threat posed by the US Navy's Polaris submarines — thirteen boats were completed in 1964 alone! In addition to this, the absence of any credible open-water ASW capability in the Soviet Navy was causing one of those major tremors that periodically disrupt Soviet long-term construction programmes and lead to a fundamental reorientation of strategies and a discrediting of past policies.

It was at this time that it was decided to convert the Krupny-class Rocket Ships into Large Anti-Submarine Ships. Their

Inboard Profile

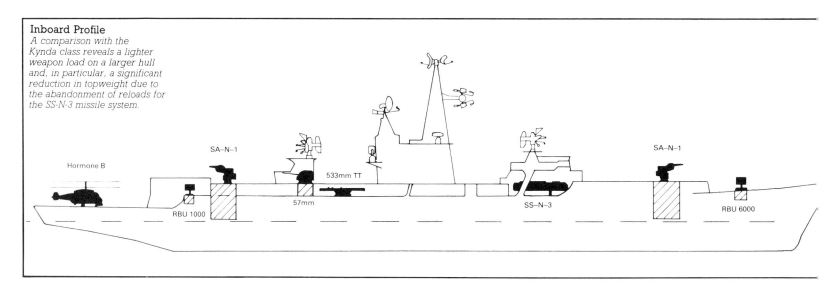

A comparison with the Kynda class reveals a lighter weapon load on a larger hull and, in particular, a significant reduction in topweight due to the abandonment of reloads for the SS-N-3 missile system.

Hormone B

SA-N-1

533mm TT

SA-N-1

RBU 1000

57mm

SS-N-3

RBU 6000

Left: *An aerial view of Vitse Admiral Drozd underway in the Caribbean during the major Soviet Exercise 'Okean 70'. (US Navy)*

Opposite page, top: *A photograph of a Kresta I at anchor in the Mediterranean. The helicopter hangar was the first installed in a Soviet surface combatant. It is exceptionally high by West European standards because of the clearance needed by the Ka-25 Hormone with its superimposed coaxial rotors. (US Navy)*

Opposite page, bottom: *A Kresta I on deployment in 1975. This ship has exchanged her earlier Don-2 and Don-Kay navigation radars for two Palm Frond, carried on the yardarms. Note the broad funnel uptakes with the Big Net air search radar between them. (C-in-C Fleet)*

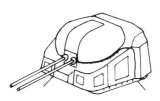

57mm gun (twin)
In service: 1963.
Barrel length: 80cal.
Angle of elevation: +85°
Rate of fire: 120rpm per barrel.
Projectile weight: 2.8kg (6lb).
Muzzle velocity: 1,000m/sec (3,280ft/sec)
Range: 10km (5.4nm) max.; 5–6km (2.7–3.2nm) effective
   AA.
Fire control: Muff Cob.

anti-ship missile launchers and magazines were removed and replaced by a twin SA-N-1 launcher for Goa surface-to-air missiles, three RBU 6000 anti-submarine rocket launchers, and quintuple torpedo tubes. Data for the latter weapons was provided by a new medium-frequency bow sonar. The modernization was so extensive that subsequently they received the new NATO designation 'Kanin'.

The Krestas were the first of the new major combatants to be affected by the Soviet re-evaluation; possibly they had to be reclassified as Large Anti-Submarine Ships in order to justify their continued construction. Moreover, construction of the original Kresta design had been terminated by about 1967 in favour of a modified anti-submarine variant known as the Kresta II. The ASW capability of the Kresta I, however, remained only on a par with the Kashin. No stand-off weapons were fitted, although the FRAS-1 missile was in service aboard the helicopter cruiser *Moskva* before the second Kresta-class vessel was completed. The helicopter carried by the ships is the Hormone B variant, which is designed specifically for missile targeting and lacks the weapons bay and dipping sonar of the Hormone A ASW version, which was put into production simultaneously. The relatively short-ranged rocket launchers and anti-submarine torpedoes are matched by the same short-ranged high frequency sonar fitted in the Kyndas and Kashins.

It is not altogether surprising, therefore, that some ten years later, when large numbers of purpose-built anti-submarine vessels had been completed for the Soviet Navy and the anti-surface role had once again become 'respectable', the Kresta I class was again being referred to as a Rocket Cruiser (Raketny Kreyser). A close analysis of her capabilities suggests that she was indeed designed as such, and that the 'anti-submarine' label was imposed for political rather than military reasons.

The qualities of the Kresta I class are worthy of closer consideration, as they reflect changing Soviet philosophy with regard to anti-ship operations. The Kresta I differs from the Kynda class in general configuration largely for reasons of construction, but there is also a significant shift in the balance of her armament. The anti-submarine capabilities of the Kresta I are only marginally greater than those of the Kynda class. Air defence capabilities, on the other hand, show a two-fold increase, while the number of anti-ship missiles carried is reduced by 75 per cent. Air defence is enhanced by the provision of a second SA-N-1 launcher for Goa missiles, by improvements in search and tracking as a result of the adoption of the Big Net/Head Net C combination and of additional sensors such as Plinth Net, and by the vastly more capable ECM outfit. The SS-N-3 launchers, on the other hand, are paired, not quadruple. They can fire only on forward bearings and have no reload provision. The elimination of reloads is admittedly not too great a loss, as they apparently proved something of a liability on the Kynda class, both in terms of topweight and the difficult nature of the transfer operation. Moreover, the concept of reloads made little sense in the context of the 'one-shot' coordinated strikes against NATO task forces envisaged by the Soviets. The reduced number of ready rounds is also mitigated by the provision of a helicopter for missile targeting. Kyndas operating in the eastern Mediterranean in the late 1960s and early 1970s were compelled to employ destroyers — usually a Kashin — as shadows for the carriers of the US Sixth Fleet, because of the difficulty of mounting continuous aerial surveillance operations so far from Soviet land bases. The reduced number of anti-ship missiles carried by the Kresta class is, therefore, partly compensated by improvements in targeting and, consequently, in accuracy.

Forward Deployment
The changes in the balance of the armament outlined above, taken together with the larger hull and consequent improvements in sea-keeping and endurance, suggest that the Kresta class was intended to operate farther outside Soviet waters than the Kynda. The enhanced air defence capabilities would compensate to some extent for the increased difficulty of providing adequate air cover in areas far from Soviet land bases, and would allow the new cruisers more autonomy in anti-carrier operations. Also, although reconnaissance was still largely in the hands of the lumbering Bear D bombers, there was now an integral over-the-horizon targeting capability in the form of the Hormone B helicopter. Exercise 'Okean 70', involving more than 200 surface ships and submarines, demonstrated the ability of the Soviet Navy to make near-simultaneous coordinated strikes involving aircraft, surface ships and submarines at a number of points in the Atlantic and the Pacific. One of the new cruisers, *Vitse Admiral Drozd*, operated in the western Atlantic out of Cuba in conjunction with Bear Ds operating from Havana. The extreme forward location in which the *Drozd* operated in the course of this exercise would certainly have been untenable in a war situation. Nevertheless, Soviet attempts to confirm the feasibility of long-distance anti-carrier operations coordinated from land-based command positions reveal growing Soviet ambitions in this direction, leading ultimately to the construction of the Kirov-class 'battlecruiser'.

Service Life
The Kresta-class cruisers, completed at the rate of one per year at the Zhdanov Yard (Leningrad), joined the fleet between 1967 and 1970. Three were allocated to the Northern Fleet, and *Vladivostok* went to the Pacific. The significance of these deployments must be seen in context with those of the Kynda class. The Northern Fleet now had three of the most modern Rocket Cruisers, the Pacific Fleet had a single

Kresta-class vessel and two Kyndas, while the remaining pair of Kyndas operated in the Black Sea and Mediterranean.

The deployments give an interesting indication of Soviet anti-carrier priorities, and also of Soviet assessments of the various capabilities of these units. The Northern Fleet required ships with greater range and autonomy than the other fleets, as NATO carriers operating in the southern reaches of the Norwegian Sea could be employed against a variety of Soviet military targets. In the Pacific and the eastern Mediterranean, on the other hand, the range factor was of less significance, as the surface action groups (SAGs) would generally be picking up enemy carriers and amphibious forces only when they entered the areas in which Soviet surface forces were concentrated. Moreover, the two Kyndas operating with the Mediterranean Squadron could more easily be supported by smaller missile-armed units, such as the then-new Nanuchka class, and by destroyers armed with air defence weapons.

It is equally significant that from the beginning of the 1970s no Rocket Cruisers served in the Baltic. NATO strategy did not envisage risking carriers in these constricted and dangerous waters, so there was little point in retaining anti-carrier units in the Baltic Fleet. The latter was now composed almost exclusively of light forces — fast attack craft armed with missiles and torpedoes, and anti-submarine corvettes — and amphibious vessels, backed up by a handful of older Sverdlovs, Kotlins and Skorys and a few modern missile-armed destroyers. The Baltic, because of its traditional naval associations and its concentration of key shipyards and maintenance facilities, also became the major training and work-up area for surface combatants that had recently entered service or had undergone refit. The Northern Fleet, in particular, was largely maintained by the Baltic shipyards. Although this presented a neat and logical solution to a problem that was at once historical and geographical, it also begged the question of how effectively these units could be maintained in the Northern Fleet area in the event of hostilities, when the straits that separate Denmark and Norway would certainly be closed by NATO forces. In 1980, *Sevastopol* joined *Vladivostok* in the Pacific Fleet. The transfer was made possible by the impending entry into service of the large nuclear-powered Rocket Cruiser *Kirov*, which would replace *Sevastopol* in the Northern Fleet.

Vitse Admiral Drozd
One unit of the Kresta I class, *Vitse Admiral Drozd*, underwent from 1973 to 1975 an extensive refit in which pairs of 30mm Gatling guns were installed on either side of the ship immediately forward of the tower mast at the level of the first superstructure deck. Bass Tilt fire control radars replaced the Tee Plinth electro-optical sensors in the bridge wings. The Gatling installation involved an extension of the first superstructure deck on both sides to provide magazines. The installation resembles that of the later Kresta II anti-submarine variant, and provides greater protection against anti-ship missiles.

Other modifications include re-siting the lower Side Globe radomes in order to accommodate the 30mm Gatlings, and the construction of a large two-deck structure between the bridge and the tower mast. The latter modification is not connected with the Gatling installation and probably provides additional crew accommodation (or space for electronics) in what remains a very tight design.

Right: Leningrad *on her way to the amphibious exercise 'Zapad 81' held in the Baltic. Soviet perceptions of the role and capabilities of this class is defined as 'to seek, discover, intercept and destroy enemy submarines'. One method of detection mentioned is the dropping of 'hydro-acoustic buoys', which 'make it possible to determine, from a helicopter, the place and movement of the submarine'. (Novosti)*

Moskva Class

The first of the Moskva-class helicopter cruisers is reported to have been laid down in 1963, with completion in early 1967. This makes *Moskva*, the name-ship, an exact contemporary of the first of the Kresta I-class Rocket Cruisers. She and her sister *Leningrad* were to receive the designation 'Anti-submarine Cruiser' (Protivolodochny Kreyser). Their construction marked an important new development in Soviet maritime strategy.

Polaris

The first American Polaris submarine, *George Washington*, went to sea in 1960. By 1963, nine further Polaris boats had entered service, and a new class comprising no less than 31 units (Lafayette class) was under construction or on order. Polaris effectively changed the nature of the nuclear threat facing the Soviet Union. Defence against the land-based nuclear forces of the United States — the intercontinental

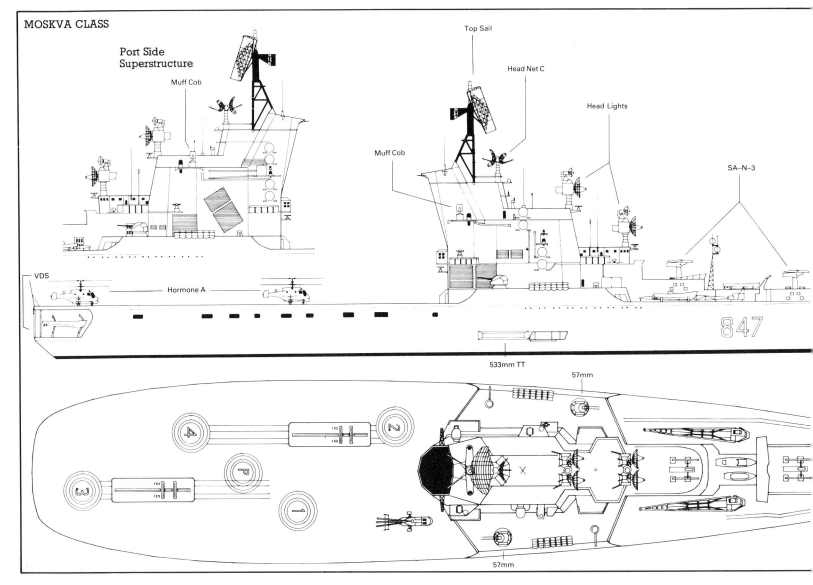

Port Side
Superstructure

Muff Cob

Top Sail

Head Net C

Head Lights

Muff Cob

SA–N–3

VDS

Hormone A

847

533mm TT

57mm

57mm

ballistic missiles (ICBMs) and the long-range strategic bombers — had never been the responsibility of the Soviet Navy. The primary mission of the latter since the late 1950s had been the defence of Soviet territory against the carrier-borne nuclear bombers of the US Navy. The A-3 Skywarrior aboard the US carriers had an operational range of about 2,000km (1,100nm) — over 3,000km (1,600nm) with in-flight refuelling — and was designed to strike at Soviet ports and other military installations with a minimum of warning. The best defence against the Skywarrior was a pre-emptive strike on the mother ship, and this line of thought provided the rationale for the Soviet anti-carrier strategy of the late 1950s, based on long-range submarines armed with torpedoes and cruise missiles, Rocket Cruisers, and land-based naval bombers.

The range of the early Polaris A-1 and A-2 missiles was remarkably similar to that of the Skywarrior, and with the entry into service of the first Polaris submarines the nuclear strike mission of the Skywarrior and of the carriers themselves was down-graded by the US Navy; the A-3 became a tanker aircraft for attack planes with less than half its combat radius, and its successor, the A-5 Vigilante, was used for reconnaissance duties. It was not, therefore, unnatural for the Soviet Navy to assume that the forward-based nuclear strike mission of the Skywarrior was being transferred to the Polaris submarine.

This new development was regarded by the Soviets with considerable alarm, as it effectively short-circuited the extensive anti-carrier system being built up by the Soviet Navy and the Naval Air Force. Moreover, the transfer of the forward-based nuclear threat from the air to beneath the waves placed the threat in an area where the Soviet Navy was particularly badly-equipped to deal with it because of its previous neglect of anti-submarine warfare. This deficiency

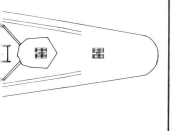

N-1

RBU 6000

MOSKVA CLASS
Soviet designation: Protivolodochny Kreyser (PKR — Anti-Submarine Cruiser)

Construction

Ship	Builder	Laid down	Launched	In service
Moskva	Black Sea Shipyard,	1962	1964	July 1967
Leningrad	Nikolayev	1964	1966	1968

Displacement
Standard: 14,500 tons. Full load: 19,200 tons.

Dimensions
Length: 191m (625ft), overall.
Beam: 34m (112ft), flight deck; 26m (85ft), water-line.
Draught: 7.6m (25ft).

Armament
ASW: 15–18 Ka-25 Hormone A helicopters; 1 twin SUW-N-1 launcher (20? FRAS-1 missiles); 2 12-barrelled RBU 6000 rocket launchers; 2 quintuple banks of 533mm (21in) torpedo tubes (removed late 1970s).
AAW: 2 twin SA-N-3 launchers (44 Goblet missiles); 2 twin 57mm guns.

Electronic equipment
Surveillance radar(s): 1 Top Sail, 1 Head Net C; 3 Don-2.
Fire control radar(s): 2 Head Lights (SA-N-3); 2 Muff Cob (57mm guns).
Sonar(s): 1 keel-mounted low-frequency sonar; 1 medium-frequency VDS.
ECM: 8 Side Globe; 2 Bell Clout, 2 Bell Slam, 2 Bell Tap, 2 other Bell.

Machinery
2-shaft geared steam turbines; 100,000shp = 30 knots maximum.

Complement
850.

Below: Moskva *in 1969. The white-painted Ka-25 helicopter is probably a specially-fitted air/sea rescue model designed to act as plane guard. The variable depth sonar is fully streamed from the stern. (Novosti)*

could be overcome only by instituting an anti-submarine programme on a massive scale.

The Development of Soviet ASW

The new emphasis on anti-submarine warfare demanded fundamental changes, not only in the type of vessel built but also in the orientation of Soviet naval weapons technology. Ships would have to be built to operate at greater distances from their own fleet areas than was previously the case, and would require more capable air defence systems in order to survive enemy air attack. They would also require underwater detection systems and anti-submarine weapons of greater range and sophistication than those fitted to the Rocket Cruisers and their escorts. Short-range anti-submarine defence was no longer adequate. The new ships would have to be able to hunt, detect and eliminate the Polaris boats in order to perform their mission.

Soviet anti-submarine weapons and sensors of the early 1960s were primitive by Western standards. A massive investment programme was therefore required to put the Soviet Navy on the same footing. The Moskvas were the first major units to benefit from this programme.

The Eastern Mediterranean

Both *Moskva* and her sister *Leningrad* were built at the Black Sea Shipyard, Nikolayev. This in itself is significant, as they were the first major modern units to be completed outside the Baltic, where all the Rocket Cruisers had been built. An expanded shipbuilding programme would require a spreading of the shipbuilding load. The Soviets clearly wished to build-up expertise in the Black Sea yards, which had building ways of the requisite dimensions and were already involved in the construction of modern missile destroyers of the Kashin class. But there were other factors. The eastern Mediterranean provided some of the best launch points for Polaris against Soviet military and civilian targets. Access to the eastern Mediterranean from the Polaris base at Rota (Spain) involved the transit of narrow 'choke-points' in the central Mediterranean, which offered possibilities for the monitoring of SSBN movements to and from their patrol stations. The early 1960s saw persistent efforts by the Soviets to secure port facilities in Egypt from President Nasser after the loss of their foothold in Albania in 1961. These facilities were conceded only after the defeat of their Arab client in the 1967 Middle East War, but from that moment on the Soviet Union had access not only to the naval base of Port Said but also to airfields in Egypt and Libya. The massive injections of military aid to rebuild the Egyptian armies after 1967 were an indication of the price the Soviets were prepared to pay in order to secure these concessions.

On completion, both *Moskva* and *Leningrad* joined the Black Sea Fleet, and since that time they have rotated between the Black Sea and the Mediterranean on a regular basis. Although they have on occasions sortied into the North Atlantic for major exercises, these operations have generally been concerned with the evaluation of the Anti-Submarine Cruiser concept in distant waters. As most of the deployments took place in the early 1970s, it seems likely that operational experience was being gained for incorporation in the succeeding Kiev class, which was designed for these waters. There is every indication, therefore, that the Moskva class was built in the Black Sea for a specific anti-SSBN role in the eastern Mediterranean.

Aspects of the Design

In opting for a helicopter cruiser to serve at the centre of an ASW hunting group, the Soviet Navy was following a precedent set by other Mediterranean powers during the 1960s. ASW carriers had been in operation with the Western navies since the 1950s, but those in service in the Atlantic were generally ex-fleet carriers of Second World War vintage. The early 1960s, however, saw the completion of novel purpose-built helicopter cruiser designs for the French and Italian navies. The French *Jeanne d'Arc*, which had her superstructures forward with a long flight deck and hangar aft, could serve either as a commando carrier or as an anti-submarine cruiser, depending on which helicopters were embarked. The Italian Andrea Doria class, which could accommodate four small ASW helicopters in a conventional hangar forming part of the after superstructure, had a much heavier 'cruiser' armament comprising US Terrier missiles supplemented by eight 76mm guns and light anti-submarine homing torpedoes. By the early/mid-1960s the Italians were publishing details of a larger successor, *Vittorio Veneto* which, in addition to the heavy armament of the Dorias, had a large hangar aft for no fewer than nine small helicopters, with a lift at its forward end to connect it to the extensive flight deck.

The design of the Moskva class was, therefore, very much in line with the latest European developments and was undoubtedly influenced by the French and Italian vessels. As befitted an emergent naval super-power, however, the Soviet ships were on an altogether grander scale. The full load displacement of the Moskvas is about 18,000 tons as compared with 12,400 tons for *Jeanne d'Arc* and less than 9,000 tons for *Vittorio Veneto*. Their profile is dominated by a massive central superstructure block, which divides the ships neatly into two distinct sections. The conventional forward section carries the major weapon systems and their magazines; rocket launchers and twin-arm missile launchers rise in steps

THE EASTERN MEDITERRANEAN

YUGOSLAVIA
BULGARIA
Bosphorus

ADRIATIC

ITALY
ALBANIA
TURKEY

GREECE
AEGEAN
SEA

North-east of Cyprus
Anchorage
SYRIA

SICILY
CYPRUS
LEBANON

Hammamet
Anchorage
Kithira
Anchorage
CRETE
East of Crete
Anchorage
EASTERN
MEDITERRANEAN

TUNISIA
ISRAEL

North of Sollum
Anchorage
Alexandria
Port Said

Mersa Matruh

EGYPT

LIBYA

Two of the West European designs that undoubtedly influenced that of Moskva, *the French* Jeanne d'Arc *(left) and the Italian* Vittorio Veneto *(right). Both have a large hangar and flight deck for helicopters aft and conventional 'cruiser' weapons forward.*

towards the central superstructure block, on which the search and fire control radars are mounted, also in steps. The superstructure ends abruptly in a large pyramid-shaped uptake for the steam turbines. The after section is broad and flat, an uninterrupted expanse of flight deck with the hangar beneath. It terminates in an open stern, the flight deck extending over the fantail and supported on stanchions in the manner of Japanese carriers of the Second World War; beneath it two whalers are carried on davits.

Flight Deck and Hangar
The flight deck itself measures approximately 80m by 34m. It overhangs the after part of the hull, the side-plates being gently curved outwards to meet it. Beneath it is a single hangar, which extends from just forward of the fantail right up to the superstructure, at which point it must necessarily be terminated by the funnel uptake trunking and the magazine hoists serving the starboard gun mounting. The extent of the hangar is also indicated by the row of small openings of varying dimensions located in the hull just beneath the flight deck. These may be ventilators for the dispersal of fumes during helicopter refuelling operations. The dimensions of the hangar itself must, therefore, be about 65m by 24m.

The hangar and flight deck are served by two long narrow lifts, each about 16.5m by 4.5m, arranged en echelon with the port-side lift forward of the one to starboard. The lift surfaces are of bare steel, contrasting with the rest of the flight deck which has a brownish cladding. They have fixed rails and attachments to enable the helicopters to be securely locked onto them. At the forward end of the flight deck, inside the massive funnel structure, there is a sizeable covered bay that can be closed off by two hinged folding doors. This was originally thought to be the only lift; this initial analysis has persisted in some sources, despite photographs revealing the existence of the two lifts on the flight deck itself. Close-ups, however, suggest that this is nothing more than a garage for deck tractors; there is a similar garage forward of the flight deck on *Kiev*. The bay appears to be some 15m long and can accommodate two helicopters side by side; this presents a viable alternative to strike-down in the hangar during intensive flying operations.

Initially, four helicopter spots were provided: one fore and aft of each of the lifts. They are marked by two white concentric circles and numbered 1-4; 1 and 3 to starboard, 2 and 4 to port. In about 1970 a central spot was added, with what appears to be the cyrillic letter 'P' (letter 'R' in the Western alphabet) in place of a number. These spots are covered by

Kamov Ka-25 Hormone A
In service: 1966.
Length: 10.4m (34ft), fuselage; 12.3m (40ft), overall (rotors folded).
Rotor diameter: 16m (52ft).
Height: 5.4m (18ft).
Weight: 5,000kg (11,000lb), empty; 7,300kg (16,000lb), fully loaded.
Engines: 2 Glushenkov GTD-3 turboshafts, each 900hp.
Speed (cruising): 190km/hr (120mph) max.
Ceiling: 3,350m (11,000ft).
Operational radius: 300km (160nm).
Armament: 1–2 400mm A/S homing torpedoes, nuclear/ conventional depth charges in internal weapons bay; maximum weapons load, 1,000kg (2,200lb).
Sensors: Chin-mounted surface search radar; dunking sonar, towed MAD, sonobuoys in external boxes (later models).

A Comparison of the Ka-25 Hormone with Anti-Submarine Helicopters in Service with Western Navies

	Ka-25	SH-3 Sea King (USA)	SH-2 Seasprite (USA)	WG-13 Lynx (FR/UK)
In service:	1966	1962	1970	1976
Weight, maximum:	7,300kg (16,000lb)	9,500kg (21,000lb)	6,030kg (13,300lb)	4,760kg (10,500lb)
Crew:	2	4	3	2
Speed (at sea level):	220km/hr (135mph)	265km/hr (165mph)	265km/hr (165mph)	270km/hr (170mph)
Range, maximum:	650km (350nm)	1,000km (540nm)	680km (370nm)	630km (340nm)
Endurance:	1.5–2hrs	4.2hrs	2.5hrs	1.5hrs
Armament:	1–2 400mm torpedoes or depth charges	4 Mk. 46 torpedoes or depth charges	2 Mk. 46 torpedoes or depth charges	4 Sea Skua/ AS-12 ASMs or 2 Mk. 46 torpedoes or 2 depth charges
Sensors:	Search radar; MAD; dunking sonar; sonobuoys	Search radar; MAD; dunking sonar; sonobuoys	Search radar; MAD; sonobuoys	Search radar; sonobuoys

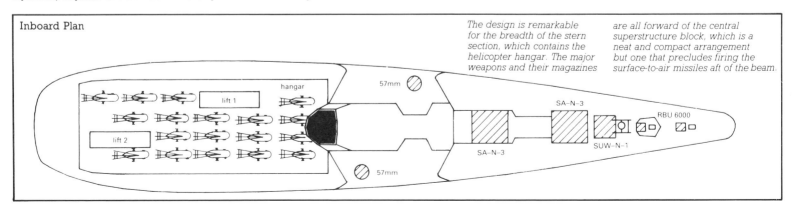

Inboard Plan

The design is remarkable for the breadth of the stern section, which contains the helicopter hangar. The major weapons and their magazines are all forward of the central superstructure block, which is a neat and compact arrangement but one that precludes firing the surface-to-air missiles aft of the beam.

hangar

lift 1

lift 2

57mm

57mm

SA-N-3

SA-N-3

SUW-N-1

RBU 6000

square mesh mats during helicopter operations to prevent the helicopter slipping on the deck.

Just above the bay doors, at the forward end of the flight deck, is a catwalk surmounted by a Don-2 navigation radar. Since two further Don-2 aerials are mounted beneath the two Head Lights radars for navigation purposes, the third radar is presumably provided for control of helicopter operations. Above it is a second catwalk, which leads round to the sides of the superstructure. This carries the flight control cabin, which is located on the centre-line. A less familiar aid to helicopter operations — but one that is standard in the Soviet Navy — is the provision of stanchions forward of the flight deck from which striped wind-socks are suspended.

Helicopters

The Ka-25 Hormone A helicopter was developed via the tiny Ka-15 Hen (in service 1958) and the pre-production Harp (first seen in 1961). It has since become the standard Soviet ship-borne anti-submarine helicopter, while other variants have been developed for missile guidance (see p. 36 for details of the Hormone B on the Kresta I) and amphibious or vertical replenishment (VERTREP) operations. The Ka-25 is intermediate in size between the small manned helicopters carried by West European ASW destroyers and frigates and the much larger Sea King in service on NATO cruisers and carriers. It has good lift characteristics but rather limited endurance, about half that of the Sea King. There is a prominent radome beneath the nose, and the sizeable weapons bay can accommodate torpedoes, depth charges and mines. A dunking sonar and magnetic anomaly detector (MAD) are standard fit. The Ka-25 Hormone is equipped for night and bad-weather operations, but not for all-weather operations.

The timing of production of the Ka-25 suggests that it was designed specifically to operate from the Moskva class. What is perhaps more surprising is that the Moskva class should have been designed specifically to operate the Ka-25. This is indicated by the shape and size of the lifts, which have slots and guide-rails to accommodate the wheels of the Hormone as part of the securing mechanism. When in 1974 *Leningrad* embarked two Mi-8 helicopters for minesweeping operations in the Suez Canal, the helicopters had to remain on deck as, at 18.3m, they were too long for the lifts. The Yak-36 Forger A, with which *Moskva* is reported to have conducted trials in the mid-1970s, must have been a very tight fit indeed, and the Forger B two-seat training version is too long to be struck down. The lifts of Western carriers, on the other hand, are generally designed to accommodate a variety of helicopters and fixed-wing aircraft, a feature that has frequently made possible a change of role. The disadvantage of the Soviet approach is that it imposes restrictions on the dimensions of future aircraft. Significantly, the new Helix helicopter, designed as the Hormone's replacement, is remarkably similar in size and general configuration to its ageing predecessor.

Original estimates of a complement of thirty helicopters were far too high. A close consideration of the hangar floor space available would suggest that a maximum of eighteen Ka-25s could be accommodated, with a more usual peace-time complement of perhaps fifteen (see diagram). Even the figure of eighteen assumes that aircraft maintenance work-shops do not encroach on the main hangar area, but are located forward of the hangar beneath the superstructure.

Anti-Submarine Missiles

Helicopters are not the only anti-submarine systems carried by the Moskva class. Soviet efforts to match Western progress in ASW demanded that stand-off weapons operating in conjunction with medium and low frequency sonars be developed to provide a medium-range all-weather capability against fast-manoeuvring nuclear-powered submarines. The Western nations had followed two lines of development; the first, represented by the American anti-submarine rocket, or ASROC (in service 1961), was that of a simple ballistic rocket carrying either a homing torpedo or a nuclear depth charge; the second, represented by the French Malafon (in service 1962) and the Australian Ikara (in service 1963), was that of a cruise missile with a mid-course guidance capability carrying a homing torpedo.

Interestingly, the Soviets chose to develop both types of missile, and apparently in the same order. The ballistic rocket, the FRAS-1 (Free Rocket Anti-Submarine), made its appearance on *Moskva* in 1967, while the cruise missile, SS-N-14, entered service three years later on the Kresta II class. The launcher for the anti-submarine missiles, designated SUW-N-1, is the first of three twin-arm launchers on *Moskva*'s fore-deck. Two slender missile arms, joined by a single cross-brace, are suspended from the top of a bulky central pillar. Beneath it are two long, narrow reload hatches, each about 4.5m by 1.25m. The shape of the hatches suggests that the missiles are run up at an angle of perhaps 45°, not vertically as one would expect. It seems likely, therefore, that the magazine is positioned immediately aft of the launcher, and that the missiles are stowed horizontally.

The FRAS-1 rocket itself is about 6m in length. It has a somewhat stubby cylindrical body with an ogival nose-cone and small cruciform tail surfaces. It is larger than ASROC and has a range estimated at 30km (16nm), three times that of the American missile. Unlike ASROC, it does not, apparently, have an alternative payload of a homing torpedo, and is restricted to a nuclear warhead. In view of the intended deployment of the Moskvas and their successor *Kiev* against Polaris submarines, a nuclear-tipped missile represents a logical development — a 'last-ditch' weapon to be used in a worst-case scenario. Moreover, the range of the missile — and hence the 'dead time' during which a hostile SSBN could attempt a high-speed escape — is such that only a nuclear warhead could guarantee a kill. The variety of anti-submarine systems available to the Moskva class give them a capability for flexible response. Helicopters and lesser weapons could be used for conventional ASW in conditions short of all-out war.

The near-simultaneous development of a cruise missile for anti-submarine use is significant in that it reveals a Soviet desire to provide a similar flexible response in smaller ASW vessels unable to operate large numbers of helicopters. The cruise missiles could receive sonar updates on a submarine's position in mid-flight, thus a conventional payload comprising a homing torpedo could be carried. It was reported for a number of years that this cruise missile, the SS-N-14, was carried by the Moskvas as an alternative loading to the FRAS-1. No one, however, has explained satisfactorily how a missile with an aeroplane configuration could be fired from a conventional twin-arm launcher. The launcher for the Australian Ikara is in the form of a cradle, while the French Malafon and all other Soviet cruise missiles are launched from ramps (open or enclosed). Such a mix would also greatly

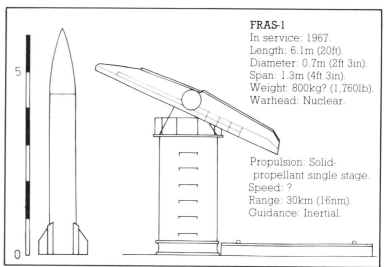

FRAS-1
In service: 1967.
Length: 6.1m (20ft).
Diameter: 0.7m (2ft 3in).
Span: 1.3m (4ft 3in).
Weight: 800kg? (1,760lb).
Warhead: Nuclear.

Propulsion: Solid-propellant single stage.
Speed: ?
Range: 30km (16nm).
Guidance: Inertial.

Opposite page, top: *An aerial view of Leningrad taken during the mine clearance operations in the Suez Canal in 1974. The helicopters at the forward end of the flight deck are mine-sweeping versions of the Mi-8 Hip, which proved too large for the aircraft lifts. (DPR, Navy)*

Opposite page, bottom: *A recent view of Moskva operating Ka-25 Hormones from her four helicopter spots. Note the mesh mats used to prevent the helicopters from slipping on the wet flight deck. (US Navy)*

Above: *The anti-submarine and surface-to-air missiles carried by Moskva. The FRAS-1 missile (left) is simply a ballistic rocket fitted with a nuclear warhead. The SA-N-3 Goblet (right) was the standard Soviet area defence missile until the advent of the vertically-launched SA-N-6 in 1980. (US Navy)*

Right: *A remarkable close-up of the starboard side of the super-structure of Moskva, taken in 1968. The fire control and surveillance radars rise in steps, terminating at the forward end of the massive canted funnel. Note the original triangular balancing vanes on the Top Sail 3-D radar. The Side Globe ECM radomes are grouped together with the smaller Bell Slam and Bell Tap antennae at the forward end of the main superstructure block. The Muff Cob fire control radar and the large Bell Clout ECM radome are on a platform projecting from the side of the funnel. This arrangement is reversed on the port side because of the different positions of the 57mm mounting and the large engine-room vents. (US Navy)*

complicate the magazine layout and handling arrangements. The shape and position of the reload hatches beneath the SUW-N-1 launcher suggest, on the other hand, a relatively simple arrangement comprising one or two horizontal magazine rings holding a total of perhaps twenty missiles, reloads being lifted from the top of the ring (or rings) and run up onto the launcher arms.

Smaller ASW Weapons

As completed, *Moskva* and *Leningrad* had the customary anti-submarine rocket launchers and torpedo tubes in addition to their helicopters and missiles, thereby reinforcing the traditional Soviet emphasis on defence in depth. Two RBU 6000 rocket launchers were sited one above the other close to the bow. The quintuple banks of torpedo tubes were concealed behind sliding hull doors amidships, immediately aft the stowage bay for the accommodation ladders. (The torpedo tubes have since been removed.)

Sonars

The appearance of the Moskva class quickly established the extent of Soviet efforts to develop first-class anti-submarine sensors to compete with those of the West. The keel-mounted sonar installed in the Moskva class is reported to be a large low-frequency panoramic model capable of long-range operation. It is accompanied by a variable depth sonar — the first such installation in a major Soviet warship — the towing apparatus for which is housed in a shallow well in the centre of the stern beneath the overhang of the flight deck. The variable depth sonar operates independently; it is not designed to integrate with the main hull sonar and it uses a higher frequency. Similar VDS installations began to appear on a variety of major Soviet surface warships from about 1971 onwards, being generally paired with a medium- or low-frequency bow sonar. These installations differed from that of the Moskvas in that the towing gear was inside a housing.

The new sonars were an impressive achievement in view of the lack of interest in ASW displayed by the Soviet Navy during the 1950s. Nevertheless, technological backwardness in the form of primitive vacuum tube and hybrid electronics would continue to place the Soviet Union some way behind NATO in anti-submarine detection. The larger sonars that the Soviets were now building would have the range necessary for the detection of fast-moving nuclear submarines, but would have more difficulty than their Western counterparts in picking out a submarine contact from the surrounding underwater noise. By the early 1970s, NATO was making exceptional progress in this area as a result of rapid advances in solid-state technology, in particular the miniaturization of components.

Air Defence

The innovatory nature of the appearance and ASW systems of the Moskva class was matched by a new air defence system, designated SA-N-3. This was thought for some time to be a derivative of the land-based SA-6 Gainful but, although the naval missile is similar in size and performance to Gainful, it has a very different configuration and has an associated set of tracking and guidance radars that bear little resemblance to those of the land-based system. Significantly, the naval missile received the NATO designation 'Goblet' from an early stage, whereas the earlier SA-N-1 Goa took its name from its land-based counterpart, the SA-3.

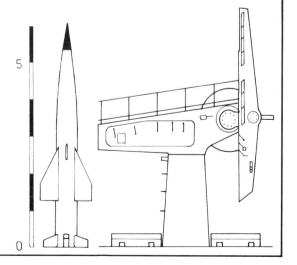

SA-N-3 Goblet
In service: 1967.
Length: 6.1m (20ft).
Diameter: 0.6m (2ft).
Span: 1.4m (4ft 8in).
Weight: 700kg (1,540lb).
Warhead: 60kg (130lb) HE.
Propulsion: Solid-propellant single stage.
Speed: Mach 2.5–3.
Range: 30km (16nm).
Ceiling: 25,000m (80,000ft).
Guidance: Radar/command.
Fire control: Head Lights.

Opposite page, top: *A sailors' concert on an anti-submarine cruiser of the Moskva class provides an excellent close-up of the forward end of the flight deck. Top left is the flying control cabin, with a Don-2 helicopter control radar just visible on the catwalk below. The hinged doors close off the large bay set between the funnel uptakes. (Novosti)*

Opposite page, centre: *An aerial view of the midships section of Moskva taken as she lay at anchor off Kithira Island, Greece in 1974. The platform fitted for trials of the Yak-36 Forger is still in place. Forward of it are two Ka-25 Hormone helicopters with their rotors folded. (US Navy)*

Right: *Leningrad on her way to the Baltic for the Warsaw Pact amphibious exercise 'Zapad 81'. The doors of the bay at the forward end of the flight deck are folded back, revealing the tail of a Hormone helicopter. The large 'fish' and towing mechanism of the variable depth sonar is sunk into the centre of the stern. Note also the newly-modified balancing vanes of the Top Sail 3-D surveillance radar. (C-in-C Fleet)*

Goblet missiles are launched from two twin-arm launchers located between the SUW-N-1 anti-submarine missile launcher and the bridge. The launchers are superimposed to eliminate mutual interference on forward arcs, and the deckhouses on which they are located have prominent blast deflectors at their forward end. The SA-N-3 launcher has a more conventional configuration than that associated with the SA-N-1 system. It is not stabilized, indicating that earlier problems with missile acquisition in Soviet naval SAM systems had been overcome by this time. In the installation aboard the Moskva class and the later Kresta IIs, there are four small square hatches beneath the launcher, which can reload while trained to port and starboard (and possibly fore and aft). This layout may have been adopted to ensure a rapid rate of fire but, as later vessels equipped with the SA-N-3 system have only two hatches beneath their launchers, it may equally well indicate that two variants of the missile are carried, fitted with different warheads. The absence of a true surface-to-surface missile in such large and valuable ships as these would tend to support the possibility that the Goblet missile can be employed in the anti-ship role, in addition to its primary air defence role.

The Goblet missile itself is quite unlike any previous Soviet land-based or naval surface-to-air missile in appearance. About 6m in length, it has a somewhat stubby cylindrical body with a tapered nose, and large cropped-delta cruciform wings with smaller cruciform tail surfaces indexed in line. The wings may fold for stowage in order to maximize magazine capacity, which is estimated at 22 missiles per launcher. Unlike Goa, it is a single-stage missile without a booster. Nevertheless, its range, estimated at some 30km (16nm), indicates significant advances in propulsion technology since the development of the earlier missile.

Command guidance was retained for the SA-N-3 system. NATO navies — and the US Navy in particular — were beginning to opt in favour of semi-active guidance for their own SAMs in order to improve accuracy at longer ranges. The Soviet Navy was faced not with the threat of long-range land-based bombers armed with stand-off weapons, but by relatively small carrier-based strike aircraft equipped with short-range anti-ship missiles. The range at which aircraft needed to be engaged was of less significance than the ability to handle a number of targets quickly and efficiently, hence the Soviet preference for double-ended SAM systems employing twin launchers.

The Head Lights radar, which provides guidance for the Goblet missile, is if anything even bulkier and heavier than its predecessor, Peel Group. It comprises two pairs of dishes of open mesh construction disposed symmetrically about a central pillar. The lower two dishes, which have a diameter of about 3.8m, are mounted on the front face of large boxes, which presumably house their electronics. The upper pair, with a diameter of about 1.8m, are mounted atop the boxes on a small lattice assembly. Between the lower two dishes is a small solid dish, which is thought to provide the command link. The whole assembly is supported from the top of the mounting pillar on a yoke structure of tubular steel construction, and can be rotated and elevated. Stabilization seems likely in view of the prominent balancing vanes that project from the rear of the electronics boxes.

It is thought that the larger dishes track the target while the smaller ones, which can be elevated independently, track the missiles. The small, solid dish transmits command signals to the missiles for course correction. Since two dishes are provided for tracking, it may be that two targets can be engaged simultaneously provided that they are reasonably close together in azimuth and elevation. A standard firing policy of two missiles per target is a more likely possibility.

The other major element of the SA-N-3 system is the massive Top Sail radar, the first Soviet three-dimensional radar to employ frequency scanning techniques. The rapid and efficient engagement of air targets within the effective range of the Goblet missile requires a tracking radar capable of giving range, bearing and height data on a number of targets at several times that distance. The development of Top Sail, with a maximum range approaching 550km (300nm), provided the Soviets for the first time with such a capability, although the shorter-range 'V'-beam Head Net C was retained in Moskva for back-up. The Top Sail antenna, which is carried at the summit of Moskva's central superstructure block immediately forward of the funnel uptakes, has a curved lattice reflector in the shape of a diamond with cropped corners, illuminated by a waveguide wrapped around a tube running parallel to its axis and supported top and bottom. The heavy framework of the main antenna body, which is tilted at about 20° to the vertical, is balanced by prominent V-shaped vanes. Originally, these were of a rigid, triangular configuration, but in 1973–74 the Top Sail antenna on Moskva was modified to resemble the installation on the Kresta II and Kara classes, with smaller vanes suspended from a lattice structure of tubular steel. This modification was a useful recognition feature until it was extended to her sister Leningrad in the late 1970s.

The electronic apparatus associated with the SA-N-3 system contributes in no small way to the impressive appearance of Moskva and her successors. The radars, however, are extraordinarily heavy and bulky, and reveal deficiencies in Soviet antenna design and metal technology. They represent a brute force approach to technological progress, whereby improved performance takes precedence over considerations such as the excessive topweight involved in shipboard installation. In a ship the size of Moskva, such considerations are clearly of less importance, but when the Soviets decided to extend installation of the SA-N-3 system to smaller units, considerable ingenuity was required in order to obviate stability problems. The system has not, in effect, been fitted to any vessel below cruiser size, and lesser ships have until recently had to be content with short-range point-defence systems. The Kanin-class destroyer conversions were receiving the earlier SA-N-1 Goa air defence systems as late as the mid-1970s, when Goa was already approaching obsolescence. The Soviet Navy, therefore, never possessed a series of area defence missiles designed to match vessels of different sizes comparable to the US Navy's '3-T' series (Talos/ Terrier/Tartar).

Other Air Defence Systems

Apart from her main air defence system, Moskva has an identical AAW (anti-aircraft warfare) outfit to that of the Kresta I class. On either side of the main superstructure block, twin 57mm AA guns are disposed en echelon to give coverage over a full 360°. The Muff Cob fire control directors are located on platforms projecting from the sides of the superstructure and the funnel respectively. Tee Plinth electro-optical sensors are mounted at a lower level.

The ECM outfit comprises eight of the large Side Globe

antennae plus four per side of the customary Bell series. These are disposed asymmetrically on either side of the main superstructure block. The asymmetry appears to be an indirect consequence of the layout of the machinery which, as on the Kresta I class, is concentrated amidships beneath and immediately forward of the massive central funnel. The exact location of the boiler rooms is indicated by the provision of prominent air vents on either side of the superstructure. The vents to starboard are at the after end of the superstructure, whereas the port-side vents are more central, suggesting that the boiler rooms themselves are en echelon. The port-side Side Globe ECM antennae are mounted in pairs one above the other on the side of the funnel. Those to starboard are mounted centrally on the superstructure. The two smaller jammers of the Bell series are mounted with the Side Globe antennae on either side. The larger Bell Clout radome is mounted close to the Muff Cob director.

The waveguides for these antennae are in conduits on the outside of the superstructure, as in the Kresta I class, and lead to a central point high in the main superstructure block, which presumably houses a centralized operations room. The latter is not particularly close to the navigation bridge, which is at a lower level forward of the main block and, incidentally, is poorly situated in terms of all-round vision.

Replenishment

The Soviet predilection for using lengths of 'railway track' for handling missiles, torpedoes, smaller munitions and stores during replenishment is well illustrated on *Moskva*. Lengths of track run from either side of the foremost RBU 6000 rocket launcher up to the main superstructure block, and are served by two large cranes which are generally stowed flat on the deck. The track runs outside every weapon system on the forecastle, with 'branch lines' leading off towards the strike-down hatches of the SUW-N-1 launcher.

Besides stores and munitions, the cranes handle the ship's boats, which are located between the two SA-N-3 launchers and on the upper deck forward of the superstructure.

Service History

Below: The British Type 21 frigate HMS Avenger *shadowing* Leningrad *in the English Channel, 10 August 1981. (C-in-C Fleet)*

The deployment cycle of *Moskva* and her sister *Leningrad* since completion has generally involved service with the Mediterranean Squadron for one ship while the other undergoes refit and work-up in the Black Sea. Deployments are frequently made in company with other anti-submarine units. It is thought that it was originally intended that the ships should also deploy to the Indian Ocean via the Suez Canal, but this option was no longer available after the closure of the latter in 1967, and Soviet naval forces in the Indian Ocean had to be supported from the Pacific Fleet, Interestingly, it was *Leningrad* that headed the Soviet force deployed in 1974 to assist in the mine-clearance operations in the Suez Canal. She embarked two specially-configured Mi-8 Hip helicopters for this mission. Useful experience in helicopter minesweeping techniques was gained, but it is reported that the Soviet part in the operation was not a conspicuous success.

At about the same time that *Leningrad* deployed to the Suez Canal, *Moskva*, stationed in the Black Sea, was fitted with a raised platform about 20m square and 1m high with ramps leading up to it. The platform was installed at the after end of the flight deck and covered the after lift. Photographs were released showing Ka-25 helicopters operating from this platform, but these probably amounted to little more than an attempt to obscure its true purpose, which was to enable trials of the Yak-36 Forger VTOL aircraft to be conducted prior to its operational debut on *Kiev*. The need for the construction of such a platform probably stems from the unsuitability of *Moskva*'s flight deck cladding for fixed-wing VTOL operations, given the intense heat generated by the two vertical lift engines of the Yak-36. *Kiev*'s own flight deck is covered with special heat-resistant tiles and it seems likely that the platform observed on *Moskva* had a similar covering.

The possibility that one or both of these ships might be penned in the Black Sea at the outbreak of hostilities has not been lost on the Soviets. *Moskva* is reported to have conducted helicopter operations in support of amphibious landings in the Black Sea shortly after completion. In the summer of 1981, *Leningrad* took part in a similar, but larger-scale exercise in the Baltic in company with *Kiev* and other major units.

Both ships have remained largely unmodified since their completion, except for the removal of their torpedo tubes during the late 1970s. It would not have been an easy matter to update their air complement in view of the problems noted regarding the restricted size of the lifts and the unsuitability of the ships for fixed-wing VTOL operations. The Ka-25 Hormone will presumably be replaced eventually by the new Helix, but the operational capability of the Moskvas must be expected to remain largely unaltered.

Kresta II Class

In 1970 a new variant of the Kresta class emerged when *Kronshtadt* deployed to the Mediterranean for her shakedown cruise. In dimensions and general layout she was virtually identical to the four ships of the Kresta I group, but she carried a completely new generation of weapon systems. (A comparison of the Kresta I and Kynda classes, which carried exactly the same weapon systems on a very different basic design, reveals a development process which is exactly the reverse.)

Air Defence

The most obvious external difference between the two sub-groups of the Kresta class is the replacement of the SA-N-1 area defence system, together with its associated tracking and guidance radars, by the SA-N-3 system that had first seen service three years earlier on *Moskva*. Adoption of the latter involved accommodating the massive Top Sail three-dimensional air surveillance radar on a relatively small hull, which necessitated major structural alterations amidships. The broad pyramidal tower that dominates the appearance of the Kresta I class was scaled down in an effort to keep top-weight within limits; the main body of the tower is only two-thirds the height of that on the Kresta I, and terminates in a tall central pillar on which the Top Sail antenna is mounted. In contrast, the funnel uptakes had to be heightened in order to keep the corrosive gases clear of the after Head Lights missile guidance radar, which is some two metres taller than the Peel Group radar it replaced. The shape of the funnel was changed and, above it, the Head Net C general-purpose air search antenna was fitted in place of Big Net. Otherwise, the various components of the SA-N-1 system were replaced on a one-for-one basis; SA-N-3 launchers were fitted fore and aft in place of the SA-N-1 launchers, and Head Lights guidance radars replaced Peel Group atop the smaller radar towers on either side of the central tower/funnel structure. The smaller weapons of the Kresta I class — the twin 57mm gun mountings, the RBU 6000 and RBU 1000 rocket launchers and the quintuple torpedo tubes — remained unchanged.

Point Defence

The appearance of *Kronshtadt* marked the operational debut of the Soviet Navy's first point defence system for use against air-launched anti-ship missiles. Previously, Soviet anti-missile defence had relied exclusively on electronic counter-measures, and ECM provision on the Kresta II was little different to that of the previous group of ships. Additional back-up was now provided in the form of small automatic quick-firing guns, mounted in pairs on either side of the ship between the main radar tower and the bridge structure. The deckhouse on which the guns are located, and which also contains their magazines, is built out to the sides of the ship at the level of the first superstructure deck. Close-up photo-

graphs of the mounting quickly revealed that there were six rotating barrels, operating on the Gatling principle and capable of a very rapid rate of fire. The exact calibre of the weapon was in dispute for a number of years, being variously quoted as 23mm or 30mm. The latter figure now appears to be generally accepted.

The development of such a weapon years ahead of any Western equivalent — the US Navy's Phalanx entered service only at the beginning of the 1980s — is a remarkable achievement. One of the essential features of the American weapon, however, is its on-mounted radar, which ensures a quick reaction time and a high degree of accuracy. Not only is the equivalent Soviet fire control radar mounted separately, thereby increasing problems of coordination, but there appear to have been problems with its production; *Kronshtadt* and some of her successors of the Kresta II and Kara classes were completed with only the gun mountings in place. When fitted, the Bass Tilt radars occupied the after end of the bridge wings, the Tee Plinth electro-optical sensors being displaced to a position abreast the pedestal of the Head Lights guidance radar. Bass Tilt can be distinguished from the smaller Drum Tilt, which is employed as a fire control radar for the similar-sized twin 30mm mountings on smaller craft, by the prominent triangular base from which, presumably, it takes its NATO codename.

ASW Capabilities

There are three other important features that distinguish the Kresta II from its near-sister, the Kresta I. The first is the

Opposite page: Admiral Isachenkov, *photographed by an RAF Nimrod north of the Hebrides in 1977. (MoD)*

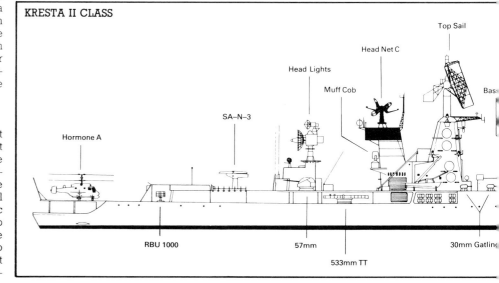

KRESTA II CLASS

Top Sail · Head Net C · Head Lights · Muff Cob · Bass[s] · Hormone A · SA-N-3 · RBU 1000 · 57mm · 533mm TT · 30mm Gatling

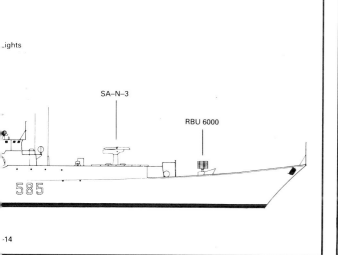

Lights

SA–N–3

RBU 6000

585

-14

30mm Gatling gun (6-barrelled)
In service: 1970.
Barrel length: 60cal?
Angle of elevation: +85°.
Rate of fire: 3,000rpm (mount).
Projectile weight: ?
Muzzle velocity: 1,000m/sec (3,280ft/sec).
Range: 3km (1.6nm) max.; 2.5km (1.3nm)
 effective AA.
Fire control: Bass Tilt/remote visual.

KRESTA II CLASS
Soviet designation: Bol'shoy Protivolodochny Korabl' (BPK — Large Anti-Submarine Ship)

Construction

Ship	Builder	Laid down	Launched	In service
Kronshtadt	Zhdanov Yard,	1966	1967	1970
Admiral Isakov	Leningrad (all units)	1967	1968	1971
Admiral Nakhimov		1968	1969	1972
Admiral Makarov		1969	1970	1973
Marshal Voroshilov		1970	1971	1973
Admiral Oktyabrsky		1970	1972	1974
Admiral Isachenkov		1971	1973	1975
Marshal Timoshenko		1972	1974	1976
Vasily Chapaev		1973	1975	1977
Admiral Yumashev		1974	1976	1978

Displacement
Standard: 6,000 tons. Full load: 7,600 tons.

Dimensions
Length: 158m (518ft), overall.
Beam: 17m (56ft).
Draught: 5.5m (18ft).

Armament
ASW: 2 quadruple SS-N-14 launchers (8 missiles); 1 Ka-25 Hormone A helicopter; 2 12-barrelled RBU 6000 rocket launchers; 2 6-barrelled RBU 1000 rocket launchers; 2 quintuple banks of 533mm (21in) torpedo tubes.
AAW: 2 twin SA-N-3 launchers (44 Goblet missiles); 2 twin 57mm guns; 4 30mm Gatlings.

Electronic equipment
Surveillance radar(s): 1 Top Sail, 1 Head Net C; 2 Don-Kay, 1 Don-2.
Fire control radar(s): 2 Head Lights (SS-N-14, SA-N-3); 2 Muff Cob (57mm guns); 2 Bass Tilt (30mm Gatlings).
Sonar(s): 1 bow-mounted medium-frequency sonar.
ECM: 8 Side Globe; 1 Bell Clout, 2 Bell Slam, 2 Bell Tap, 2 other Bell.

Machinery
2-shaft geared steam turbines; 100,000shp = 34 knots maximum.

Complement
380.

shape of the bow, which has considerable overhang. The position of the anchors, which are well forward, suggests the presence of a bow sonar dome — probably the first example of its type in the Soviet Navy. The size and power of the model fitted in the Kresta II class is almost certainly greater than that installed in earlier ships of cruiser size, but is probably not as great as that of the sonar fitted in *Moskva*, which is keel-mounted. It operates probably at medium frequency, and may be the same model fitted in the Kanin conversion.

The second distinguishing feature is the helicopter, which is not the Hormone B version carried by the Kresta I class for missile targeting, but the Hormone A model employed by *Moskva* for anti-submarine warfare. Handling arrangements for the helicopter have also been modified, presumably because of problems experienced in operating the helicopter from the low quarterdeck of the Kresta I in rough weather. The forecastle deck has been extended aft beyond the hangar, and leads directly onto a helicopter platform supported on stanchions above the stern.

The new arrangement placed the hangar on the wrong level, and considerable ingenuity had to be applied in order to compensate for this. It was impossible to raise the hangar itself, as it would then have obstructed the after arcs of the SA-N-3 missile launcher, so the hangar is fitted with a hinged roof that is raised as the helicopter is wheeled in. The hangar floor serves as a lift between forecastle- and quarter-deck level. This is a complex and somewhat clumsy arrangement that places an additional maintenance load on the ship's complement and is vulnerable to breakdown. It is, however, a solution to the problem of providing a 'double-ended' ship of limited displacement with a helicopter hangar without exceeding topweight limits. Similar arrangements were adopted for the succeeding Kara class, even though the latter was a larger type of a new design. On the after end of the second Head Lights radar tower is a second Don-Kay navigation radar. This installation follows a precedent set by *Moskva* in providing a radar specifically for helicopter control.

SS-N-10 and SS-N-14

The third modification was perhaps the most significant of all. It was to become the centre of a lengthy controversy in which Western assessments, not only of the primary purpose of the new ships but of the overall direction of Soviet maritime strategy, were in the balance. The modification itself was simple enough. In place of the large twin launchers for SS-N-3 missiles fitted abreast the bridge structure of the Kresta I, there were shorter four-tube 'box' launchers. The missile housed in these launchers was assumed, not unnaturally, to have the same anti-ship function as the larger SS-N-3, and was duly christened SS-N-10. The length of the tubes suggested a missile of longer range than the 20–35km (11–19nm) SS-N-2 Styx fitted to fast patrol craft, but of shorter range than the intermediate SS-N-9, which had just appeared on the Nanuchka-class missile boat. The SS-N-10 was credited with a range of 55km (30nm) and was described as a 'horizon-range' missile.

These first assumptions were not unreasonable, as the anti-ship mission of the Soviet Navy was well established in Western perceptions, and it seemed inconceivable that the Soviets would build a ship of this size and importance equipped only with defensive weapons. The regression from the 300km (170nm) SS-N-3 to a relatively short-ranged missile could be explained by the difficulty of providing targeting

and mid-course correction beyond the horizon in areas where the Soviet Navy could not rely on land-based aircraft, combined with the abandonment of an on-board missile guidance helicopter in favour of an ASW model.

Initial doubts about the primary role of the SS-N-10 missile began to surface in the mid-1970s, when some commentators suggested that the SS-N-10 might be designed for use against submarines. This view was not fully accepted in Western defence publications until 1977, although there is evidence to suggest that the American intelligence services were in no hurry to dispel the illusion that the SS-N-10 was an anti-ship missile for domestic reasons; notably, the need to secure Congress funding for the US Navy's own anti-ship missiles under development at that time. The new NATO number assigned to the Soviet missile, SS-N-14, suggests that the reassessment of the missile's primary role took place in about 1973, at roughly the same time as the trials of the SS-N-13

SS-N-14
In service: 1970.
Length: 6.5m (21ft).
Diameter: ?
Span: ?
Weight: 2,500kg (5,500lb).
Payload: Anti-submarine homing torpedo.
Propulsion: Liquid-fuel motor.
Speed: Mach 0.95.
Range: 45km (25nm).
Guidance: Radar/command.
Fire control: Eye Bowl or Head Lights.

Left: *A bow view of* Admiral Oktyabrsky, *taken in the English Channel in 1974. The quadruple SS-N-14 launchers are particularly prominent beneath the cantilevered bridge wings. Just aft of the SA-N-3 launcher, protected by blast shields, are twin-barrelled chaff launchers for anti-missile defence. (Skyfotos)*
Opposite page: *This stern view, taken during Exercise 'Ocean Safari' in 1975, shows clearly the complex helicopter handling arrangements of the Kresta II. The twin doors of the hangar are open and the hinged roof section is raised ready to receive the Hormone, which is positioned in the centre of the landing pad. In the centre of the hangar is the lift, which lowers to become the hangar floor. Note the mesh mat covering the landing pad to prevent slippage. (HMS* Ark Royal*)*

Helicopter Hangar Arrangement

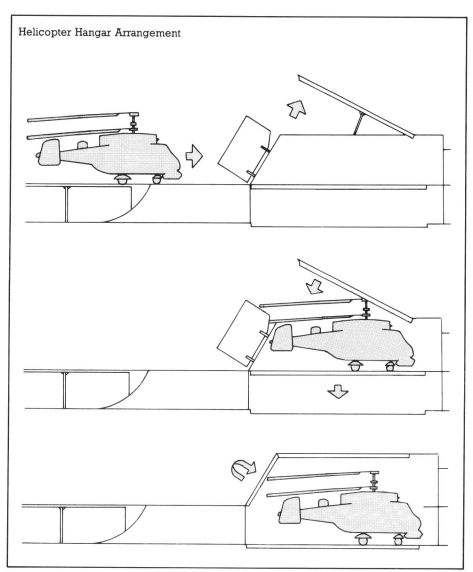

Inboard Profile

Although the weapons themselves have changed, they occupy identical positions to those of the Kresta I class. There is little difference, therefore, in their overall distribution and the hull-volume they occupy.

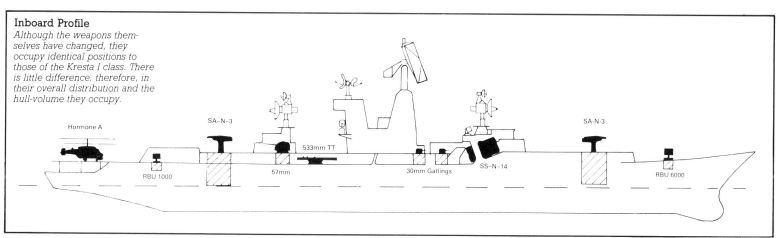

Hormone A   SA–N–3   533mm TT   SA–N–3

RBU 1000   57mm   30mm Gatlings   SS–N–14   RBU 6000

terminally-guided SLBM and the entry into service of the Soviet equivalent of SUBROC, the SS-N-15.

Although no photograph of the SS-N-14 has been released, it is reported to have a conventional cruise missile configuration and a payload that comprises a homing torpedo. It is not unlike the Australian Ikara in conception, although it is much larger. The range of the missile is reported to be 45km (25nm), although this may well be an over-estimate in view of the weight of the homing-torpedo payload. It can be guided in flight, like Ikara, with the necessary missile tracking and command link being provided by one of the Head Lights guidance radars.

The range of the SS-N-14 is such that serious questions have been asked about Soviet ability to provide target data for its effective employment. The range of the US Navy's ASROC missile (11km/6nm) was deliberately tailored to match the maximum detection range of the contemporary SQS-23 sonar. The latter was a low-frequency model, so it is unlikely that the medium-frequency Soviet sonar fitted in the Kresta II class could match it in long-range performance. The effectiveness of the SS-N-14 out to its maximum range appears to depend on sources of targeting data other than the ship's own sonar. In the case of the Kresta II, this presumably means the use of its own helicopter, which is fitted with a dipping sonar and could supply position updates on a hostile submarine contact even during the flight of the missile. We must also not discount the possibility of combined operations in which the Kresta II would work in conjunction with other surface units, submarines and possibly ASW aircraft, such as the Il-38 May. The long range of the SS-N-14 would enable the ship to respond to data inputs passed on by ships spread over a broad area.

The First Purpose-Built BPK

In spite of the similarity in layout of the Kresta I and Kresta II designs, the weapons systems installed in the latter provided evidence of a dramatic shift away from the anti-ship mission in the direction of anti-submarine warfare. If we set aside the air defence systems, which simply enable both types to operate outside Soviet sea-space in the face of NATO carrier aircraft, the essential change in the main armament of the ships from long-range anti-ship missiles backed up by a missile guidance helicopter to anti-submarine missiles backed up by an anti-submarine helicopter becomes more readily apparent. The Kresta I was conceived as a Rocket Cruiser — and has now reverted to that classification — while the Kresta II variant was designed from the start as a Large Anti-Submarine Ship and, subsequently, became the standard Soviet ocean-going ASW type outside the Mediterranean.

Service Life

The ten ships of the Kresta II class were constructed at the same Zhdanov Yard (Leningrad) that had built the Kresta I. Built at the rate of roughly one unit per year from the mid-sixties onward, the Kresta II continued in production well after the introduction of the Kara class, the first of which entered service in 1973. The length of the production run, which contrasts with the truncated construction programmes of the Kresta I and Kynda classes, is indicative both of a successful design and of a more settled Soviet maritime strategy.

The only significant modification to the more recent ships is a progressive build-up of the superstructure between the bridge and the central tower, suggesting that internal volume has proved inadequate to accommodate new electronics. Significantly, the size of the bridge structure of the Kara class is twice that of the Kresta II, and the increased displacement of the Kara indicates an acceptance of the need for hull growth to eliminate some of the constraints of the original Kresta design.

Seven ships of the Kresta II class have operated with the Northern Fleet, with regular deployments to the Mediterranean and more occasional deployments to the Caribbean and West Africa. These units usually return to the Baltic for refit and work-up. The ships generally operate singly or in pairs; a Kresta II has frequently accompanied the anti-submarine cruiser *Kiev* on deployments and during exercises. Two ships, *Marshal Voroshilov* and *Admiral Oktyabrsky*, were transferred to the Pacific Fleet in 1974, and were the only major anti-submarine units to serve with that fleet until 1978, when they were joined by a third ship, *Vasily Chapaev*. The deployment of most of the earlier units of the class to the Northern Fleet is significant in that they provided the major anti-submarine capability in that area in the period before *Kiev* entered service. The intention appears to have been to provide ASW hunting groups in both the Norwegian Sea and the Mediterranean, based on air-capable Anti-Submarine Cruisers (PKR) and Large Anti-Submarine Ships (BPK) armed with anti-submarine missiles and a single helicopter. The construction of the cruisers *Moskva* and

Below left: *A close-up of the after Head Lights missile guidance radar of a Kresta II. Beneath it is the port-side twin 57mm/80cal mounting. To the left of the picture are the quintuple torpedo tubes, decorated with red stars. The starboard Muff Cob fire control radar is located on the platform projecting from the after end of the funnel; the on-mounted TV sensor is clearly visible. (US Navy)*

Opposite page, left: *These two photographs, both taken in the Northern Fleet area in July 1980, are interesting not so much for their portrayal of Soviet sailors in action and at leisure as for the close-ups they provide of the electronics of a Kresta II class ship. There is a Bell Clout ECM jammer on a platform projecting from the face of the central tower mast. Smaller Bell Slam and Bell Tap antennae are located on platforms between the large Side Globe radomes on the sides of the mast; a further pair of ECM radomes is sited atop the yardarms. There is a Don-2 navigation radar just below the Top Sail 3-D radar, in addition to a Don-Kay surface search/navigation radar above the bridge. (TASS)*

Opposite page, top right: *A Large Anti-Submarine Ship of the Kresta II class shadows NATO warships during Exercise 'Ocean Safari' in 1975. The photograph was taken by a helicopter from HMS Ark Royal. (HMS Ark Royal)*

Opposite page, centre right: *Admiral Isachenkov in heavy seas. Both Head Lights missile guidance radars are facing aft. (C-in-C Fleet)*

Opposite page, bottom right: *Admiral Makarov shadows HMS Ark Royal during the NATO exercise 'Northern Wedding' in 1978. Ships of the Kresta II class are frequently seen during exercises in northern waters. (HMS Ark Royal)*

Leningrad for the Black Sea/Mediterranean operational theatre preceded that of the Kara-class Large Anti-Submarine Ships in the Mediterranean, but the ASW programme designed to provide ships for the Northern Fleet operated in reverse, with the BPKs of the Kresta II class preceding the air-capable *Kiev*. The reason for this may lie in the desire to provide an air intercept/limited strike capability based on VTOL fixed-wing aircraft in the Northern Fleet area, thereby delaying the entry into service of the air-capable components of that fleet.

The allocation of the most modern Soviet ASW units to the Northern and Black Sea Fleets was a logical step, as all 31 of the latest Polaris submarines of the US Navy's Lafayette class were operating in the North Atlantic and the Mediterranean and, in particular, from the forward bases at Rota (Spain) and Holy Loch (UK). The land-locked Baltic, as we have seen, was by this time only a maintenance and training area for the larger units. The Pacific Fleet faced only a handful of older Polaris boats fitted with missiles incapable of hitting the European area of the Soviet Union, and operated under the threat of limited access to the seas outside the ring of the Japanese Islands. Both were starved of modern ocean-going ASW ships during this period. Only when Soviet ASW strategy changed from an offensive stance, directed against Polaris, to a defensive stance, in support of the Soviet Navy's own missile submarines, did attention turn once again towards the Pacific.

Krivak Class

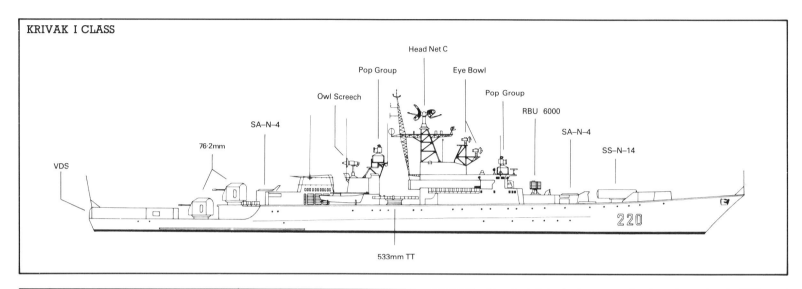

KRIVAK I CLASS

Labels: VDS · 76·2mm · SA–N–4 · Owl Screech · Pop Group · Head Net C · Eye Bowl · Pop Group · RBU 6000 · SA–N–4 · SS–N–14 · 533mm TT · 220

KRIVAK I CLASS
Soviet designation: Storozhevoy Korabl' (SKR — Patrol Ship)

Construction

Ship	Builder	In service
Bditelny, Bodry, Druzhny, Leningradsky Komsomolets, Letuchy	Zhdanov Yard, Leningrad;	1971 onwards
Pylky, Razumny, Razyashchy, Retivy, Silny, Storozhevoy, Svirepy, Zadorny, Zharky	Kaliningrad Shipyard	
Bezzavetny, Buzukoriznenny, Deyatelny, Doblestny, Dostoyny, Ladny	Kamysch-Burun Shipyard, Kerch	1972 onwards

Displacement
Standard: 3,300 tons. Full load: 3,575 tons.

Dimensions
Length: 125m (410ft), overall.
Beam: 14.3m (47ft).
Draught: 5m (16ft).

Armament
ASW: 1 quadruple SS-N-14 launcher (4 missiles); 2 12-barrelled RBU 6000 rocket launchers; 2 quadruple banks of 533mm (21in) torpedo tubes.
AAW: 2 twin SA-N-4 launchers (36 Gecko missiles); 2 twin 76.2mm (3in) guns.

Electronic equipment
Surveillance radar(s): 1 Head Net C;
1 Don-2, 1 Don-Kay or Palm Frond.
Fire control radar(s): 2 Eye Bowl (SS-N-14); 2 Pop Group (SA-N-4); 1 Owl Screech (76.2mm guns).
Sonar(s): 1 bow-mounted medium-frequency sonar; 1 medium-frequency VDS.
ECM: 2 Bell Shroud, 2 Bell Squat.

Machinery
2-shaft COGAG; 2 gas-turbines, each 25,000bhp; 50,000bhp = 31 knots maximum.

Complement
200.

The first Krivak-class vessel entered service in 1971, and series production followed. The Krivak, like the Kresta II, was designated Large Anti-Submarine Ship by the Soviet Navy. It shared with the Kresta II a number of common weapons and sensors. Neat, compact and well-armed for its size, the Krivak created an immediate impression among Western commentators, who made favourable comparisons with contemporary NATO frigates and destroyers. The role and capability of the new ships was, of course, obfuscated for some years by the mistaken belief that the missile tubes on the forecastle housed the SS-N-10 missile, not the SS-N-14 (see p. 58). This meant that the Krivaks were being assessed by Western commentators for a role they were not designed to perform (that of a 'fighting destroyer' with a primary armament of anti-ship missiles), not in terms of the ASW capability that constituted their true purpose. Western perceptions of Soviet maritime strategy, and the part these ships were intended to play in it, were therefore distorted.

Opposite page, top left: *A Patrol Ship of the Krivak I class photographed from a helicopter belonging to HMS Ark Royal. On either side of the large 'flat four' launcher for SS-N-14 anti-submarine missiles are prominent steel circles set into the deck, the purpose of which is unclear. It is conceivable that they are associated with some mechanism that facilitates reloading of the missile tubes while alongside. (C-in-C Fleet)*
Opposite page, top right: *This stern shot of a Krivak I gives an excellent view of the 'T'-shaped housing for the variable depth sonar, and of the mine-rails that run on either side of the quarterdeck. (C-in-C Fleet)*
Opposite page, bottom: *A Krivak I of the Northern Fleet. (US Navy)*

Aspects of the Design

The Krivak class has the typical full waterplane common to all modern Soviet warships. There is a long forecastle deck breaking onto a low quarterdeck and considerable sheer forward. A prominent knuckle runs from just forward of the bridge structure to the break in the forecastle. It is a hull better designed for sea-keeping than that of the larger Kashin class, and with significantly higher freeboard amidships.

The superstructure is altogether more modern in appearance than that of earlier Soviet vessels. The bridge structure comprises a single rectangular block two decks high surmounted by a broad, angular lattice mast carrying a Head Net C 3-D radar and platforms for fire control radars. Farther aft there is a lower structure incorporating the intakes and uptakes for the propulsion machinery, and additional platforms for electronics. The low, squat funnel, which is positioned well aft, contributes to the sleek, racy appearance of the Krivak class. In the manner of the Kynda class, which favoured the same block superstructures, the weapons are carried on the centre-line fore and aft, with the sole exception of the torpedo tubes, which are amidships.

Gas Turbines

The shape and position of the single funnel are clear evidence of gas-turbine propulsion. All delicate electronic apparatus is placed forward of the funnel in order to prevent damage from the hot exhaust gases, and there are prominent intakes at the funnel base. Since the Kashin class, gas-turbine installations had become common in Soviet warships below cruiser size. Successive anti-submarine corvettes — the Poti, Petya, Mirka and Grisha classes — had been so fitted. The adoption of gas-turbines rather than conventional steam plant to power the Krivaks therefore came as no surprise.

Although there is universal agreement about the nature of the Krivak's propulsion system, there is less agreement as to its size and power. Some early estimates automatically assumed a four-turbine COGAG installation of similar size to that of the Kashin class, with a total installed horsepower of as much as 112,000bhp and a maximum speed of 38 knots. More moderate assessments were of four gas-turbines with a total horsepower of 70–80,000bhp, while the lowest estimates — generally from American sources — were of only 50,000bhp. It will be readily apparent that such diverse assessments have considerable implications for the machinery layout of the Krivak class and the space occupied not only by the turbines themselves but also by the additional intake and uptake trunking required by a multi-turbine installation.

One frequently neglected factor regarding gas-turbine propulsion plants is that the turbines available are of fixed size and power. Any installation based on a particular turbine must have a total combined horsepower which is a multiple of the power of that turbine. Given the conventional two-shaft arrangement common to virtually all vessels of cruiser/destroyer size, this means multiplying by a factor of two or four in order to simplify gearing. The other relevant factor is that where navies have entered into the development of gas-turbines for naval use, the expense involved in adapting industrial or aero-derived turbines to a maritime environment has been so great that development has been concentrated on relatively few models. Throughout the 1970s, for example, there were only three models available in the West: the British TM 3B Olympus (25–28,000bhp) and the American LM 2500 (20–25,000bhp), the only prime movers in production;

and the small British RM 1A Tyne (4–5,000bhp), which was employed only as a cruise turbine to improve fuel economy. It seems unlikely that Soviet practice would be significantly different in this respect. There is every indication, in fact, that Soviet gas-turbine ships of the 1960s were powered by one of two basic models. The corvettes of the Poti, Petya and Mirka classes employ gas-turbines rated at about 12,000bhp for boost in combination with diesels in a CODAG or CODOG arrangement; while the COGAG plant of the Kashin class is based on a larger model of about 24,000bhp. It is important to note that both models are used as prime movers, the one being developed for large ocean-going vessels and the other for coastal and zonal defence vessels in the 500–1,100 ton range. There is no evidence that small gas-turbines similar in conception to the British Tyne were developed for cruise operations, the latter function being performed by diesels in the corvettes built for the Soviet Navy.

Two years after the completion of the first Krivak in 1971, another all-gas-turbine major surface warship entered service. It was generally agreed that the much larger Kara class was powered by four large turbines for a total combined horsepower of about 120,000bhp, as this sort of figure would be necessary in order to give a speed in excess of 30 knots. However, the near-simultaneous construction of the Krivak and Kara classes — the first ships of each class were probably laid down in the same year — suggests that both are powered by the same turbine. It has been reported that this is an aero-derived turbine developed from the NK-144 engine associated with the Tupolev Tu-144 supersonic transport. This would seem an entirely logical development as it establishes an exact parallel with the contemporary British marine Olympus turbine, which was derived from the aero-engine used to power the Tu-144's commercial rival, Concorde. It would also place the Soviet marine gas-turbine somewhere in the 25–30,000bhp bracket.

This last figure fits comfortably into Western assessments of the nature and power of the propulsion machinery of the Kara class, but must cast doubts on some of the higher figures given for the total power output of the Krivak class. A four-turbine plant based on the NK-144 is clearly out of the question for the Krivak class, which are relatively small ships — their overall length is some 20m less than that of the Kashin class, and 50m less than the Karas — and do not appear to have intakes and uptakes of sufficient capacity to accommodate such a plant. The early figure of 112,000bhp, moreover, appears to have been based on assumptions of a maximum speed approaching 40 knots, and there is no evidence to

suggest that the Krivaks have achieved much more than 30 knots in service. Erroneous assessments of the nature of the ship's primary armament may be partly to blame, as high speed would be a more important tactical requirement in a ship designed for hit-and-run attacks on shipping than it would in an anti-submarine unit armed with stand-off weapons.

There is every reason to believe that the Krivak is powered by only two major turbines for a total of 50–60,000bhp, adequate for a maximum speed of 30–32 knots. The only issue that remains to be discussed is the theory that the Krivak class also employs two smaller turbines in a COGOG arrangement for operations at cruise speed, in the manner of contemporary British and Dutch ships. While this proposition is more acceptable in terms of available hull-space and cannot be discounted, it must be stated that such an arrangement would constitute a break with previous Soviet practice, in which gas-turbines have been used only as prime movers with the cruise role being performed by diesels. Moreover, one of the most important aspects of the Krivak design is its simplicity, a simplicity that was intended to make mass-production possible in shipyards with no experience of building large, complex warships. The weapons, as we shall see, are largely modular installations that make few demands on internal volume; many can simply be bolted onto the deck. It seems unlikely, therefore, that a complex four-turbine plant comprising two large and two small gas-turbines (even if a suitable small turbine were available) would have been a more attractive proposition than a simple two-turbine installation. The consequences in terms of fuel consumption and reduced endurance are, of course, less favourable, but the gains in terms of economy of hull-space and of simplified construction and maintenance are considerable.

ASW Weapons

The main armament of the Krivak class comprises four SS-N-14 anti-submarine stand-off missiles, which are housed in a distinctive 'flat four' launcher close to the bow. The launcher, unlike the fixed box launchers fitted beneath the bridge wings of the larger BPKs, can be trained and elevated. No reloads are carried. Missile tracking and mid-course guidance is provided by a pair of Eye Bowl radars mounted one above the other on platforms immediately in front of the foremast. Eye Bowl is not dissimilar in configuration to the upper (small) dishes of the Head Lights radar, which performs the same SS-N-14 guidance function on ships equipped with the SA-N-3 air defence system.

The relatively small size of the Krivak class precluded the embarkation of a Hormone ASW helicopter, but the customary anti-submarine rocket launchers and long 533mm torpedo tubes are fitted. Two twelve-barrelled RBU 6000 rocket launchers are mounted forward of the bridge. The torpedo tubes are mounted in two quadruple banks amidships, between the bridge structure and the funnel. Shortly after completion, the Krivaks had an angled bulwark constructed immediately forward of the torpedo tubes, presumably to prevent damage in heavy seas.

The exaggerated overhang of the bow is indicative of a bow sonar, which is almost certainly the same medium-frequency model fitted in the Kresta II and Kanin classes. In addition, there is a variable depth sonar, the towing mechanism being located inside a prominent housing on the quarterdeck. The variable depth sonar is probably the same model that was experimentally mounted in the Moskva-class Anti-Submarine Cruisers, although in the Moskvas the VDS was in an open installation. It operates almost certainly independently of the bow sonar, neither sharing the same electronics nor combining with it for underwater search, but it does provide the redundancy favoured by the Soviet Navy.

The same problem of utilizing the full 45km (25nm) range of the SS-N-14 missile noted in connection with the Kresta II is applicable to the Krivak. Indeed, the problem is made more acute by the absence of an on-board system, such as a helicopter, capable of making detections outside the range of the ship's own sonar. The Krivak class is heavily dependent on detection from another source — another surface ship or submarine, for example — in order to exploit the full range of its anti-submarine missiles. Tactics such as these fit logically into the Soviet pattern of combined operations, although the communications problem — especially in ships with austere tactical data systems and lacking computerized data links — must put a question mark against the effectiveness of such operations in a wartime situation. Combined operations would compensate in part for the small number of missiles carried by the Krivak class in comparison with NATO anti-submarine vessels. Ships of the US Navy generally carry a minimum of eight ASROC, while European frigates equipped with Malafon and Ikara generally carry twelve to thirteen missiles.

Air Defence

Unlike the larger BPKs, the Krivaks are not fitted with an area defence missile system. The small size of the ships and their construction in smaller, less capable shipyards precluded such an installation. Instead, the Krivak class has the short-range SA-N-4 missile, which had entered service on the Grisha-class corvette in 1969.

The SA-N-4 is a low-altitude system thought to have been developed in parallel with the land-based SA-8 Gecko, a theory supported by the close physical resemblance of the Pop Group guidance radar to the Land Roll radar that guides the SA-8. This suggests that the naval version of the missile has a maximum range of about 8–10km (5–6nm) with an effective ceiling of perhaps half that figure. It may have a limited capability against anti-ship missiles, although this is by no means certain. The SA-N-4 missile has a slim cylindrical body with a tapered nose cone and small cruciform tail surfaces. It is not unlike the land-based Gecko in appear-

ance, except that the latter also has small canards close to the nose.

The twin-arm 'pop-up' launcher is housed in a distinctive circular bin; few photographs have been released showing it in the raised position. The launcher is unusual in that the central pillar, which is broader at its top than at its base, protrudes above the launcher arms. The top of the pillar, which is of hexagonal cross-section, forms the centre of the bin lid when in the lowered position. Twin hinged flaps then close around it to provide a weatherproof cover. The arms of the launcher must be horizontal in order for the flaps to close.

The bin containing the launcher is cylindrical and can be fully sunk into the ship's hull or a deckhouse. On the Krivak class, one SA-N-4 bin is installed forward between the SS-N-14 launcher and the RBU 6000 anti-submarine rocket launchers, and the other is located immediately aft the funnel, giving full 360° coverage. The internal arrangement of the missile bin remains a matter for conjecture. It appears to be installed as a complete module with both the pop-up launcher and the magazine housed within the bin itself. A comparison of the various installations of the missile suggests that the bin itself is some 5m high and about 3.7m in diameter, and that the launcher, when lowered, occupies the central part of it. The missiles, which have a length of about 3.2m, are probably stowed vertically in concentric rings around the base of the launcher. They could then be loaded onto the launcher arms only when the hinged flaps of the bin lid are open and the launcher arms are in the vertical position. It is estimated that each launcher has a magazine capacity of eighteen missiles.

The rationale for a 'pop-up' launcher appears to be that the entire launcher/magazine complex is weatherproof, thereby improving reliability in what is essentially a quick-reaction system. The intricate reloading arrangements, however, must result in a system that is rather less robust and more vulnerable to breakdown than the multiple box launchers adopted for equivalent NATO systems such as Sea Sparrow and Sea Wolf.

The Pop Group guidance radar, mounted on a platform immediately forward of the funnel on the Krivaks, comprises a box housing, about 2.2m square, with a variety of radar antennae mounted on top and on its front face. The box itself presumably contains the transmitter/receiver units, power supplies and the turning mechanism. The whole assembly can be rotated in azimuth. On top of the box is a small elliptical reflector of open mesh construction which provides

Opposite page, top: The Palm Frond surface search/navigation radar just below the Head Net C air search radar of the Deyatelny, and a Don-2 navigation radar above the bridge. The ECM equipment is not yet fitted. (TASS)
Opposite page, bottom: *A Krivak I of the Northern Fleet, photographed from the Large Anti-Submarine Ship Marshal Timoshenko of the Kresta II class in 1980. The Krivaks would support the larger BPKs in anti-submarine operations in the event of a conflict. (TASS)*

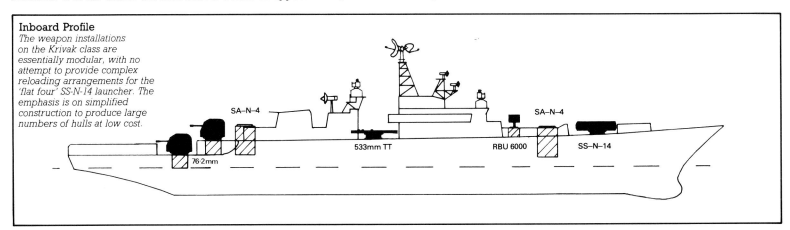

Inboard Profile
The weapon installations on the Krivak class are essentially modular, with no attempt to provide complex reloading arrangements for the 'flat four' SS-N-14 launcher. The emphasis is on simplified construction to produce large numbers of hulls at low cost.

SA–N–4

SA–N–4

76·2mm

533mm TT

RBU 6000

SS–N–14

target search. The reflector is about two metres across and can rotate independently of the main assembly. On the front face of the box are two circular arrays, the larger of which is for target tracking and the smaller for command guidance of the missiles. Between the two circular arrays there appears to be an electro-optical or low light television (LLTV) device to provide an additional missile channel and for back-up in hostile ECM conditions.

The SA-N-4 system has become the most widely deployed of all Soviet surface-to-air systems since its first appearance in 1969. It is used as the principal anti-air weapon on all major vessels in the Patrol Ship (SKR) and Anti-Submarine Corvette (MPK) categories, and as a secondary air defence system on the larger ocean-going units of the Kara, Kiev and Kirov classes.

76.2mm and 100mm

The air defence capabilities of the Krivak class are completed by medium-calibre gun mountings, mounted one above the other at the after end of the ship. As designed, the ships carried the twin 76.2mm mounting, which had become standard in Soviet warships since its first appearance on the Kynda class. Fire control was provided by an Owl Screech director located just below the Pop Group guidance radar on a platform forward of the funnel. In 1976, however, a new Krivak variant appeared in which the twin 76.2mm mountings were replaced by single 100mm mountings of a new design, and the Owl Screech fire control director was replaced by a new model, designated 'Kite Screech'. The new variant, which received the NATO designation 'Krivak II', appears to have superseded the original design at the Kaliningrad Yard in the Baltic.

The additional weight involved in fitting the larger 100mm gun mounting appears to have resulted in a shifting of the centre of longitudinal buoyancy. All modified ships appear trimmed by the stern. This does not seem to have affected ship-handling, and the Krivak II continues in production up to the time of writing.

Super-Destroyer or Utility Frigate?

The high praise that the Krivak design attracted in the West in the early 1970s has, in the past few years, been modified to a more realistic assessment. Once it was realized that the ships had a primary anti-submarine mission rather than one directed against other surface ships, the Krivak class was

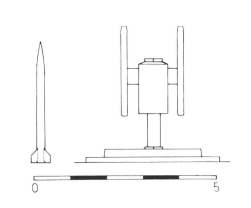

SA-N-4 Gecko
In service: 1969.
Length: 3.2m (10ft).
Diameter: 0.22m (0ft 9in).
Span: 0.55m (1ft 10in).
Weight: 190kg (420lb).
Warhead: ? kg HE.
Propulsion: Solid-propellant single stage.
Speed: Mach 2.
Range: 9km (5nm).
Guidance: Radar/command.
Fire control: Pop Group.

100mm gun (single)
In service: 1976.
Barrel length: 60cal.
Angle of elevation: +80°.
Rate of fire: 40rpm.
Projectile weight: 16kg (35lb).
Muzzle velocity: 850m/sec (2,790ft/sec).
Range: 15km (8nm) max.; 8km (4.3nm) effective AA.
Fire control: Kite Screech/local.

regarded with a more critical eye. This progressive downgrading of the Krivaks, which is particularly noticeable in the lowly position they occupy now in reference books, was reinforced when in about 1978 they were reclassified by the Soviet Navy as Patrol Ships (Storozhevoi Korabl' or SKR) — a category generally associated with the Soviet concept of zonal defence rather than with ocean-going construction.

Whilst an armament of four anti-ship missiles seemed formidable in the early 1970s, when few NATO surface ships in the destroyer and frigate categories carried any anti-ship weapons other than guns, an armament of four anti-submarine missiles was rather less formidable, not only because anti-submarine missiles presented no threat to NATO sea control in the North Atlantic and Mediterranean, but also because the average NATO ASW frigate carried two or three times this number. Moreover, the Krivak class carried no anti-submarine helicopter, whereas helicopters were now standard on modern NATO vessels.

ASW systems apart, the Krivak class carries only air defence weapons, and these, too, are of limited capability compared with those fitted in the larger BPKs of the Kresta II and Kara classes. The contemporary Kara vessel has a powerful SA-N-3 area defence system, SA-N-4 systems similar to those of the Krivak class for back-up at closer ranges and for low-level interception, and 30mm Gatlings for point defence against missile attack. A further important factor is the disparity in ECM; the powerful batteries of electronic jamming and deception devices found on the Kresta II and Kara classes are virtually non-existent in the Krivak class.

The design of the Krivak is very austere indeed in comparison with the larger, more complex Soviet missile cruisers. It fits exactly into a traditional pattern of Soviet ship-design, in which small numbers of first-line units are complemented by second-rate or 'utility' ships which, by virtue of being easy to build, are affordable in greater numbers. While the construction of Kresta II and Kara-class cruisers proceeded simultaneously at the rate of one per year in the major warship-building yards, the smaller, less specialized shipyards of Kaliningrad in the Baltic and Kamysch-Burun in the Black Sea were between them turning out three Krivaks per year — yet all three classes shared the same BPK (Large Anti-Submarine Ship) designation until 1978.

The deployment of the Krivak class is of interest in that it sheds considerable light on Soviet perceptions of the general missions of these ships. Whereas the larger BPKs have been deployed primarily to the Northern and Black Sea Fleets, most of the early units of the Krivak class were allocated to the Baltic Fleet. Figures given in *Jane's Fighting Ships, 1975–76* suggested that, of the first nine Krivaks completed, six were serving in the Baltic. Figures from the same source five years later credited the Baltic Fleet with no less than ten out of a total of 28 Krivaks completed up to that time. Even allowing for the possibility that these figures include ships recently completed in Baltic yards and still working up, they are still significant in that they present a deployment picture that is very different from that of the BPKs of the Kresta II and Kara classes.

There appear to be two basic missions envisaged for the Krivak class. The first is that of providing a major ASW capability in the Baltic. The Krivak class has become the largest Soviet surface unit to be deployed in any numbers in that sea, and appears to have the primary mission of long-

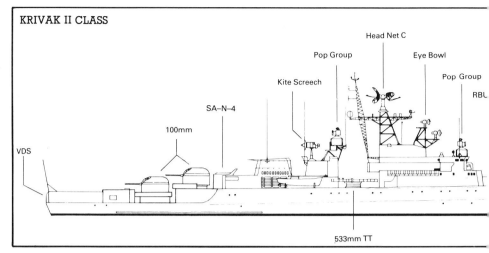

KRIVAK II CLASS

KRIVAK II CLASS
Soviet designation: as Krivak I

Construction

Ship	Builder	In service
Bessmenny, Gordelivy, Gromky, Grozyashchy, Neukrotimy, Pytlivy, Razitelny, Revnostny, Rezky, Rezvy, Ryany	Kaliningrad Yard (all units)	1976 onwards

Displacement
as Krivak I.

Dimensions
as Krivak I.

Armament
ASW: as Krivak I.
AAW: 2 twin SA-N-4 launchers (36 Gecko missiles); 2 single 100mm (3.9in) guns.

Electronic equipment
Surveillance radar(s): as Krivak I.

Fire control radar(s): 2 Eye Bowl (SS-N-14); 2 Pop Group (SA-N-4); 1 Kite Screech (100mm guns).
Sonar(s): as Krivak I.
ECM: as Krivak I.

Machinery
as Krivak I.

Complement
as Krivak I.

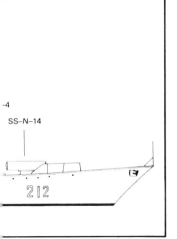

Above: *The Patrol Ship
Bessmenny of the Krivak II
group, which can be
distinguished from the Krivak I
design by the single 100mm
guns fitted aft in place of the
standard twin 76.2mm. The
quarterdeck mounting has been
located on a new deckhouse,
possibly to clear the enlarged
housing for the variable depth
sonar, but it is equally possible
that the hull-depth was inadequate to accommodate the
100mm magazine. (C-in-C Fleet)*

range escort to the large amphibious forces that have been built up there over the past fifteen years. These amphibious forces would be employed in offensive operations against Denmark (and, in particular, against the offshore islands that guard the only exit from the Baltic) in the event of hostilities between NATO and the Warsaw Pact. The lack of a major air defence system is of less consequence in these waters, as massive air cover could be provided for such an operation from air bases in East Germany, Poland and the Soviet Union. A low-level quick-reaction system such as the SA-N-4 is, on the other hand, particularly well suited to Baltic operations. Hence its installation on large numbers of minor combatants serving with the Baltic Fleet.

The Soviet decision to 'up' the calibre of the guns of the Krivak class from 76.2mm to 100mm may well have been influenced by a move on the part of NATO Baltic powers, such as Denmark and the Federal Republic of Germany, who, during the 1970s, started to build large numbers of fast patrol craft armed with the OTO-Melara 76mm gun — surface craft that would pose the greatest threat to a Soviet amphibious assault. The 100mm is far superior to the twin 76.2mm as a dual-purpose weapon, although it is almost certainly less effective in the anti-aircraft role. By choosing the 100mm the Soviet Navy would appear to have deliberately sacrificed some anti-aircraft capability in favour of providing an effective counter to the NATO fast attack craft, together with an improved fire support capability.

Another feature that makes the Krivak class particularly well suited to Baltic operations is the provision of mine rails aft for an estimated total of 28 mines. The mine rails run on either side of the variable depth sonar housing and terminate in small indentations in the stern.

The other mission originally envisaged for the Krivak class appears to have been that of supplementing the larger BPKs which, because of their complexity, could be built only in relatively small numbers. The compatibility of key weapons and sensors, such as the SS-N-14 missile and the hull and variable depth sonars with the ASW outfits of the Kresta II and Kara classes, provides a useful back-up to the larger ships, in terms both of total sonar coverage and of the availability of additional anti-submarine missiles that can then be fired from a number of separate platforms covering a broad surface area. Krivaks would be expected to operate in ASW hunting groups comprising, perhaps, three or four units, of which at least one would be a larger BPK or an Anti-Submarine Cruiser of the Moskva or Kiev class. Group operations would also mean the availability of helicopters from the larger units for the localization of submarine contacts, thereby compen-sating for the lack of an on-board helicopter on the Krivak class.

The Krivak as an SKR

The redesignation of the Krivak class from BPK (Large Anti-Submarine Ship) to SKR (Storozhevoi Korabl'/Patrol Ship) by the Soviet Navy in 1978 has been seen by some Western commentators as a 'demotion' of the ships, as recognition by the Soviet Navy that the Krivak was previously over-rated and has somehow proved inadequate for the tasks it was designed to perform. All other evidence points to the contrary; the people who over-rated the capabilities of the Krivak class were the Western commentators themselves. Evidence suggests that the Soviet Navy never regarded the Krivak as anything other than a second rate design (in the

strictly naval sense of that term), which would deliver large numbers of hulls for open-ocean ASW in a short period of time. The Krivak class has continued in production longer than either the Kresta II or the Kara classes, disproving the theory that it failed in some way to live up to Soviet expecta-tions. Even the suspected low endurance of the Krivaks does not appear to have given the Soviet Navy undue concern, as deployments to the Caribbean, West Africa and the Indian Ocean were common during the 1970s.

We must, therefore, regard the change in classification from BPK to SKR in the same light as previous changes, which have tended to reflect not so much a reassessment of the status and general capabilities of the ship itself, as of the mission that the ship is required to perform. It is not to the Krivak design itself that we should look in order to find a reason for the reclassification, but to changes in Soviet maritime strategy during the early and mid-1970s.

The key change in that strategy has been a shift in emphasis away from offensive open-ocean hunting operations directed against NATO Polaris submarines in favour of supportive ASW operations to secure the safe transit of Soviet submarines of all categories through NATO anti-submarine barriers and in defence of the new Soviet SSBN bastions. (This change in strategy is discussed more fully in the chapter on the Kiev class on p. 94.) The support of Soviet submarines in distant and hostile areas, such as the Greenland/Iceland/United Kingdom (GIUK) Gap, would require larger, more powerful ships than the Krivak class, fitted with more capable air defence systems (including ECM) and larger reserves of missiles; ships with better sea-keeping and endurance. However, the new requirement to secure the total exclusion of NATO forces from vast areas of sea in the Arctic and the north-west Pacific, thereby provid-ing a safe haven for Soviet SSBN operations, necessitated an expansion of Soviet zonal defence concepts beyond the traditional operating areas. The answer to the problem appears to have been an equally dramatic expansion of the SKR (variously translated as Guard Ship or Patrol Ship) category, which sucked in not only the Krivaks but the MPKs (Small Anti-Submarine Ships) of the Petya and Mirka classes and the ageing T-53 ocean minesweepers. Since the threat to these bastions would come from NATO attack submarines rather than surface forces, the Krivaks were particularly well-equipped for this mission. Holding a line drawn from the North Cape to Spitzbergen in the Arctic, and patrolling the gaps between the islands in the Kurile chain in the north-west Pacific, the Krivaks would work in conjunction with shore-based ASW aircraft, such as the Il-38 May, possibly with assistance from data produced by underwater hydrophones. The Petya and Mirka-class corvettes would then become the 'second rate' ships of the type, providing back-up on the perimeters and performing more general ASW and patrol duties within the exclusion zones.

This reorientation of Soviet naval missions must, of course, remain a matter for conjecture, but it would be consistent with what we have come to expect of the Soviet Navy as a result of the frequent changes of course over the past three decades. It is of interest to note that since the mid-1970s, when the change in direction was already well-established, no less than ten Krivaks, including several of the latest Krivak IIs, have transferred to the Pacific, whereas prior to that time few of their modern anti-submarine units were operational with that fleet.

Kara Class

During 1971 and 1972 reports filtered through to the Western press of the construction of two new major classes of warship at Nikolayev in the Black Sea. One of these, building at the 61 Kommuna Shipyard, which had previously built Kashin-class destroyers, was a 9,000-ton cruiser. The other, under construction at the nearby Black Sea Shipyard, which had built the Moskva class, was a carrier-type vessel. The first of the new cruisers, which received the NATO designation 'Kara', was to be named *Nikolayev*, after the shipbuilding town where she was built. The carrier was, of course, *Kiev*. The construction of two such important classes in the Black Sea served to underline a significant shift away from the traditional Baltic yards as builders of major units.

The Kara and the Kresta II

When *Nikolayev* was finally completed in 1973, her derivation from the Kresta II class was readily apparent. Although a larger ship, there are many important similarities. The hull-form follows the pattern established by the Kresta, with low freeboard amidships and prominent flare and sheer forward. The exaggerated overhang of the bow is indicative of a large, bow-mounted sonar. The transom stern with helicopter pad supported on stanchions above it is identical to that of the Kresta II. Twin launchers for SA-N-3 missiles are mounted on deckhouses fore and aft, the second superfiring above a sunken hangar for a Hormone A ASW helicopter. Quadruple box launchers for the SS-N-14 anti-submarine missiles are fitted at a fixed angle beneath the cantilevered bridge wings. They are complemented by two RBU 6000 and two RBU 1000 anti-submarine rocket launchers, disposed in identical fashion to those of the Kresta II class, and by quintuple banks of long 533mm torpedo tubes. The centre part of the Karas is dominated by a massive tower surmounted by a Top Sail three-dimensional search and tracking radar and carrying the customary ECM arrays, of which the most prominent are the eight Side Globe antennae disposed in pairs on either side. The funnel uptakes are immediately aft the tower mast, as on the Kresta class. The Head Lights guidance radars for the SA-N-3 area defence system are carried above the bridge and on a small tower aft respectively. Not only are the major weapons and sensors of the Kara and the Kresta II classes identical, therefore, but they are disposed in similar fashion on a similar hull with a similar complex system of deckhouses and towers.

In no way can the Kara class be regarded as superseding the Kresta II in the same way that the Kresta II superseded the Kresta I and the Kresta I superseded the Kynda. Whereas these other classes were constructed in strict sequence, the Kresta II continued in parallel production to the Kara at the Zhdanov Shipyard in the Baltic at an identical rate of construction — one ship per year. Parallel construction of two different designs with similar missions and capabilities marked a significant break with previous Soviet practice. The conventional cruisers and destroyers of the Sverdlov, Skory and Kotlin types, which constituted the first Soviet post-war ship-building programme, were built in all four fleet areas. This pattern changed in the late 1950s, when construction of the new generation of missile cruisers was concentrated in the Baltic. When the more numerous Kashin class went into production, construction was once more shared between the Zhdanov Yard in the Baltic and Nikolayev in the Black Sea. The Krestas, like the Kyndas, were built in the Baltic, but the

Below: *An early view of* Nikolayev *in the Mediterranean. The large number of side-mounted weapons systems is a distinguishing feature of the class. Note the empty platform for the Bass Tilt fire control radar at the after end of the funnel. (C-in-C Fleet)*

Above: *An overhead view of* Nikolayev, *taken in the Black Sea in 1977. (Novosti)*

until 1970, the basic Kresta design was much older than that. The adaptation of the Kresta class to carry the new generation of anti-submarine and air defence weapons was not, as we have seen, without problems. The ships are very short on internal volume, as is evidenced by the progressive build-up of superstructure between the bridge and the central radar tower. Many of these problems appear to have been resolved in the Kara design, which is an altogether bigger ship with a much-enlarged bridge structure.

The apparent difference in build between the Kara and the Kresta II is the result of the insertion of an extra 15m section between the bridge and the central radar tower; this has the effect of shifting the 'balance' of the Kara aft. The distance from the central radar tower to the stern is virtually the same in both classes, as is the distance between the bow and the forward end of the bridge, and — significantly — it is the fore and after sections where weapon and sensor layout is identical. The modifications to the Kresta weapon/sensor fit that were made in the Kara design are, therefore, closely related to the insertion of the extra section amidships.

There appear to have been two reasons for this extra section. The first was the need to increase internal volume in order to improve habitability — an important consideration in Mediterranean deployments — and to provide for better command and control spaces; the second factor was the adoption of gas-turbine propulsion, which necessitated some revision of the sensor layout.

Propulsion

The Kara was the first Soviet warship of cruiser size to adopt gas-turbines for its main propulsion machinery. All previous cruisers, including the Kynda, Kresta and Moskva classes, had steam propulsion. The four large gas-turbines of the Kashin class produced a total horsepower that was not far short of that of the steam plant adopted for the cruisers (96,000bhp as opposed to an estimated 100,000shp in the steam-powered ships), but this form of propulsion evidently was not considered suitable for the larger ships. One possible reason for this is the amount of internal volume taken up by the intake and uptake trunking of the COGAG plant of the Kashin class and its effect on topsides layout. The Kresta design, on the other hand, is notable for the compactness of its steam propulsion machinery, which is compressed into a relatively small centre section of the hull in such a way as to leave both ends of the ship free for both anti-ship and air defence weapons and magazines.

If the pattern of gas-turbine development followed by the Western navies during the 1960s and early 1970s is any guide, we must assume that the new generation of Soviet aero-derived turbines fitted in the Krivak and Kara classes made fewer demands on space, required a lesser volume of intake trunking, and were more economical in terms of fuel consumption. These factors would make possible the design of a large cruiser-sized ship with gas-turbine propulsion giving adequate power for a maximum speed of over 30 knots and, at the same time, adequate internal volume and deck space for a full outfit of anti-submarine and air defence weapons.

The four gas-turbines of the Kara class are grouped together in such a way that the exhausts are trunked together into a single massive square funnel. This suggests a machinery layout similar to that of the British and Dutch COGOG destroyers and frigates, in which the first pair of

Krivaks were again shared between the two major ship-building areas. There was, therefore, no precedent for the simultaneous construction of similar units, such as the Kresta II and the Kara, in different shipyards.

One factor in the decision to build the new Black Sea cruisers to a fresh design may have been the desire to utilize to the full the design teams that had presumably been responsible for *Moskva* and her sister *Leningrad*. The Black Sea had increased in importance as a centre of Soviet naval activity since the 1967 Middle East War and the subsequent deployment of a Soviet squadron to the Mediterranean. It made sense, therefore, to increase ship design and building expertise in this area in order to support a rapidly-growing Soviet surface fleet.

Given the decision to open up the construction of missile cruisers in the Black Sea, there was something to be said for a new design that would incorporate items of technology, such as the SA-N-4 short-range surface-to-air missile system and high-powered second-generation gas-turbines, that had only recently become available. It must be remembered that while the first ship of the Kresta II group was not completed

turbines is located immediately forward of the funnel facing aft, and the second pair is aft the funnel facing forward. The gearing, in this arrangement, is between the two pairs of turbines; in the case of the Kara class, it may be in a separate machinery room. (In the British and Dutch ships the gearing is in the same machinery room as the smaller cruise turbines.) The air intakes are around the base of the funnel.

The Kara appears to be the first Soviet design to have a centralized, fully-automated machinery control room. The Soviet Navy has taken sufficient pride in this achievement to release a photograph depicting the large control panel. Centralized control of the machinery has probably resulted in some reduction in the ship's complement, thereby further easing the pressures on accommodation.

The change from steam to gas-turbine propulsion in the Kara class necessitated the repositioning of some items of equipment. The Kresta had its funnel uptakes divided into two so that an air search radar could be fitted on a platform between them. This was no longer possible with the Kara because of the intense heat of the gas-turbine exhausts. The Head Net C 'V'-beam radar has, therefore, been re-sited farther forward, atop a short lattice mast mounted at the after end of the enlarged bridge structure. The lattice mast is similar to that of the Krivak, and has the same distinctive high frequency direction finder (HF/DF) mast angled aft. Additional ECM and ESM antennae, including the customary Cross Loop medium-frequency direction-finder, are carried on the lattice mast. The removal of the Head Net C aerial from

the funnel has enabled the second Don-Kay navigation radar — used, in addition, for helicopter control — to be re-sited on the after side of the central radar tower, with a consequent increase in horizon range. (In the Kresta II it was mounted low on the after Head Lights tower.) Concern about the effect of the hot funnel gases on the delicate electronics apparatus is also evident from the height and configuration of the funnel, which is designed to take the exhaust clear of the after Head Lights radar.

Command, Control and Communications
The small size of the bridge structure of the Kresta was dictated in part by the need to accommodate SS-N-3 and SS-N-14 missile launchers alongside, but also perhaps by a desire to reduce topweight after the unhappy experiences with the Kynda class. However, the requirement for more extensive command facilities, and the move towards computerized weapons control and coordination, brought with them the need for an increase in superstructure volume in order to accommodate the necessary electronics. The original Kresta bridge proved inadequate and later ships of that class had additional superstructure built up forward of the radar tower.

The greater length and beam of the Kara class made possible a bridge structure that is nearly twice the length, a deck higher and a metre wider than that of the Kresta class. The additional space available may have made possible the installation of a computerized operations room for the co-

Right: Nikolayev *being overflown by a Wessex Mk.5 helicopter from HMS* Intrepid *while operating in the Mediterranean in 1979. Her guns and Head Lights missile guidance radars are trained, and the SA-N-3 launchers and RBU 6000 rocket launchers are fully elevated in the reloading position. The Bass Tilt fire control radar for the 30mm Gatlings has now been fitted, and can be seen at the base of the funnel. (MoD)*

KARA CLASS
Soviet designation: Bol'shoy Protivolodochny Korabl' (BPK — Large Anti-Submarine Ship)

Construction

Ship	Builder	Laid down	Launched	In service
Nikolayev	61 Kommuna	1969	1971	1973
Ochakov	Yard, Nikolayev	1970	1972	1975
Kerch	(all units)	1971	1973	1976
Azov		1972	1974	1977
Petropavlovsk		1973	1975	1978
Tashkent		1975	1976	1979
Tallinn		1976	1977	1980

Displacement
Standard: 8,200 tons. Full load: 10,000 tons.

Dimensions
Length: 174m (571ft), overall.
Beam: 18.3m (60ft).
Draught: 6.2m (20ft).

Armament
ASW: 2 quadruple SS-N-14 launchers (8 missiles); 1 Ka-25 Hormone A helicopter; 2 12-barrelled RBU 6000 rocket launchers; 2 6-barrelled RBU 1000 rocket launchers (except *Petropavlovsk* — see text); 2 quintuple banks of 533mm (21in) torpedo tubes.
AAW: 2 twin SA-N-3 launchers (44 Goblet missiles); 2 twin SA-N-4 launchers (36 Gecko missiles); 2 twin 76.2mm (3in) guns; 4 30mm Gatlings.

Electronic equipment
Surveillance radar(s): 1 Top Sail, 1 Head Net C; 1 Don-2, 2 Don-Kay.
Fire control radar(s): 2 Head Lights (SS-N-14, SA-N-3); 2 Pop Group (SA-N-4); 2 Owl Screech (76.2mm guns); 2 Bass Tilt (30mm Gatlings).
Sonar(s): 1 bow-mounted low-frequency sonar; 1 medium-frequency VDS.
ECM: 8 Side Globe; 1 Bell Clout, 2 Bell Slam, 2 Bell Tap, 2 other Bell (first two ships); 4 Rum Tub, 2 Bell series (*Kerch* onwards).

Machinery
2-shaft COGAG; 4 gas-turbines each 25,000bhp; 100,000bhp = 32 knots maximum.

Complement
520.

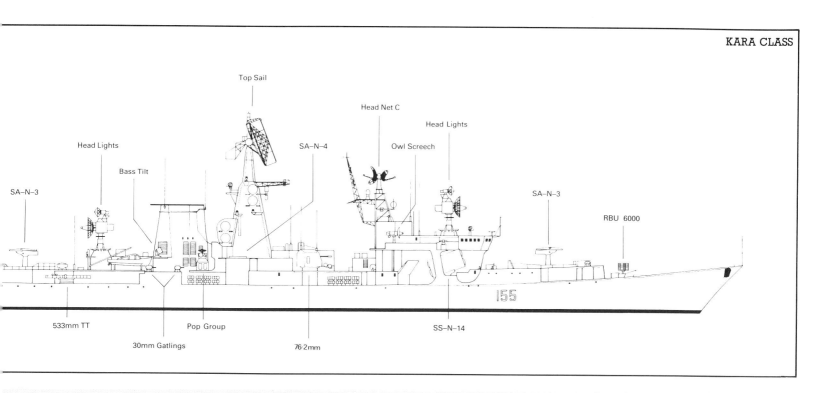

Top Sail

Head Net C

Head Lights

Head Lights

SA–N–4

Owl Screech

Bass Tilt

SA–N–3

SA–N–3

RBU 6000

155

533mm TT

Pop Group

SS–N–14

30mm Gatlings

76·2mm

741

ordination of action data and weapons control. This had previously been an area of naval operations in which the Soviet Navy seriously lagged behind NATO, partly because of inferior electronics technology and partly because of the centralized command and control techniques favoured by the Soviets. Centralized command and control placed the responsibility for data analysis and coordination with the shore command post rather than aboard Soviet ships, which were consequently less self-sufficient in this respect than their Western counterparts. However, the growing complexity of the larger Soviet surface units made it imperative that they should have a system capable of coordinating and controlling their own weapons, which were increasingly numerous and sophisticated and provided for overlapping capabilities; for example, area defence/point defence/ECM.

The weapons computers installed in the Kara class are, if all available evidence regarding Soviet electronics is to be believed, large and heavy, a generation behind those being installed in NATO warships of the same period. There is almost certainly no computerized data link capable of data transfer to other warships. Nevertheless, the Karas appear to represent a marked advance on the Krestas in their ability to display and analyse target data for their own purposes and to coordinate and control their own weapons.

New Weapons

The additional deck space created by the insertion of the new hull section has enabled twin 76.2mm AA mountings to be fitted in place of the 57mm mountings carried by the Kresta II. The increased size of the twin 76.2mm as compared with the 57mm mountings has necessitated their removal to a position between the radar tower and the bridge structure, a position that is occupied in the Kresta II class by the four 30mm Gatlings. The Owl Screech fire control directors for the 76.2mm have been installed in the bridge wings, displacing the Bass Tilt directors for the Gatlings. The latter have been moved aft to a position abreast the funnel, with their directors just above them. This in turn has resulted in the quintuple 533mm torpedo tubes being moved farther aft.

A more significant addition to the already considerable armament of the Kresta II, however, is the new SA-N-4 short-range surface-to-air missile system. SA-N-4 launcher bins are fitted on either side of the central radar tower. The bins are not sunk into the hull, as they are in the Grisha, Nanuchka and Krivak classes, but are in a particularly exposed position above the level of the upper deck. This must be seen as a somewhat hazardous arrangement, particularly as it places the SA-N-4 magazine amidships directly beneath the prominent tower mast/funnel complex, one of the most likely points of contact for a hostile anti-ship missile.

Nor is the SA-N-4 the only side-mounted weapon of the Kara. Unlike equivalent Western types, which tend to have their weapon magazines on the centre-line fore and aft, the sides of the Karas are lined with missile launchers and guns, all with their magazines in exposed positions. Besides the SA-N-4 bins, there are quadruple launchers for the SS-N-14 anti-submarine missile abreast the bridge, twin 76.2mm mountings between the bridge structure and the tower mast, pairs of point-defence Gatlings abreast the funnel, and quintuple torpedo tubes farther aft. The location of these weapons and magazines poses a serious threat to the ship's survival in the event of a hit by an anti-ship missile; even splinter damage from a near-miss or a proximity-fused air-

launched weapon could result in serious fires. These risks are taken in order to cram enough weaponry into Soviet ships to enable them to have a good chance of avoiding action damage, either through a superior first-strike capability (the SS-N-3/12/19 long-range cruise missiles) or, as in the Kara class, by having a variety of weapons with overlapping ranges and capabilities able to provide in-depth defence. In the air defence role, the Kara class has no less than five systems, each of which is duplicated at either end or on either side of the ship, to provide this in-depth defence: the SA-N-3 medium-range missile, the SA-N-4 short-range missile, the 76.2mm medium-range AA gun, the 30mm Gatling point-defence gun, and ECM (jammers and chaff-launchers). Each individual gun mounting or missile launcher has its own individual fire control radar — a total of eight without including dedicated air search and tracking radars — to enable the maximum number of targets to be engaged. Provision is made for local control of many of these weapons, and frequently there is electro-optical back-up to the guidance and fire control radars. Damage control, on the other hand, does not appear to be highly developed — a fact illustrated with grim clarity by the loss of the Kashin-class BPK Otvazhny in the Black Sea in 1974, together with most of the ship's complement.

A further consequence of mounting the SA-N-4 launchers on the beam amidships in the Kara class is that other sensitive equipment has had to be protected from blast by an elaborate system of screening. Large curved blast shields have been interposed between the SA-N-4 launcher bins and the missile's own Pop Group radars. Blast protection also seems to be the reason for the removal of the lower pair of Side Globe ECM antennae from the sides of the main radar tower; they have been mounted on protruding panels immediately behind the tower.

The blast shielding severely restricts the arcs of the two SA-N-4 launchers, especially at lower angles. Even when the arcs of both launchers are combined, there is a blind arc of a full 50° astern, whereas the blind arc on forward bearings is only 20°. Poor arcs are a common feature of side-mounted weapons as compared with centre-line installations, and the twin 76.2mm mountings also suffer from this problem, albeit to a lesser extent. The effects can best be illustrated by comparing the arcs of the SA-N-4 launchers on the Kara with the single Sea Sparrow launcher that performs the same function in the US Navy's Spruance class. The latter's single launcher, mounted aft on the centre-line, has arcs of 330° at low angles. The combined arcs of the two side-mounted launchers of the Kara, on the other hand, amount to no more than 290°. It should be remembered, of course, that the Kara class has excellent arcs for its centre-line SA-N-3 launchers fore and aft, while Spruance does not have an area defence system. Nevertheless, the comparison does reveal that the total capability of a ship with large numbers of missile launchers and guns may be less than the sum of its constituent parts.

Improvements in Underwater Detection

The outfit of anti-submarine weapons carried by the Kara class is identical to that of the Kresta II, but significant improvements were made in underwater detection. Visible evidence of this is provided by the fitting of a variable depth sonar, housed in a prominent casing beneath the helicopter landing pad. The VDS, which operates independently of the

Opposite page, left: A close-up of the centre section of Nikolayev, displaying most of the features that distinguish the Kara class from the Kresta II class. On the right-hand side of the picture is the distinctive bin containing the SA-N-4 'pop-up' launcher and its magazine. Twin 76.2mm mountings occupy the centre of the picture. To the left, mounted high in the bridge wings, is the port-side Owl Screech fire control radar. The lattice mast is another distinguishing feature. It is similar to that of the Krivak class, and was fitted in order to reposition the Head Net C 3-D air surveillance radar away from the hot exhaust gases from the funnel. (US Navy)
Opposite page, right: Kerch, the third ship of the Kara class, was the first to be fitted with Rum Tub ESM antennae, which can be seen on the platforms projecting from the tower mast between the Side Globe ECM radomes. (DPR, Navy)

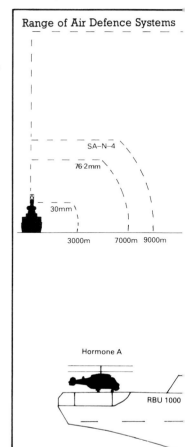

Range of Air Defence Systems

SA-N-4
76.2mm
30mm
3000m 7000m 9000m

Hormone A
RBU 1000

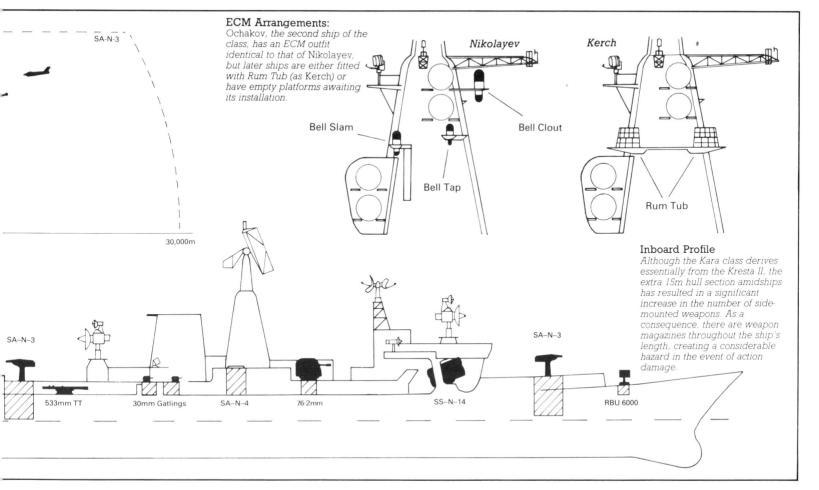

ECM Arrangements:
Ochakov, *the second ship of the class, has an ECM outfit identical to that of Nikolayev, but later ships are either fitted with Rum Tub (as Kerch) or have empty platforms awaiting its installation.*

Nikolayev

Kerch

Bell Slam

Bell Clout

Bell Tap

Rum Tub

SA-N-3

30,000m

Inboard Profile
Although the Kara class derives essentially from the Kresta II, the extra 15m hull section amidships has resulted in a significant increase in the number of side-mounted weapons. As a consequence, there are weapon magazines throughout the ship's length, creating a considerable hazard in the event of action damage.

SA-N-3

SA-N-3

SA-N-3

533mm TT   30mm Gatlings   SA-N-4   76·2mm   SS-N-14   RBU 6000

main hull-mounted sonar, is probably the same model installed in the Krivak class. It is also generally agreed that the bow sonar of the Kara is a large, low-frequency model developed as a result of experience with the Moskva class.

Large bow-mounted sonars tend to pull down the stem of a ship when operating at higher speeds. This may explain the additional flare and height of the bow section of the Kara as compared with the Kresta II. The freeboard amidships, on the other hand, has remained at about 5m. The height of the bow is therefore double that of the hull amidships. This is an unusual ratio in a flush-decked ship of this size, but it is by no means uncommon in Soviet construction. The low freeboard amidships enables more topweight — ie, weapons systems — to be carried, while the sheer and flare of the bow give the vessels good sea-keeping qualities. An interesting side-effect of the considerable sheer forward is that the SA-N-3 deckhouse/magazine also rises at a slight angle. On previous classes with SAM launchers similarly arranged — notably the Kashins and Krestas — the top of the forward deckhouse was strictly horizontal.

Modifications to the SA-N-3 Launcher

Whereas the SA-N-3 launchers on the Kresta II and Moskva classes have four reload hatches beneath them, those on the Kara have only two. This is a more conventional arrangement, and corresponds to standard practice on NATO vessels equipped with area defence missiles. But it does raise again the question of why four hatches were provided in earlier cruisers fitted with the SA-N-3 system. If four hatches were considered an advantage in terms of rapid reloading, why did the Kara revert to two? Also, if the two sets of hatches on Moskva and the Kresta II were provided in order to accommodate two different missiles, one of which had a warhead better suited to the anti-ship role, does this mean that the Kara carries only the surface-to-air version of the missile?

There are no easy or obvious answers to these questions. Although anti-ship missiles were an important feature of Soviet ship construction in the 1960s, there is no reason why this should have remained so in the early 1970s, when the emphasis was on anti-submarine operations and adequate numbers of Rocket Ships and Cruisers with an anti-surface mission were already in service. Moreover, it has been pointed out that any surface-to-air missile has some anti-ship capability, especially if it employs command guidance. It may simply be a matter of reverting to a less complex reloading system that would be more reliable and require less maintenance than the four-hatch system of the earlier launchers. The two-hatch arrangement was retained for the later Kiev class, even though the four-hatch system was still being installed in Large Anti-Submarine Ships of the Kresta II class in the late 1970s, when construction of the Karas and Kievs was already well-established.

Service Life

The first four units of the Kara class all entered service with the Black Sea Fleet. The first ship, *Nikolayev*, passed through the Bosphorus soon after completion and since that time has rotated with her sisters *Ochakov* and *Kerch* on deployments to the Mediterranean. Operations in company with an Anti-Submarine Cruiser (PKR) of the Moskva class are not uncommon, reinforcing the suggestion that the Kara was designed as the major Large Anti-Submarine Ship (BPK) element in Mediterranean sub-hunting groups comprising a single PKR and one or more BPKs, complementing a similar set-up in the Northern Fleet area where the groups would comprise a PKR of the Kiev class and one or more BPKs of the Kresta II class. The relative proximity to NATO air bases and the inevitable presence of the US Sixth Fleet, with its two big super-carriers, may provide the rationale for the close attention paid to air defence qualities in the Kara design.

In the spring of 1979, *Petropavlovsk* and *Tashkent*, the fifth and sixth units, transferred to the Pacific in company with the new Anti-Submarine Cruiser *Minsk*. The arrival of this powerful task force in the Far East virtually doubled the strength of the Pacific Fleet at a stroke, reaffirming the growing importance of this area to Soviet SSBN operations under the new 'bastion' concept (see also pp. 69 and 96). It is reported that a third ship, *Tallinn*, joined the Pacific Fleet in 1981.

Azov

The fourth ship, *Azov*, has never emerged from the Black Sea. The only photograph of her published openly is of poor quality, but reveals that she is being employed, like *Provorny* of the Kashin class, as a trials ship for new surface-to-air missile systems. Whereas *Provorny* is a relatively old ship that has only recently been modified, *Azov* had the experimental systems aboard at her completion. The allocation of such a large modern unit to the role of trials ship is in itself evidence of the importance of the equipment being tested.

The system that has been tested aboard *Azov* since 1977 is almost certainly the vertical launch SA-N-6 area defence system now installed in the cruiser *Kirov*. The only visible modifications to *Azov* are the suppression of the after SA-N-3 launcher and the after Head Lights radar; in place of the SA-N-3 launcher there is simply a flat expanse of deck — suggesting the installation of a vertical launch system — but the Head Lights guidance radar has been replaced by a larger unidentified model. The latter has a different configuration to the Top Dome radar in *Kirov*, and is presumably a prototype from which Top Dome was developed.

ECM and ESM

Nikolayev and *Ochakov*, the first two ships of the class, were given an ECM outfit identical to that of the Kresta II class. Besides the distinctive Side Globe antennae there is a large Bell Clout radome on a platform projecting from the forward face of the tower mast, and two pairs of smaller radomes — Bell Slam and Bell Tap — are fitted at the four corners of the tower mast below the upper pairs of Side Globe radomes. *Kerch* appeared in 1976 with the smaller Bell antennae replaced by Rum Tub ESM antennae (see p. 92). *Petropavlovsk* and *Tashkent*, the fifth and sixth ships, were completed with large empty platforms for Rum Tub, which had not been fitted when the ships made their transit to the Pacific Fleet in early 1979 but was installed soon afterwards. In addition, *Petropavlovsk* carries two drum-shaped antennae on platforms projecting from either side of the helicopter hangar aft. These have since appeared on the large cruiser *Kirov* and the new Large Anti-Submarine Ship *Udaloy* and are apparently designated 'Round House'. They may be ESM antennae, but a more likely possibility, in view of the recent expansion of Soviet naval air operations, is that they are for tactical air navigation (TACAN). Their installation on *Petropavlovsk* necessitated the removal of the after RBU 1000 anti-submarine rocket launchers.

Kiev Class

Experimental Soviet VTOL (vertical take-off and landing) aircraft made their first public appearance at the air display at Domodedovo in July 1967. The date is significant as it would have been during this period that the final plans were being prepared for the next generation of Soviet air-capable cruisers. The emergence of *Kiev* from the Black Sea nine years later with a development squadron of Yak-36 Forgers in addition to a large complement of anti-submarine helicopters marked the culmination of Soviet efforts to get fixed-wing VTOL aircraft to sea. In the same way that the design of the Moskva class was influenced by the latest European — and, in particular, Mediterranean — thinking about independent sub-hunting operations employing ship-based helicopters, that of *Kiev* reflected the latest British ideas for providing small air-capable ships with their own fighter protection.

The British were the first to develop VTOL technology based on aero-engines with vectored thrust. The experimental Hawker P.1127 Kestrel was engaged in flight trials as early as 1961, and these trials extended to operations from the carrier *Ark Royal* in 1963. By 1962 there were plans for an ambitious follow-up aircraft that would meet the needs both of the RAF and the Royal Navy, the Hawker P.1154. The revolutionary VTOL principle opened up the possibility of operating sophisticated, high-performance jet aircraft from much smaller air-capable platforms than had hitherto been contemplated. The development of such an aircraft came at a crossroads for carrier development. The Royal Navy, faced with the problem of attempting to operate the latest heavy jet aircraft from a generation of aircraft-carriers designed during the Second World War, was on the verge of ordering a new series of larger vessels that would prove very

Left: An early view of Kiev in the Atlantic on her way to join the Soviet Northern Fleet. The size and 'spikiness' of the island superstructure and the comparatively low freeboard distinguish her from Western air-capable vessels. Note how close the port-side Gatling sponson is to the water. (MoD)

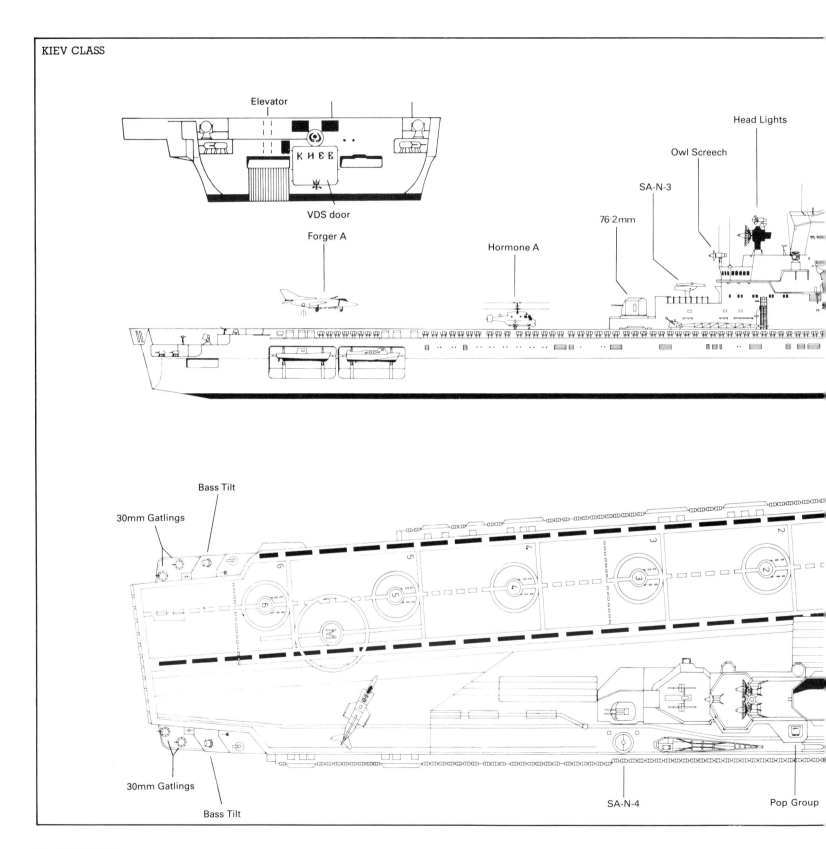

Elevator

Head Lights

Owl Screech

SA-N-3

76·2mm

VDS door

Forger A

Hormone A

К И Є В

Bass Tilt

30mm Gatlings

6 5 4 3 2

30mm Gatlings

Bass Tilt

SA-N-4

Pop Group

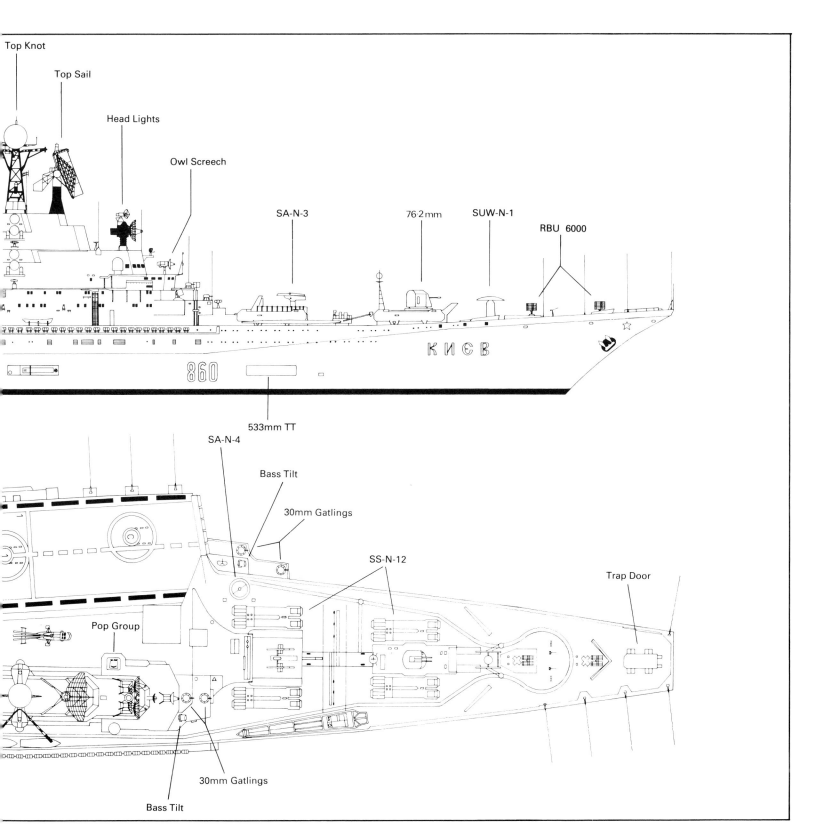

Top Knot

Top Sail

Head Lights

Owl Screech

SA-N-3

76·2 mm

SUW-N-1

RBU 6000

860

КИⒺB

533mm TT

SA-N-4

Bass Tilt

30mm Gatlings

Pop Group

SS-N-12

Trap Door

30mm Gatlings

Bass Tilt

expensive; in the end, prohibitively so. It was also becoming very difficult to fund the wide range of specialist aircraft required for a fully-fledged attack carrier, given the small number of each type that would be required. A new strike aircraft, the Buccaneer, was now coming off the production lines, but for a supersonic interceptor the Royal Navy would have to turn to the American F-4 Phantom. As for airborne early warning (AEW), the elderly Gannet was in urgent need of replacement. A joint Anglo-French project for a new aircraft would come to nothing, leaving the Royal Navy to soldier on with the Gannet until the late 1970s and the Marine Nationale without any sort of AEW aircraft. The French, too, were experiencing similar problems to those of the Royal Navy, having completed two relatively small attack carriers in the early 1960s. Unable to fund a home-built interceptor, they had to turn to the American F-8 Crusader, which was essentially a lightweight day fighter with a limited all-weather capability.

In the early 1960s, VTOL aircraft seemed to many the only way out of the US-led development spiral of bigger and better carriers, and larger and heavier jet aircraft. VTOL aircraft did not need a large flight deck from which to operate, requiring neither 90m steam catapults to launch them nor arrestor wires to enable them to land. They could, therefore, be operated from smaller carriers, offering the possibility of an increase in the number of operating platforms for a given financial outlay. The British Harrier, which became the production aircraft after the demise of the P.1154, was to be operated experimentally from the widest possible variety of ships, including naval auxiliaries fitted with helicopter decks.

There were, however, certain disadvantages inherent in vertical take-off operations that would have to be taken into account in assessing the maritime role to which VTOL aircraft would be best suited. The major disadvantage was that of reduced payload in comparison with conventional aircraft using catapult-assisted take-off; the latter could carry more weapons and — of equal importance, particularly in a maritime scenario — more fuel. VTOL aircraft would be hampered in the strike role by their small weapons payload and by their lack of range, and in the interceptor role by their limited endurance. There was also a significant reduction in high-altitude performance, but this was more acceptable in a maritime environment, where hostile strike aircraft would generally have to come in low in order to attack their targets. VTOL aircraft gained in manoeuvrability (because of their use of vectored thrust) much of what they lost in high-speed performance. On balance, it appeared in the early 1960s that the VTOL aircraft had potential as a naval interceptor, provided that some solution could be found to the problem of endurance. In opting for an interceptor (in the form of the P.1154) rather than a strike aircraft, the Royal Navy was simply confirming contemporary assessments of the capabilities of VTOL aircraft in a maritime role.

The appeal of VTOL aircraft for the Soviet Navy was of a different order to that which influenced developments in the British Royal Navy, at least in these early stages. The British were, after all, still toying with the idea of fully-fledged attack carriers in which the P.1154 would be but one of the components making up the air group. The Soviet Navy, on the other hand, had no intention of building attack carriers on the US Navy pattern, in which squadrons of attack planes constituted the anti-ship component, with fighter squadrons providing protection not only for the carrier but also for the long-range attack squadrons themselves. The Soviet Navy had opted for long-range air- and ship-launched missiles to perform the anti-ship mission. By the mid-1960s it was well on the way to building up the surveillance systems that would provide the necessary target data for the ships and aircraft that served as platforms for those missiles.

What the Soviet Navy did require was an interceptor capable of fleet air defence. Shipborne interceptors would enable the Soviet sub-hunting groups to operate in hostile, open expanses of ocean where support from land-based fighters was out of the question. This consideration was of particular relevance in the all-important Northern Fleet area, as Soviet sub-hunting forces operating in the Norwegian Sea would have to contend not only with NATO carriers but also with NATO strike aircraft operating from land bases around the periphery. It is significant that the first of the new Soviet VTOL cruisers, *Kiev*, deployed to that area immediately after completion of her trials and work-up. The gap of fully nine years between the commissioning of *Moskva* and her successor can, therefore, almost certainly be attributed to the necessary development and redesign of the VTOL aircraft that were to be operated by the latter.

The Yak-36

The first experimental Soviet VTOL aircraft, the Yak-34 Freehand, employed similar vectored-thrust techniques to those of the British Kestrel. Two turbojet engines (the Kestrel had only one) were mounted side by side at the bottom of the front fuselage, which had a divided ram air intake in the nose. The exhaust from each engine was vectored through a large-diameter louvred and gridded nozzle. However, while the British retained the basic elements of the Kestrel design in its production successor, the Harrier, the Soviets made a number of fundamental changes in the configuration of the Yak-36 during its development. The Yak-36 Forger, which ran ship-board trials from the cruiser *Moskva* in 1973–74 before making its first public appearance on *Kiev* during the latter's first deployment to the Northern Fleet area, has similar dimensions to Freehand, but employs very different VTOL techniques. Power is provided by a single large turbojet of about 7,700kg (17,000lb) thrust, exhausting through a single pair of vectoring side-nozzles to the rear of the wing; the large lateral intake ducts are level with the after part of the cockpit.

In addition, there are two small vertical lift jets each of about 2,500kg (5,500lb) thrust immediately aft the cockpit under a rearward-hinged louvre door. The lift-jets are angled aft, the exhaust effluxes combining with those of the main engine to form a 'V' beneath the fuselage for take-off and landing operations.

It is not clear why the Soviets abandoned the relatively simple vectored-thrust principle on which the Freehand was based in favour of a combination of vectored thrust and vertical lift, except that similar multi-engine alternatives to the British Kestrel had been proposed in Western Europe from the outset and had led to other relatively unsuccessful aircraft — notably, the French Mirage IIIV and the German VAK 191. The aim was for a more stable aircraft during the crucial take-off and landing phases, but this was achieved only at great cost to the overall performance of the aircraft concerned; this is as true of the Forger as it was of the abortive West European designs. The use of three separate engines for

---

Yakovlev Yak-36MP Forger
In service: 1976.
Length: 15m (50ft).
Span: 7m (24ft).
Height: 3.8m (13ft).
Weight: 7,250kg (16,000lb), empty; 9,000kg (20,000lb), fully loaded.
Engines: 1 Lyul'ka vectored-thrust turbojet, 7,650kg (16,900lb) thrust; 2 lift jets, each 2,500kg (5,500lb) thrust.
Speed: 1,170km/hr (725mph=Mach 1.1) at high level; 1,125km/hr (700mph) at sea level.
Ceiling: 12,000m (40,000ft).
Combat radius: 185km (100nm) as interceptor (includes 75 minutes loiter time); 370km (200nm) in high-level attack role; 230km (125nm) in low-level attack role.
Armament: As interceptor, 2 AA-2-2 'Advanced Atoll' AAMs (possibly also AA-8 Aphid); 2 23mm cannon. As strike aircraft, 2 AS-7 Kerry, or bombs, or 16–32 rockets. All stores, munitions, fuel tanks are carried on four underwing pylons; maximum weapons load 1,360kg (3,000lb).
Sensors: Small ranging sight; passive warning system.

KIEV CLASS

Soviet designation: Taktychesky Avionosny Kreyser (TAKR — Tactical Aircraft-Carrying Cruiser)

Construction

Ship	Builder	Laid down	Launched	In service
Kiev	Black Sea Shipyard, Nikolayev (all units)	Sept 1970	31 Dec 1972	May 1975
Minsk		Dec 1972	May 1975	Feb 1978
Novorossiysk		Oct 1975	Dec 1978	1981
Kharkov		1978		

Displacement
Standard: 36,000 tons. Full load: 42,000 tons.

Dimensions
Length: 275m (902ft), overall; 250m (820ft), between perpendiculars.
Beam: 50m (164ft), flight deck; 38m (125ft), water-line.
Draught: 9m (30ft).

Armament
Tactical aircraft: 12 Yak-36 Forger A.
ASW: 18 Ka-25 Hormone A helicopters; 1 twin SUW-N-1 launcher (20? FRAS-1 missiles); 2 12-barrelled RBU 6000 rocket launchers; 2 quintuple banks of 533mm (21in) torpedo tubes.
ASuW: 4 twin SS-N-12 launchers (24 missiles); 2–3 Ka-25 Hormone B missile targeting helicopters.
AAW: 2 twin SA-N-3 launchers (72 Goblet missiles); 2 twin SA-N-4 launchers (36 Gecko missiles); 2 twin 76.2mm (3in) guns; 8 30mm Gatlings.

Electronic equipment
Surveillance radar(s): 1 Top Sail, 1 Top Steer; 2 Palm Frond.
Fire control radar(s): 1 Trap Door (SS-N-12); 2 Head Lights (SA-N-3); 2 Pop Group (SA-N-4); 2 Owl Screech (76.2mm guns); 4 Bass Tilt (30mm Gatlings).
Carrier-controlled approach radar: 1 Top Knot.
Sonar(s): 1 bow-mounted low-frequency sonar; 1 medium-frequency VDS.
ECM: 8 Side Globe; 12 Bell series; 4 Rum Tub.

Machinery
4-shaft geared steam turbines; 140,000shp = 32 knots maximum.

Complement
1,800.

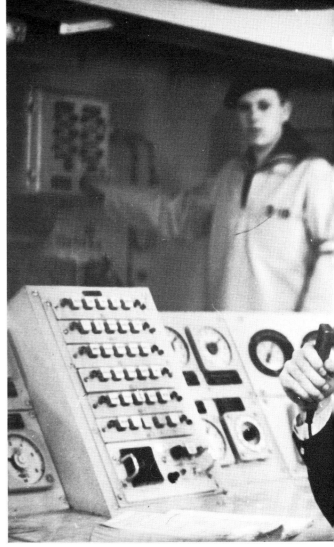

Left: Kiev *in heavy seas in the Atlantic. Her low freeboard and stabilizers make her a very steady platform for VTOL operations, but the Soviets have shown little enthusiasm for operating the Yak-36 Forger in marginal weather conditions. (C-in-C Fleet)*
Above: *The machinery control room of* Kiev. *Although the monitoring equipment looks somewhat dated by contemporary Western standards, the photograph suggests that all the ship's propulsion machinery, and possibly the auxiliary generating machinery, is controlled centrally. (TASS)*

Above: *An overhead view of Minsk, taken at the same time as the previous photograph. Note the after aircraft lift, which is in the 'down' position. The only visible difference between Minsk and Kiev lies in the deck markings. On Minsk, the broken line that marks the centre of the angled deck is not deflected to pass through the centre of the forward helo-circle, which is offset to port. The large circle aft, which may be used for Forger landings, is positioned farther away from the deck park and has an 'M' at its centre. (DPR, Navy)*

Right: *An overhead view of Kiev, with a Ka-25 Hormone on the forward helo-circle and two Yak-36 Forgers on the deck park aft. Note the burn marks behind the after helo-circle, caused by the lift-jets of the Forgers. (MoD)*

Left, top and centre: *These two photographs show Yak-36 Forger aircraft parked on the forward area of Kiev's flight deck. In the upper photograph the large forward aircraft lift is in the 'down' position, revealing a conventional hoist mechanism. The flying control gallery can be seen at the extreme right of the picture. In the lower photograph, the aircraft numbered 04 is the two-seat training version of the Yak-36, the Forger B. It has an extended nose section, which is angled down to improve vision from the double cockpit. (US Navy; MoD)*

Left, bottom: *The after deck part of Kiev, showing the 'railway track' running beneath the tails of the Forger A aircraft; missiles, bombs and rockets are brought up to the flight deck via three small elevators aft of the island superstructure and are wheeled across the deck park on trolleys. (MoD)*

Opposite page, top: *A close-up of three Yak-36 Forger A VTOL aircraft on the after deck park of Kiev. A 23mm gun pod is fitted on the outer pylon of the first aircraft. The intake and outlet doors for the vertical lift jets are in the open position. (TASS)*

Opposite page, centre: *Three Forger pilots in conversation on the flight deck of Minsk. They appear to be wearing immersion suits beneath their coveralls and are equipped with backpack parachutes. (TASS)*

Opposite page, bottom: *A Yak-36 Forger takes off on a mission. The vertical lift engines give added stability at the cost of heavy fuel consumption. There are four underwing pylons, and two of these would generally be occupied by fuel tanks on combat missions. If gun pods are fitted, they have to be carried on the underwing pylons, too, as use of the under-fuselage position utilized for that purpose on the British Sea Harrier is precluded by the operation of the lift jets and their outlet doors. (TASS)*

take-off and landing does not mean that the Forger is more able to survive the failure of a single power unit than a single-engine VTOL aircraft. The reliable operation of all three engines is crucial to the aircraft's stability during these phases. Moreover, the likelihood of engine failure in one of the three power units is between six and eight times greater than that of a single-engine aircraft. This problem is exacerbated by the dependence on a successful relight of the two lift engines, which are shut down during the horizontal flight phase.

The Forger employs only VTOL operation. Short rolling take-offs, which are commonly used by the Harrier, would be possible only if complex control systems were fitted to synchronize the vectored thrust nozzle rotation with the thrust of the vertical lift engines. Even so, the Forger would attain a speed of only 60–80 knots at the end of its run. (The Harrier attains 100–120 knots in the same distance.) The latter factor has important consequences for payload, as wing lift depends on speed squared. There is no evidence to suggest that the Forger is capable of anything but a standing take-off, which makes payload comparisons with the British Sea Harrier even less favourable. This particular performance gap has been further widened by the British development of the ski-jump, which has yielded tremendous benefits in terms of the take-off weight of the aircraft.

The lengthy transition from vertical to horizontal flight makes for a slower reaction time, increased vulnerability and high fuel consumption. The Forger takes approximately 90 seconds to accomplish its transition — three times as long as the Harrier — and consumes an estimated ten times as much fuel in the process. Finally, there is only a very limited VIFF (vectoring in forward flight) capability, because the Forger has only a single pair of vectored thrust nozzles for its main propulsion engine compared with two pairs for the Harrier. This limits combat manoeuvrability, and, consequently, the effectiveness of the Forger as an interceptor.

There is every indication that, in choosing a multi-engine configuration, the Soviets jumped the wrong way, and that the Yak-36 Forger operated by *Kiev* has almost certainly failed to live up to initial Soviet expectations. Its capability as an interceptor is limited by low endurance and other performance factors. It also appears to lack the search radar that enables the British Sea Harrier to perform so well in the fleet air defence role. Moreover, the delicate nature of the take-off operations observed on *Kiev* and her sister *Minsk* makes it difficult to envisage a rapid scrambling of VTOL fighters to counter an air attack. These problems are compounded by the absence of on-board airborne early warning aircraft, which could detect incoming strike aircraft flying at any level at the sort of range that would enable the Forgers to get into the air in time to meet the attack.

The capabilities provided by the Forger are primarily those of air strike against isolated NATO ASW units of frigate size and against small craft, the support of amphibious assault operations, reconnaissance, and the pursuit of hostile reconnaissance aircraft or ASW aircraft, such as the P-3 Orion.

A Carrier/Cruiser Configuration

In adopting a hybrid carrier/cruiser configuration for *Kiev* and her sisters, the Soviet Navy was simply following a pattern of development already established by the Moskva class. An angled flight deck similar to those of NATO carriers was adopted, but this terminated at the after end of a conven-

tional forecastle, on which most of the 'cruiser' weapons were located. The flight deck was angled not because an angled deck was essential to air operations, as it was on the NATO carriers, but out of weight and space considerations. The massive island superstructure to starboard, carrying air defence weapons and all of the major surveillance and fire control radars, encroaches on the flight deck to such an extent that the latter had to be angled out to port in order to create sufficient space for aircraft lifts and deck parking outside the line of the take-off and landing area. The overhang to port also compensates in part for the weight of the superstructure. Whilst having more of the appearance of a conventional aircraft-carrier than the Moskva class, *Kiev* continues to maintain the strict division between air component and conventional cruiser capabilities established by her predecessor.

Hull-Form

Kiev has a very full, low hull aft, but the forecastle, which carries most of the cruiser weapons, rises sharply, and the considerable flare of the bow is carried right forward by the squaring-off of the stem at the level of the upper deck. The combined effect of the finely tapered bow with its large sonar dome, and the transom stern (which is submerged only at high speed), is to shift the longitudinal centre of buoyancy forward, presumably with the aim of keeping the forecastle dry even in heavy seas. This effectively corrects a tendency observed in the Moskvas for the ships to bury their bows in a swell.

The lack of freeboard aft is quite remarkable — 13m compared with 19m for the big US Navy carriers. The full waterplane and active fin-stabilization combine to give the ship much greater stability than the traditional fixed-wing carrier. *Kiev* has been observed to have very low overall motions in a seaway, and these are clearly critical for the VTOL operations for which she has been designed. One disadvantage of the low freeboard is that side lifts were out of the question. Both aircraft lifts in *Kiev*, therefore, occupy valuable hangar space. A further problem is the height of the Gatling sponson on the port side forward, which is so close to the water that some loss of speed in heavy weather must result if damage is to be avoided.

There are numerous scuttles in the ship's sides forward, and these are complemented by rectangular ventilation grilles, similar to those on the Moskva class, alongside the hangar deck. Quintuple banks of 533mm torpedo tubes are set into the hull behind sliding doors just forward of the island superstructure, and there are open recesses for acommodation ladders amidships. There are deeper recesses aft for the

ship's boats, two of which are slung on radial davits on either side of the stern.

The wide transom stern has been the subject of much comment and speculation. There is a large central door bearing the ship's name, behind which the variable depth sonar is housed. Above the variable depth sonar door, just below the level of the flight deck, are two small recesses that may house a night approach radar or lights.

To port and to starboard there are longer, deeper recesses of identical dimensions. The starboard recess contains an outlet for a refuse incineration plant. It has also been used for stern refuelling with the ship at anchor. Beneath the recess on the port side is a dark grey, deeply ribbed vertical surface that extends to below the level of the waterline. Various functions have been suggested for this 'ribbed' door to port, including the possible operation of landing craft. This latter suggestion can be safely discounted on the grounds that there is inadequate space available aft for any sort of well-deck; the hangar deck is only some 5.5m above the waterline. A more likely suggestion is that it gives access to a loading area able to accept bulky goods from fleet tenders or other small boats. This theory is supported by the siting of a narrow 5m by 1m elevator directly above it at flight deck level, enabling munitions and, presumably, personnel, to be transferred between the two.

Flight Deck

The flight deck is offset to port, and is angled out at about 4°. Helo-circles 7m across and numbered one to six, are marked out along the centre-line of the angled deck, with a further circle at the forward end offset to port. The latter is marked with the cyrillic 'C' (Western alphabet 'S') and presumably has a different function to the others. It may be that this spot is reserved for the helicopter used for plane guard duties during flying operations. There is, in addition, a much larger circle some 11m in diameter aft. In *Kiev*, this circle is centred on the line that marks the outer edge of the flight deck, but in her sister *Minsk* it has been moved inboard some 5m, presumably to clear the deck park aft. The circle has an 'M' at its centre and appears to be used for Forger landings.

Squeezed between the island superstructure and the angled deck is a large lift 18.5m by 10m, capable of accepting two Forgers or two Hormones. There is a second aircraft lift of the same length, but only half as wide, tucked away behind the island. In terms of width, it can only just accommodate the Forger and suffers the same limitations as the aircraft lifts in *Moskva* with regard to its ability to accept future aircraft. The problem is rather less acute in *Kiev* because of the size of the forward lift, which is large even by Western standards.

Below: *A starboard-side view of Kiev in 1976. Note the clean hull-lines and the vents immediately beneath the flight deck. (US Navy)*

Opposite page, top: *A stern quarter view of Kiev. A single Ka-25 Hormone is operating from the flight deck, and there are two pairs of Yak-36 Forgers on the forward and after deck parks respectively. (C-in-C Fleet)*

Opposite page, centre: *An early view of Minsk in the eastern Mediterranean in February 1979, shortly after she passed through the Bosphorus. A Ka-25 is positioned on the after helo-circle and four others are lined up on the after deck park. (Royal Navy)*

Opposite page, bottom: *Kiev in the North Atlantic in the early 1980s with a Royal Navy Sea King overhead. On deck are four Ka-25 Hormones and two Yak-36 Forgers. (C-in-C Fleet)*

There is a third elevator, 6m square, just abaft the large triangular deckhouse that separates the flight deck from the forecastle area. The deckhouse itself appears to serve as a 'garage' for deck tractors (see p. 49 for comparison with *Moskva*) and a large self-propelled vacuum cleaner used to clear the flight deck of foreign objects that might be ingested by the aircraft engines. The purpose of the elevator appears to be to transfer tractors and stores between hangar and flight deck levels. It seems likely, therefore, that the forward end of the hangar serves as a 'parking space' for tractors, fork-lifts and stores, as it does in the big US Navy carriers. On the outboard side of the after aircraft lift there are three munitions elevators, each about 5m by 1m and connected to the ship's 'railway system'. They indicate that extensive magazines for aircraft ordnance are sited directly below in the ship's hull.

There are two major areas available for deck parking. The first is alongside the superstructure forward of the main aircraft lift, and can accommodate two pairs of Hormones or Forgers. Steel rings disposed in circular fashion are set into the deck for securing purposes. (Similar rings are provided for each of the helo-circles.) There is also what appears to be a grid running beneath the inner two aircraft spaces, the purpose of which may be to provide an electrical supply for heating or power. The other deck-park is on the starboard side aft. It can accept about four aircraft of either type, angled inboard towards the flight deck, and is frequently used by the Forgers. This is a convenient arming point for the ship's aircraft because of the proximity of the three munitions elevators, which are served by a pair of railway lines for wheeled trolleys.

The after deck-park and the entire angled portion of the flight deck is covered with brownish heat-resistant tiles about 0.5m square. These are made necessary by the intense heat generated by the lift engines of the Forger during VTOL operations. The extent of the tiling indicates that, while the larger circle aft may generally be used for Forger landings, it is intended that any of the other seven spots can be used by this aircraft, suggesting that air operations involving multiple Forger take-offs were envisaged as part of the ship's operational concept.

Air Group and Hangar

The number of aircraft that *Kiev* can accommodate can only be a matter for conjecture. Initially, there were considerable discrepancies between European estimates of up to 50 aircraft, and the US Navy's figure of 25 — nine Yak-36 Forger A, one Yak-36 Forger B, fourteen Ka-25 Hormone A and one Ka-25 Hormone B — which was based on observation of *Kiev*'s air group during her first deployment. In view of the largely experimental nature of air operations on that first deployment — evidenced by the presence on board of a Forger B two-seat trainer — it seems likely that *Kiev* was carrying less than her full complement of aircraft. Nevertheless, the European figures were clearly well adrift, and have since been progressively reduced to around the 35 mark.

Unlike the US Navy, which is happy to keep half the air group of one of its big carriers permanently on deck, the Soviets keep all their aircraft in the hangar when they are not involved in flying operations — hence the lack of parking space on the flight deck. This may be due in part to the relatively low freeboard of the Soviet ASW cruisers, but the main reason appears to be the severe weather conditions

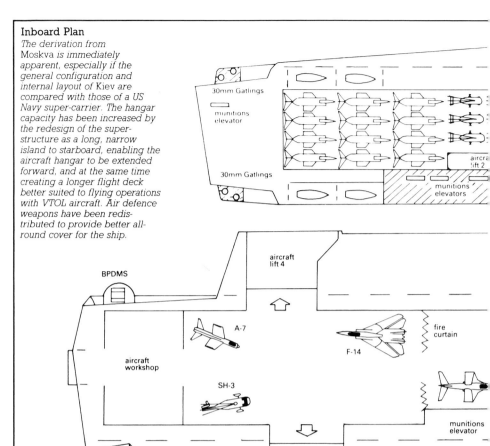

Inboard Plan

The derivation from Moskva *is immediately apparent, especially if the general configuration and internal layout of* Kiev *are compared with those of a US Navy super-carrier. The hangar capacity has been increased by the redesign of the superstructure as a long, narrow island to starboard, enabling the aircraft hangar to be extended forward, and at the same time creating a longer flight deck better suited to flying operations with VTOL aircraft. Air defence weapons have been redistributed to provide better all-round cover for the ship.*

under which the ships would be expected to operate for much of the year from their bases in the Arctic and the northwest Pacific.

The aircraft capacity of *Kiev* is determined by the available hangar space. The contours of the hangar itself can be ascertained from certain visible features, such as the position of aircraft lifts, munitions elevators, side recesses and weapon magazines. The single hangar is enclosed, on the British pattern, and stretches from the forward end of the superstructure to the after end of the ship. The width of the forward part of the hangar is limited by the large island superstructure, the inner edge of which is some 15m inboard. (US Navy. carriers have their island placed on the flight deck overhang, with access via the supporting sponson, thereby maximizing hangar space.) The hangar widens aft of the superstructure, but the positioning of the three munitions elevators just outside the starboard edge of the after aircraft lift suggests that the latter marks the outer limit of the hangar to starboard. It would seem logical that the port side of the hangar follows the inner edge of the recess for the ship's boats aft, with aircraft workshops to the side on the British pattern. This would give convenient hangar widths throughout; 15m for three Hormones or Forgers forward, and 21m for

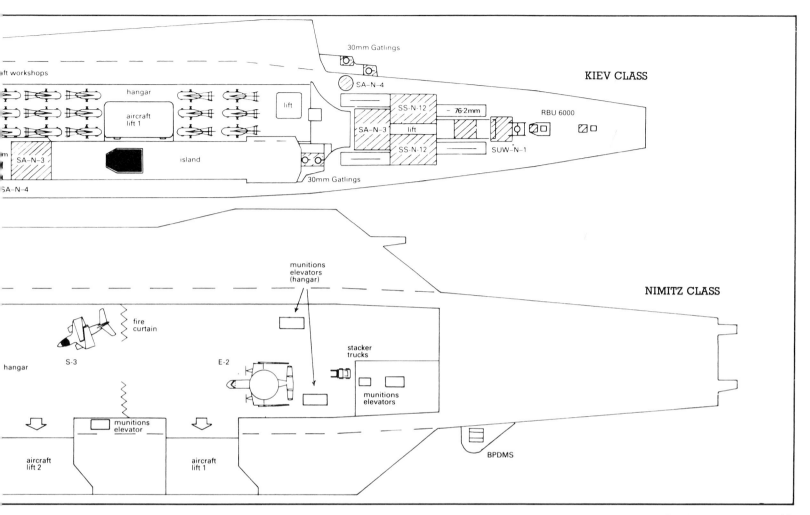

KIEV CLASS

NIMITZ CLASS

four of either aircraft aft. To determine exactly where the hangar ends is not so easy. It does not extend to the stern, as the space is occupied by the bulky variable depth sonar installation. Therefore, it seems likely that the end of the hangar coincides with the narrowing of the flight deck just forward of the Gatling sponsons.

If the preceding assumptions hold good, we would have a forward hangar section of about 25m by 15m between the cargo elevator and the larger of the two aircraft lifts, a centre section of the same width but about 55m long extending from the forward aircraft lift to the after end of the second lift, and an after section 45–48m long and 21m wide. These three sections could be isolated from one another by fire curtains for damage control purposes. Such a hangar could accommodate a squadron of twelve Yak-36 Forger As, an ASW helicopter squadron of eighteen Ka-25 Hormone As, a detachment of two or three Hormone B helicopters for missile targeting and a Hormone C for search-and-rescue. The accompanying drawing shows how such an air complement could be accommodated.

The after aircraft lift is almost certainly supported at the corners, as on the Moskva class, which allows loading from the side or the rear. Photographs of the forward lift on *Kiev*, however, show a more conventional arrangement, with cables and wheels set into the vertical 'wall' constituted by the continuation of the side of the island below decks to starboard. If the port side of the lift is supported in the same way, the lift-well would divide the hangar into two separate parts, with access only from forward and aft.

Flying Operations

There are a number of interesting differences in the way flying operations are conducted aboard *Kiev* as compared with Western practice. US Navy observations of *Kiev*'s first deployment established a distinct lack of ground-crew participation in launching and landing procedures. All instructions for movement, including taxiing, take-off and landing, appear to be directed by radio from the spacious flying control station, which is sited beneath the after Head Lights guidance radar. No external electrical power or ground support is used by the Forger during its start-up sequence, and all maintenance work is performed on the hangar deck. Chocks and chains are removed prior to engine start, after which the ground crew retires. On landing, chocks and chains are re-secured after engine shut-down. Re-spotting is done by a deck tractor.

All Forger take-offs and landings are in the VTOL mode. The lift-off sequence is smooth and is, undoubtedly, greatly assisted by the twin vertical-lift engines. The transition from vertical to horizontal flight is carried out very slowly and carefully, and appears to be more susceptible to turbulence. The latter factor is aggravated in *Kiev* by the height and spikiness of the island, which must result in a poor airflow pattern over the flight deck. Flying operations with the Forger appear to be undertaken only in relatively calm conditions. The landing sequence starts far astern, with a steady descent until the last 500m. The Forger then decelerates smoothly at a steady 30m above sea-level. The final approach is made at 10–15m above the flight deck at an aircraft speed of five knots. The Forger then enters its hover-phase, and lands vertically. Lining up the angled flight deck with the wind direction is assisted by the provision of the customary striped wind-sock suspended from a short mast above the tractor garage. Throughout flying operations, a Hormone is stationed in the 'angel' position with an escort two miles aft as a plane guard.

ASW and Air Defence

The anti-submarine weapons carried by *Kiev* to complement her helicopter squadrons are those that appeared on the Moskva class some nine years earlier: two RBU 6000 rocket launchers are fitted in line well forward, with a twin-arm SUW-N-1 launcher for FRAS-1 nuclear-tipped missiles just aft the second rocket launcher. Target data for these weapons is provided by a large panoramic bow sonar, and by an independent variable depth sonar set into the stern. The bow sonar, which is a long-range model operating at low frequency, was probably developed from the keel-mounted sonar installed in the Moskva class, while the variable depth sonar appears to be a larger model than those previously fitted in the Krivak I and Kara classes.

The area defence system is the well tried SA-N-3, backed up by the short-range SA-N-4, twin 76.2mm mountings and point-defence Gatlings. In accordance with previous practice each system is duplicated, but in contrast to the weapons layout of *Moskva*, which has all her major systems on the forecastle, *Kiev* has her own air defence weapons divided equally between forward- and after-firing positions. The first SA-N-3 launcher is atop a large deckhouse at the after end of the forecastle, and a twin 76.2mm mounting is located on a separate deckhouse farther forward. To port of the SA-N-3 launcher at upper-deck level is an SA-N-4 'bin', with a pair of 30mm Gatlings located on a sponson just below it. A second pair of Gatlings is mounted to starboard at the forward end of the island superstructure.

The other set of major air defence weapons is located at the after end of the island. The SA-N-3 launcher is superimposed above a second 76.2mm mounting, with the SA-N-4 'bin' on the outer deck edge, abreast the 76.2mm deckhouse. The after Gatlings are in the stern quarter positions, just below the level of the flight deck.

Kiev is credited by some reference sources with an improved version of the Goblet missile, having a range stated to be 55km (30nm) as compared with only 30km (16nm) for the earlier model. This seems a remarkable improvement in performance for a missile of substantially the same configuration with no apparent change in the system of guidance.

The same sources suggest a greater magazine capacity for *Kiev* than for other Soviet ships fitted with the SA-N-3 system. This theory appears to be based on the increase in hull-

Opposite page, top: *A close-up of Ka-25 Hormone A helicopters operating from* Kiev, *August 1979. These models have a prominent box mounted on the after end of the fuselage which is thought to contain sonobuoys. This photograph gives an excellent view of the size and texture of the heat-resistant tiles that cover the flight deck. (TASS)*

Opposite page, bottom: *Ka-25 Hormone A anti-submarine helicopters on the forward part of* Kiev's *flight deck. The three helicopters with rotors folded are on the small forward deck park area. A grid, possibly for power supply, runs parallel with the island superstructure. Forward of the deck park is the tractor garage. Note the steel rings set into the deck around No. 1 helo-circle for securing the aircraft. (Royal Navy)*

Top right: *Helicopter crews respond to an alarm signal aboard* Minsk. *Note the sonobuoy packs mounted on the rear fuselage of the Ka-25s. (TASS)*

Right: *A close-up of the island superstructure of* Minsk, *taken in the East China Sea in 1979. The major air surveillance and tracking radars are Top Sail (right) and Top Steer (left), with the distinctive Top Knot precision approach radar between. The other antennae, disposed vertically in line with the central lattice mast are, from top to bottom: one Top Hat (?) ECM, two Rum Tub ESM, two Side Globe ECM, two Bell Bash ECM, one Palm Frond navigation radar, two Side Globe ECM, two Bell Thump ECM, and a Tee Plinth electro-optical sensor. (US Navy)*

depth, which would enable a second feeder magazine to be placed beneath the first. Since previous classes are generally credited with 22 missiles per magazine, the total figure of 72 suggested for *Kiev* presumably takes into account the additional space occupied by the mechanism that transfers the missile rounds from the lower to the upper magazine, given that the missiles are stowed vertically beneath the launcher.

Fire control radars for the air defence weapons are located, together with the air surveillance and tracking radars, atop the large island superstructure. Head Lights and Owl Screech fire control radars are superimposed one above the other at either end of the superstructure, and the Pop Group guidance radars for the SA-N-4 launchers are mounted on platforms projecting from its sides. The platforms are diagonally opposite one another, reflecting the position of the launchers themselves. The small Bass Tilt radars for the Gatlings are mounted with each pair of guns.

Surveillance Radars

Between the major fire control radars atop the superstructure are the air search and tracking radars, which are mounted on separate pillar masts forward of the massive funnel. The first is the large Top Sail antenna, which is an essential part of the SA-N-3 area defence system. The other radar, smaller but of similar configuration to Top Sail and making its first appearance on *Kiev*, has received the NATO designation 'Top Steer'. It comprises a curved lattice scanner with a rectangular frontal aspect, mounted back-to-back with a Head Net A antenna. Top Steer is thought to employ frequency scanning to give three-dimensional surveillance and tracking. It provides a useful back-up for Top Sail in the event of damage or mechanical failure, thereby reinforcing traditional Soviet practice and ensuring that *Kiev* can maintain control of her aircraft and defend herself against hostile air attack at all times. Top Steer also provides the additional tracking capacity essential in a ship operating large numbers of aircraft. Between the Top Sail and Top Steer antennae is a tall lattice mast surmounted by a large radome designated 'Top Knot'. The radome is thought to house a precision approach radar, enabling the Forgers and Hormones to home in on their mother-ship.

ECM

The ECM outfit of *Kiev* is exceptionally complete. The various antennae are arranged vertically on either side of the island superstructure in line with the central lattice mast. Beneath each pair of Side Globe radomes there are platforms for smaller ECM jammers of the Bell series. The upper platform on either side carries two radomes, designated 'Bell Bash', while the lower platform carries two larger radomes, designated 'Bell Thump'. A third, still larger radome is installed on platforms projecting from either side of the central lattice mast. At the base of the lattice mast are four antennae of distinctive configuration, designated 'Rum Tub'. *Kiev* was the first Soviet ship to be fitted with these antennae, but they have since appeared on at least two ships of the Kara class and on the large cruiser *Kirov*. Rum Tub resembles the segments of the upper part of a spirits barrel, hence its name. It is always fitted as a four-piece installation, each antenna covering a separate 90° quadrant around the ship. The directional element is clearly essential to its function, suggesting that its purpose is to gather and analyse radar emissions from other ships. Between the ECM antennae on either side of the superstructure are small elliptical scanners, designated 'Palm Frond', which serve as navigation radars. Below the ECM antennae are the customary Tee Plinth electro-optical sensors, which provide fire control back-up for the air defence systems.

Anti-Ship Weapons

Moskva was the first major Soviet warship to abandon the long-range anti-ship cruise missile. From the late 1960s, a clear division began to emerge between those ships designed with an anti-surface mission and those with an anti-submarine mission. The last ships to be fitted with long-range anti-ship weapons were the Rocket Cruisers of the Kresta I class. These were succeeded by a series of Large Anti-Submarine Ships in which the SS-N-3 anti-ship missile was replaced by the SS-N-14 anti-submarine missile. The early 1970s saw the conversion to Large Rocket Ships of a number of vessels of the Kildin and Kashin classes, but these conversions were intended to perform a limited, specialist mission (see p. 31), and the anti-ship missile fitted was a horizon-range model. It came as something of a surprise, therefore, when *Kiev*, initially typed by the Soviets as an Anti-Submarine Cruiser (Protivolodochny Kreyser), emerged from the Black Sea with large elevating launchers that clearly housed a new long-range anti-ship missile.

The SS-N-12 is thought to be a development of the SS-N-3 fitted in earlier Soviet cruisers. It has an overall length of about 12 metres. Advances in propulsion technology are probably responsible for an increase in maximum range from an estimated 300km (170nm) for the SS-N-3 to about 450km (250nm).

The eight launchers on *Kiev* are arranged in four pairs on either side of the SA-N-3 and 76.2mm deckhouses forward. The launchers are elevated to about 30° for firing. The blast from the forward group is deflected by hinged plates set into the deck, while the after group have the deckhouse behind them specially shaped for that purpose. The launchers can be reloaded from a below-decks magazine located between them. The reloads appear to be stored on either side of a narrow elevator from which they are moved sideways to the launcher on a system of athwartships rails. Most reference publications agree that sixteen reloads are carried. This

Opposite page: *This Soviet photograph of sailors running to action stations aboard* Kiev *gives an excellent view of the electronics on the inboard side of the island superstructure. The numerous ECM radomes and ESM antennae are mounted centrally, and duplicate the arrangements on the outboard side of the island. In the foreground is the port-side satellite communications terminal, housed in a prominent radome. The port-side Pop Group guidance radar for the SA-N-4 missile can be seen in the background. On platforms projecting from the lower catwalk are two Tee Plinth electro-optical sensors, used as back-up for the radar fire control systems. (TASS)*

Top right: Kiev *and her sisters still rely on the Bear D long-range reconnaissance aircraft to locate and identify hostile surface forces, and to provide a relay for their SS-N-12 anti-ship missiles. This aircraft is being escorted away from the USS* Nimitz *during the NATO exercise 'Teamwork 80' by one of the carrier's F-14 Tomcats; the F-14s of the combat air patrol (CAP) would pose the major threat to the Bear in the event of hostilities. (US Navy)*

Right: *A close-up of the fore-deck area, on which most of the 'cruiser' weapons are located. The forward SA-N-3 launcher is to the right and the twin 76.2mm mounting to the left. The massive paired launchers for SS-N-12 anti-ship missiles are on either side of the two central deckhouses. Between them can be seen the narrow centre-line lift that brings up additional missile rounds from the magazine, and the rails running athwartships from the lift on which the missiles are moved in line with the tubes for reloading. (US Navy)*

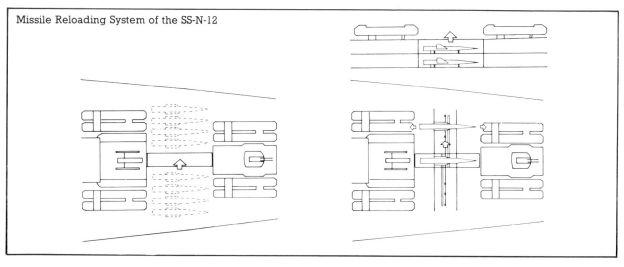

Missile Reloading System of the SS-N-12

figure would suggest a magazine on two deck-levels, with four reloads on either side of the elevator.

The distinctive Scoop Pair radars carried by cruisers equipped with the SS-N-3 missile have been replaced by a single retractable antenna, designated 'Trap Door', which is housed in a rectangular box close to the stem. The height at which the antenna is mounted does not appear to be critical, suggesting that the 'cruise' phase of the SS-N-12 is conducted at high altitude.

The SS-N-12 missile is the major offensive system carried by *Kiev*, and performs the same mission as the fixed-wing attack squadrons of the big US Navy carriers. However, its maximum range of 450km (250nm) does not compare favourably with an operational radius of about twice that figure for the A-7 Corsair and A-6 Intruder strike aircraft currently in service with the US Navy. *Kiev* carries no airborne early warning aircraft capable of detecting surface targets at long range, and is equipped only with short-range helicopters (Hormone Bs) for missile targeting. Targeting data and mid-course correction at these longer ranges would have to be provided by a combination of Bear D bombers and reconnaissance satellites. (Current Soviet satellite capabilities are dealt with in more detail on p. 106.)

The offensive, defensive and reconnaissance capabilities of the US carrier battle group are essentially self-contained, enabling the US carrier to operate in any area of the world without any degradation of its operational effectiveness. The effective employment of *Kiev* is limited, in comparison, by constraints such as the proximity and availability of land-based aircraft (in the form of the Bear D for missile targeting) and the maintenance of adequate satellite surveillance over the operating area in question. Efficient long-range communications are also essential, and *Kiev* is particularly well-equipped in this respect.

Long-Range Communications

Projecting from the top of the central lattice mast are two distinctive Vee Bar high frequency antennae similar to those fitted in the two Sverdlov-class cruisers modified as command ships, and in some submarine depot ships. (The latter apparently serve as flagships of submarine squadrons.) Between the after SA-N-3 launcher and the second of the twin 76.2mm mountings is a radio sextant, designated 'Bob Tail', housed in a box covered by a hinged lid.

Satellite communications terminals are fitted — for the first time in the Soviet Navy — providing the secure ship-to-shore link essential for distant ocean operations. The terminals, which are housed within radomes, are located on platforms projecting from the sides of the superstructure directly opposite each of the Pop Group guidance radars for the SA-N-4 missile system.

A Change of Policy

Fitting long-range SSMs in a ship the size of *Kiev* created few problems from a design point of view. There are, however, indications that there were more important reasons for this departure from previous Soviet practice than the mere availability of the necessary weight and space. Although the attempts to counter the Polaris submarine resulted in major advances in Soviet anti-submarine warfare capabilities, it seems likely that they achieved little other than to hasten the development of American submarine-launched ballistic missiles (SLBMs) with increased range, thereby freeing US submarines from the need to operate in areas such as the eastern Mediterranean and the Norwegian Sea. In the West, too, the sub-hunting groups favoured for open-ocean sub-hunting operations in the late 1950s and early 1960s had been largely discredited, and expert opinion was shifting in favour of the creation of ASW barriers in bottlenecks, or 'choke

Left: Minsk, *with three Yak-36 Forgers on the after part of the flight deck. (TASS)*

points', through which submarines would have to pass in order to reach their patrol areas. The most important of these barriers was in the Greenland/Iceland/United Kingdom (GIUK) Gap, where NATO surface units would combine with diesel patrol submarines, nuclear-powered hunter-killers, and P-3 Orion and Nimrod ASW aircraft to exclude Soviet submarines from the North Atlantic. A fixed underwater detection system based on passive hydrophones, known as SOSUS (Sound Surveillance System), was developed and extended during the 1950s and 1960s. By the early 1970s it was providing high-quality information about Soviet submarine movements through the GIUK Gap and in the North Atlantic area. It was envisaged that the barrier would be further strengthened by the development of the Captor mine — essentially an encapsulated homing torpedo — which would seal off entire sections of the Gap from submarine penetration in the event of hostilities.

The creation of the GIUK ASW barrier provoked two quite distinct Soviet reactions. The first was an attempt to reduce the vulnerability of the growing force of Soviet ballistic-

missile submarines; the second reaction aimed to secure the safe deployment of Soviet attack submarines through the barrier in order to maintain the threat to shipping in the North Atlantic.

The Development of Soviet SSBN Strategy
First and second generation Soviet submarine-launched ballistic missiles had a range of only 650km–3,000km (350–1,600nm), considerably less than that of the Polaris A-3. Early Soviet philosophy concerning submarine-launched missiles appears to have stressed their use against military targets, a mission the Soviets in their turn may have attributed to Polaris (see p. 43). Lack of range was not, therefore, a major concern, as it also implied short flight-times for the missiles with the attendant likelihood of catching strategic bombers on the ground and ships in harbour. The increasing vulnerability of land-based ICBMs, given the improved accuracy (and counter-force capability) of the latest missiles, led to a shift in emphasis towards sea-based nuclear-deterrent systems, both in the United States and in the USSR.

The consequence of this for the Soviet Navy was the development of the Delta-class submarine armed with the SS-N-8 SLBM, which had almost three times the range of its immediate predecessor, the SS-N-6. Whereas the earlier Yankees, which were armed with the latter missile, had to pass through the GIUK ASW barrier in order to target the United States, the Delta — the first of which was completed in 1973 — could fire its missiles from just outside its bases in the Arctic and the north-west Pacific. This made possible the creation of extended inner defence zones, or bastions, in the areas of the Northern and Pacific Fleets, policed by Soviet ASW forces in order to prevent incursions by Western hunter-killer submarines. The range of the SS-N-8 was such that targets throughout the North American land mass could be covered by submarines operating within the bastion areas.

The Bastions*
The major Soviet SSBN bastion was to be created in the Barents Sea in the Northern Fleet area. Its boundary appears to run from the northernmost point on the Kola Peninsula, towards the island of Spitzbergen. It is understood that on the sea bed along this line the Soviets have placed a hydrophone system similar in conception to the American SOSUS. In the event of an outbreak of hostilities, ocean-going anti-submarine units backed up by ASW aircraft, such as the Il-38 May, would patrol this boundary with the aim of excluding NATO submarines.

A similar bastion has apparently been created in the Sea of Okhotsk to the north of Japan. This inhospitable sea, much of which is icebound and shrouded in thick fog for at least half the year, has never favoured surface operations, but it is very deep in places, especially at its south-eastern end, and is ringed by the islands of the Kurile chain. It is an excellent holding area for submarines, as it is totally enclosed by land with the exception of two narrow straits that lead into the Sea of Japan and the numerous deep channels that give access to the north-west Pacific. Increasing Soviet interest in this area is evidenced by a major expansion of facilities at the naval base of Magadan during the early 1970s, and the further development of Petropavlovsk on the southern tip of the Kamchatka Peninsula. Built originally as a submarine base, Petropavlovsk is used increasingly by surface ships, and now boasts four military airfields. Both these ports are isolated from the major Pacific Fleet headquarters at Vladivostok by the lack of a land transport link. They would, however, undoubtedly assume a vital importance in the event of hostilities; Pacific Fleet SSBNs would gather in the Sea of Okhotsk, and ASW forces — anti-submarine ships, patrol ships, submarines and ASW patrol aircraft — would take up patrol positions off the entrances to the channels in the Kurile chain. These ships would presumably be supported from Petropavlovsk, and would operate with the backing of a passive hydrophone system located in the channels.

Although it must be stressed that much of the above is conjecture, the assumptions on which these theories are based go a long way towards explaining developments in the north-west Pacific during recent years; in particular, the 'militarization' of the Kuriles — to the detriment of relations between the USSR and Japan — and the remarkable build-up of the surface element of the Soviet Pacific Fleet, which now

*The term 'bastion' is borrowed from Michael McCGwire, whose writings were a major influence on this and other chapters of the book.

includes seven major anti-submarine vessels, plus ten Krivaks.

Minsk, the second unit of the Kiev class, joined the Pacific Fleet in mid-1979. Since that time, a floating dock 335m by 88m with a capacity of 80,000 tons has been delivered to Vladivostok by Japanese shipyards, complementing a dock of similar size built by Sweden and delivered to Severodvinsk in the Northern Fleet area. There is every indication that the Kiev class, which will eventually number four units, will be shared evenly between the Northern and the Pacific Fleets. The primary role of the ships serving in the latter area will presumably be as the focus of Soviet anti-submarine operations in defence of the SSBN bastion, a role for which their extensive command facilities and their powerful air component make them admirably equipped. They would also be available to support the Soviet land forces around Vladivostok in the event of a serious deterioration in relations with China, and to support the Rocket Cruisers and attack submarines of the Pacific Fleet in breaking any attempted blockade of the Straits of Tsushima by units of the US Seventh Fleet.

The GIUK Gap
The creation of the SSBN bastions, together with the development of longer-range submarine-launched ballistic missiles, was one Soviet response to the GIUK ASW barrier. There remained, however, the problem of access to the North Atlantic for the Yankee-class SSBNs, the first of which had been completed as recently as 1967, and for the large numbers of nuclear-powered submarines armed with cruise missiles and torpedoes serving with the Northern Fleet; there were some 68 of the latter in 1982. These submarines would

The North-West Pacific: The Sea of Okhotsk provides a natural haven for Soviet ballistic missile submarines (SSBN) operating with the Pacific Fleet. The militarization of the Kurile Islands and the rapid expansion of the base at Magadan during the 1970s are clear indications of Soviet intentions. The major base at Petropavlovsk, which has also been extended, provides unrestricted access to Pacific waters both for attack submarines armed with cruise missiles (SSGN/SSG) and torpedoes (SSN/SS) and for surface units operating in defence of the bastion.

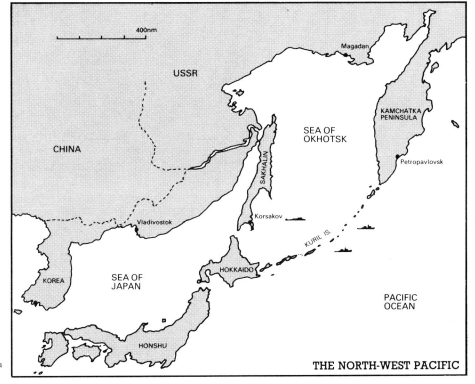

THE NORTH-WEST PACIFIC

The North Atlantic: *A Soviet view of the NATO anti-submarine barrier in the GIUK Gap. In the event of hostilities, deployment of the main offensive arm of the Soviet Navy – its submarine fleet – would involve a battle for control of these all-important waters. The Soviet Navy looks increasingly to its surface fleet, working in conjunction with aircraft and submarines, to break down the NATO defences. The long-range SS-N-12 missiles carried by Kiev would be employed to drive away NATO surface units such as anti-submarine carriers and frigates.*

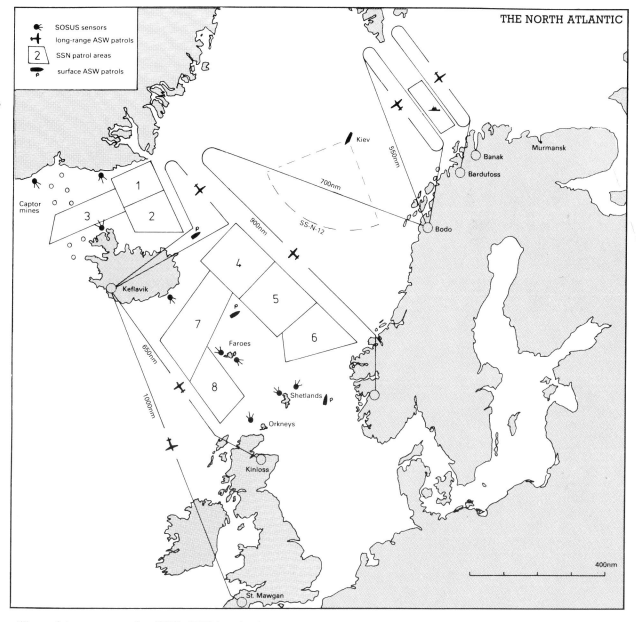

Legend:
- SOSUS sensors
- long-range ASW patrols
- 2 SSN patrol areas
- surface ASW patrols

still need to penetrate the GIUK ASW barrier in order to perform their essential sea denial role. Furthermore, the increased emphasis given by the US Army in recent years to rapid reinforcement of the European armies by air and by sea had created the need for large convoys loaded with equipment vital for the prosecution of a land campaign in Europe. NATO estimates suggest that, in an emergency, no less than one thousand ship-loads would be needed to move supplies and stores across the North Atlantic in the first month, and about half that number for every month after that. Since few Soviet submarines would already be on patrol in the North Atlantic area at the outbreak of hostilities, it would be essential to engineer a break-out of those submarines that found themselves on the wrong side of the barrier.

In his book *The Sea Power of the State*, Admiral Gorshkov has criticized the failure of the German Navy in the Second World War to support its submarine operations with other forces, and has further stated that: 'surface ships . . . remain the essential — and often the only — combat weapons for securing the deployment of the chief striking force of our navy: its submarine fleet'. The implications of these statements are that surface units would be used not only to guard the SSBN bastions, but would be employed offensively against NATO forces preventing the deployment of Soviet attack submarines to their own patrol areas. It is this new 'offensive' element in Soviet anti-submarine strategy that appears to provide the main justification for the heavy battery of anti-ship missiles carried by *Kiev*. Operating in conjunction

Left: *Two major new aircraft entered service with the AV-MF in the mid-1970s: the Tu-20 Bear F, which is an anti-submarine variant of the long-running Bear series, and the Tu-22 Backfire B, seen here. The Backfire B is a new long-range bomber, armed with the AS-4 Kitchen or the AS-6 Kingfish anti-ship missile, both of which have a range in excess of 200km (110nm). The aircraft itself has an unrefuelled radius estimated at 5,000km (2,700nm), and can, therefore, strike at targets in the North Atlantic. Both the Bear F and the Backfire B would be used in support of forward-deployed Soviet surface forces, especially in the GIUK Gap. (Swedish Air Force)*

with SSNs and SSGNs and other Soviet surface units, her role would be to clear a pathway through one of the exit points in the GIUK Gap. NATO SSNs and patrol submarines would be harassed by her Hormone helicopters, and ASW patrol aircraft would be chased away by her Yak-36 Forgers. Surface units, such as ASW frigates and helicopter carriers, would be engaged by her long-range SSMs, probably in conjunction with land-based Backfire bombers, with targeting information provided by Bear Ds.

It is questionable whether such a mission would be attempted in the presence of the big US Navy carriers, as considerable doubts must remain about the survivability of the Soviet ships in the face of an attack by Intruders and Corsairs armed with stand-off missiles. It may be, however, that Soviet surface units would only take up position once the US carriers had been engaged and taken out by the Backfire bombers and Charlie-class cruise missile submarines (SSGNs) charged with that mission. *Kiev* remains vulnerable, even so, to strike aircraft based in the UK and in Iceland, so a further requirement would be the suppression of these air bases by missile or air attack.

Kiev's mission in the Atlantic remains heavily dependent on successful combined operations, with all the attendant problems of coordination and communication. Before she could move against the barrier, she would need to have accurate information on the state of enemy land-based and sea-based air, and about the position of hostile surface units. This information could be provided only by 'external' methods of reconnaissance, such as satellites or Bear Ds. Operations in the Gap itself would depend on the ability of other arms — the Naval Air Force or the Strategic Rocket Forces — to eliminate NATO air superiority.

What cannot be doubted is that the Soviet Navy is preparing for a specific mission in support of its submarines in the GIUK Gap, and that *Kiev* and her sisters will be an important element in the execution of that mission. In July 1980, a major Soviet naval exercise began off the North Cape inside the Arctic Circle. The exercise involved a move outwards into the Norwegian Sea, ending up in the vicinity of Iceland. The surface forces taking part were centred around *Kiev*, and included four Krestas, six Krivaks, a Sverdlov and a Kotlin. The implications of this exercise are obvious: contest-

ing the GIUK barrier is becoming as important a mission for the Soviet Navy as defending it has become for the NATO navies. The renewed emphasis on anti-ship capabilities in some of the latest Soviet ships (see *Kirov* and *Sovremenny*) indicate that they will be a key element in the new strategy.

Power Projection
The suitability of the Kiev class for the power projection mission has been widely discussed in the West. In Britain, this mission has been generally taken for granted, to the point where many commentators have suggested that the Anti-Submarine Cruiser (PKR) designation initially ascribed by the Soviets to *Kiev* was simply a deception to circumvent the terms of the Montreux Convention of 1935, which governs permitted naval movements through the Bosphorus. In the United States, on the other hand, commentators have been quick to point out the significant differences in configuration and capability between the US super-carriers, which were built specifically for the projection mission, and *Kiev*, which is only half the size with an air complement heavily biased towards anti-submarine operations and a substantial 'cruiser' armament.

In the spring of 1979, after the completion of *Minsk*, the Soviet Navy assembled a large force in the Mediterranean which included both of the new Anti-Submarine Cruisers and the recently-completed amphibious transport dock *Ivan Rogov*. This force engaged in a major amphibious exercise off the coast of North Africa. In this exercise, *Rogov* was the central element of the amphibious assault force. The landings were supported by one of the Kiev-class ships, which provided additional helicopters to augment the vertical assault forces and employed her Forger VTOL aircraft in ground support operations. The second Kiev performed anti-submarine operations around the landing force.

Two years later, in the summer of 1981, *Kiev* entered the Baltic, where she joined the helicopter carrier *Leningrad* and 17 other major warships in supporting 'Zapad 81', a major amphibious exercise involving some 45 amphibious vessels. Opposed landings were made with the assistance of land-based aircraft to suppress coastal defences. Exercises such as these reveal, firstly, a capability for power projection and, secondly, an interest on the part of the Soviet Navy in the performance of the new cruisers in such operations. The re-classification of *Kiev* and her sisters as Taktychesky Avionosny Kreyser (Tactical Aircraft-Carrying Cruiser) in 1978 provides further evidence of Soviet awareness of the new possibilities inherent in the operation of fixed-wing aircraft. There can be little doubt, however, that power projection is very much a subsidiary mission of these ships, given the balance of their air complement and weapon systems. Moreover, it is important to note that the Soviet Navy frequently uses vessels in its current armoury to test future concepts. Soviet naval exercises are not staged simply to test the capabilities for which its ships were designed, but also to provide the necessary operating experience for the design of new types better suited to a particular mission that the Soviet Navy is anxious to develop.

A further important distinction needs to be established between the Soviet cruisers and the US Navy's carriers in terms of their relative capabilities for power projection. The US carriers are designed for independent operations against a distant land mass, and can operate anywhere in the world. Their big powerful fighters can create and sustain local air superiority, and their attack aircraft can undertake inter-diction missions against hostile airfields. The Soviet cruisers, however, are incapable of providing an adequate air umbrella while at the same time undertaking ground support missions; the Forgers are too limited in their capabilities and too few in number to accomplish both missions simul-taneously. There are, moreover, no long-range attack squadrons capable of taking out enemy air bases. Air superiority for operations in support of amphibious landings would have to come from Soviet land bases, and this clearly places considerable limitations on the deployment of the Kiev class in the power projection mission.

The most likely scenario for such operations in a European context would be Northern Norway, where a Kiev supported by aircraft from bases on the Kola Peninsula might assist amphibious operations aimed at outflanking NATO ground forces. Similar operations might also prove valuable in the north-west Pacific, especially in the event of a sudden deterioration in Sino-Soviet relations. In the power projection role, the Soviet cruisers are, as it were, tied to a string at the other end of which there must necessarily be a Soviet land base able to provide the requisite air superiority for successful operations.

Replenishment

Throughout the 1960s, Soviet operations were sustained by the concession of port facilities by friendly countries, and by the use of sheltered anchorages in the Mediterranean and the Indian Ocean. Ships were supplied with stores, fuel and munitions while alongside or at anchor. The Soviet merchant marine was widely employed in this task. The few naval tankers capable of underway replenishment used the slow stern refuelling method abandoned by the Western navies during the 1950s. The transfer of solid stores while underway was unknown.

The Soviet Navy began to build specialized replenishment oilers from the late 1960s, employing the latest abeam transfer techniques to supply their major warships with fuel and solid stores while underway. A number of these were already in service by the time *Kiev* commissioned.

Underway replenishment became vitally important with the envisaged extension of Soviet surface operations into the south-western reaches of the Norwegian Sea. In the Kiev design, particular attention has been paid to the transfer of stores to and around the ship. Two constant-tension transfer stations for dry stores and munitions and three probe-type stations for fuel and fresh water are provided on the outboard side of the island. There are also two large cranes on the star-board deck-edge for replenishment in port or at anchor.

Once aboard, missiles, munitions and dry stores can be moved on wheeled trolleys to any part of the ship via a 'railway track' that encircles the forecastle and runs aft along the starboard side directly beneath the transfer stations. The track has branch lines leading off to the SUW-N-1 launcher reload hatches, the SS-N-12 missile elevator, and the three smaller aircraft ordnance elevators aft. The forward crane is also capable of transferring SAMs and SSMs to the larger missile elevator, while the after crane handles the ship's boats that line the outboard side of the island.

Right: *In 1979 the first of a new class of major Soviet replenishment vessels,* Berezina, *appeared. She is much larger and more capable than the earlier naval tankers of the Boris Chilikin class. The capacity for dry stores is double that of the Chilikins. There are two sliding-stay constant-tension stations on either side, in addition to fuel transfer stations. Stores and munitions can also be transferred by the vertical replenishment method, employing two Hormone C utility helicopters. The shortage of specialist underway replenishment vessels is, nevertheless, still a hindrance to forward deployment of the Soviet Navy on a large scale in a combat situation. (DPR, Navy)*

Kirov Class

In the late 1970s, news filtered through to the West of a new type of major surface warship under construction at the Baltiisky Yard, Leningrad. The new vessel was remarkable on two counts. It was of conventional cruiser configuration, unlike *Moskva* or *Kiev*, but its length overall was about 250m with displacement an estimated 25,000 tons — more than twice that of any cruiser in service with NATO and almost three times that of the Kara class. Secondly, there was evidence that the ship would have nuclear propulsion. The Baltiisky Yard had not built major warships for some considerable period. It had, however, been responsible for the construction of the Soviets' first nuclear-powered ice-breaker, *Lenin*, and had recently completed two vessels of a new type, *Arktika* and *Sibir*, powered by two reactors each yielding an estimated 35–40,000shp. The experience of the Baltiisky shipyard in this particular field was almost certainly responsible for the decision to place the order for the new cruiser there.

A third feature of the new cruiser, which became apparent only when *Kirov* began her fitting out, is that she is the first Soviet warship to employ vertical launch techniques for her major missile systems. This particular development is more clearly linked with technological advances than the other two features, which are indicative of important changes in Soviet maritime strategy.

The Rocket Cruiser Makes a Comeback

Soviet reactions to perceived threats from NATO have never produced the sort of warships that the Western nations would have expected, and *Kirov* is no exception. From the mid-1950s until the early 1970s, when the new cruisers were designed, the Soviet Navy never wavered from its faith in the guided missile as a means of by-passing what was seen essentially as a 'reactionary' dependence in the West on aircraft carriers to project power and exercise sea control. Soviet types, therefore, followed a development pattern which had a logic all its own.

While Soviet anti-carrier operations were essentially 'defensive' in nature, as they were in the 1960s, the missile ships could be relatively simple designs with modest air defence and anti-submarine capabilities and limited endurance, not only in terms of operating radius but also in terms of magazine capacities. But the need to contest Western control of open-ocean areas, such as the southwestern extremities of the Norwegian Sea, created a requirement for ships able to operate in sea-space that was essentially the home ground of the NATO navies, whilst at the same time retaining their formidable anti-ship capabilities. These ships would necessarily be larger and more sophisticated than their predecessors. They would need air defence weapons capable of dealing with the concentrated force of NATO carrier-based and land-based attack squadrons;

Opposite page: *All the major weapons systems carried by Kirov are located in the forward part of the ship. Tucked inside the forecastle is the twin-tube launcher for SS-N-14 anti-submarine missiles. Behind it are the twelve small hatches of the SA-N-6 air defence system and the twenty larger hatches for SS-N-19 anti-ship missiles. (MoD)*
Left: *The bow wave formation created by Kirov indicates that she is fitted with a large bow-mounted sonar. (MoD)*

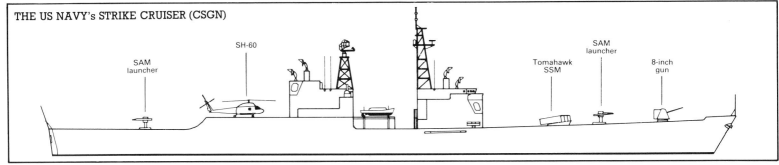

THE US NAVY's STRIKE CRUISER (CSGN)

SAM
launcher

SH-60

SAM
launcher

Tomahawk
SSM

8-inch
gun

Left: *A magnificent stern view of* Kirov, *1980, with the large door that conceals the variable depth sonar particularly prominent. (MoD)*
Opposite page: *This early photograph of* Kirov, *taken in 1980, emphasizes the high freeboard of the ship. The flare and sheer of the bow section is well-suited to rough-water operations in the Northern Fleet area. (MoD)*

improved anti-submarine capabilities, which would enable them to defend themselves against NATO SSNs; first-rate communications, to enable them to maintain secure command links with Soviet naval headquarters ashore and to coordinate the activities of other friendly units in their operating area; and much greater staying power.

Only considerations such as those outlined above make any sense of the dramatic increase in size of *Kirov* as compared with the last of the previous series of Rocket Cruisers, the Kresta I. The increase in displacement from 6,000 tons standard for the latter to a massive 20,000 tons for *Kirov* is unprecedented in a ship of basically the same type occupying a place in the same line of development. It is, on the other hand, worth pointing out that the complement of twenty long-range anti-ship missiles carried by *Kirov* is only four more than the total number of rounds carried by the much smaller Kynda class. The increase in displacement is dictated not so much by the requirement for greater anti-ship firepower as by the requirement to exercise that firepower in areas where previously the Soviet Navy was not able to operate with any great confidence; in areas such as the Greenland/ Iceland/United Kingdom (GIUK) Gap. Defensive qualities and the requirement for better communications and endurance account for the major part of the increase in displacement.

Kirov and the US Navy's Strike Cruiser

There are a number of striking similarities between *Kirov* and the now-defunct Strike Cruiser (CSGN) proposed by the US Navy in the mid-1970s. The latter was conceived as a carrier escort capable of independent operations at the centre of a surface action group (SAG). As well as being fitted with the Aegis air defence system, with its unrivalled capacity for tracking and engaging a large number of air targets simultaneously, the Strike Cruiser would have carried a powerful battery of long-range Tomahawk cruise missiles in armoured box launchers for anti-surface engagement. Air defence and anti-submarine missiles would be fired from twin-arm launchers fore and aft, a large hangar and flight deck for two Sea King or LAMPS III ASW helicopters was to be provided, and two Phalanx Gatling-type weapons were to be fitted for close-in anti-missile defence. Later drawings of the ship also show a major-calibre 8in (203mm) gun mounting for fire support operations. The overall balance and composition of the armament was therefore remarkably similar to that of *Kirov*.

The link between the two designs is not purely coincidental. All the available evidence suggests, however, that the CSGN was influenced by Soviet developments rather than the other way round. The Strike Cruiser proposal was initiated in 1975 — too late to have influenced the design of *Kirov*, which had been laid down two years previously. The proposal came, moreover, when the US Navy was particularly receptive to new concepts as a result of the fundamental reappraisal of tactical and strategic thinking begun by Admiral Zumwalt, who served as Chief of Naval Operations (CNO) from 1970 until 1974. The advent of long-range American cruise missiles prompted a serious consideration of how to multiply Soviet targeting problems by shifting more offensive power onto the decks of surface units, instead of continuing to concentrate that power on a few big carriers.

Unfortunately, the projected cost of the Strike Cruiser approached that of a nuclear-powered carrier, and since the carrier force would need an estimated two dozen escorts fitted with Aegis in the not-so-distant future the CSGN was barely affordable. Even if it were, it was unlikely that it could be released from the carrier escort role to perform the independent surface operations that would have been responsible for much of the additional cost. The proposal was therefore rejected and replaced by one for a cheaper, conventionally-powered Aegis escort (the DDG 47) which was more in line with the US Navy's traditional tactical thinking.

General Configuration

The general configuration of *Kirov* is basically what we have come to expect of a Soviet cruiser. For three-quarters of the ship's length there is no sheer, but the raised forecastle rises sharply towards the bow. The after part of the ship is characterized by the customary full waterplane, which is utilized to provide a broad flight deck for helicopters, with a hangar beneath. The main deck-line breaks at this point onto a low quarterdeck. The broad transom stern incorporates a large square door concealing a variable depth sonar. The sides of the hull are flared through the water-line throughout the ship's length, thereby maximizing available deck-space. A prominent knuckle runs all the way aft from just forward of the superstructures.

The superstructures are also typical of earlier Soviet construction, rising in gently graduated steps towards a massive central pyramid. The latter was at first assumed to be simply a radar tower for major surveillance and ECM antennae, but photographs published during *Kiev*'s sea trials revealed hitherto unsuspected exhaust vents angled upwards from the rear of the pyramid structure, throwing into question earlier assumptions about nuclear propulsion.

Forward of the pyramid is a massive superstructure block carrying one of two guidance radars for the air defence system. The navigation bridge is at the forward end of the block. Atop the after end, sandwiched between the guidance radar and the central tower is a hexagonal-shaped admiral's bridge. The navigation bridge is large and well-sited, but the admiral's bridge has poor views fore and aft. Immediately forward of the bridge structure, at a lower level, there is a tall deckhouse carrying a number of small fire control radars and direction-finding aerials. The after superstructure rises in steps occupied by a second series of fire control radars, including the second of the guidance radars for the air defence system, and culminates in a short pyramid mast mounting surveillance radars and long-range communications antennae. One of the most striking features of *Kirov* is the long flat fore-deck area, where the vertical launch systems are housed. It makes a striking contrast with the 'spiky' superstructures, which still bristle with electronic apparatus in the manner of earlier Soviet designs.

Anti-Ship Missiles

Located on this flat fore-deck is the battery of anti-ship missiles which constitute the main armament of *Kirov*. The missiles are housed in a large armoured box sunk into the hull, probably to a depth of about ten metres, immediately forward of the superstructures. Twenty hinged hatches, each 3.5m by 2.5m are arranged in four rows of five. The missiles are launched vertically and may employ a 'cold launch' technique using a sabot or ram — similar to that of the latest Soviet ICBMs — in order to avoid blast damage to the launcher silos or to the ship's superstructures.

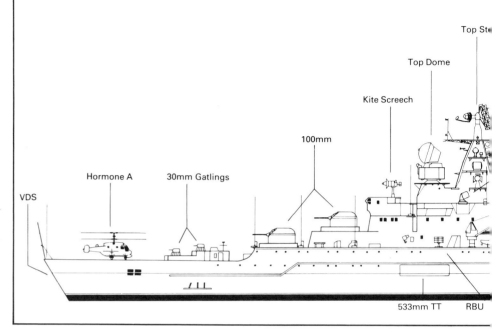

KIROV CLASS

Top St...

Top Dome

Kite Screech

100mm

Hormone A   30mm Gatlings

VDS

533mm TT   RBU

Right: *A bow three-quarter view of* Kirov *underway, 1980. The pyramid superstructure layout, culminating in the tall central tower mast, is typical of Soviet cruiser construction. (MoD)*

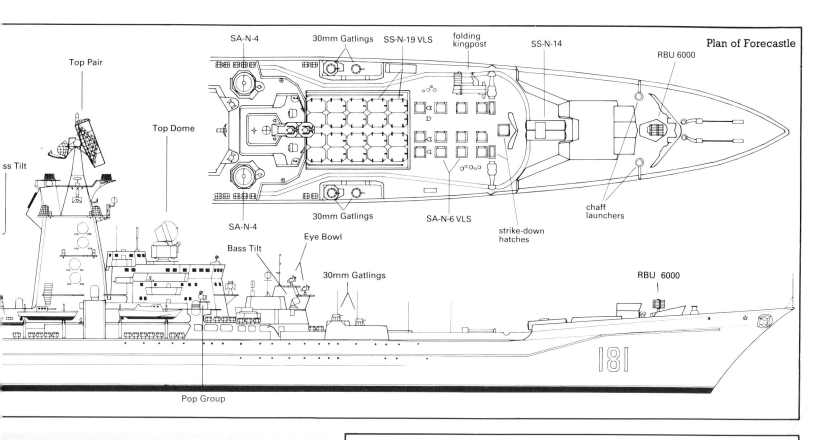

Top Pair

Top Dome

ss Tilt

SA-N-4

30mm Gatlings

SS-N-19 VLS

folding kingpost

SS-N-14

RBU 6000

30mm Gatlings

SA-N-4

Eye Bowl

Bass Tilt

30mm Gatlings

SA-N-6 VLS

strike-down hatches

chaff launchers

RBU 6000

Pop Group

KIROV CLASS
Soviet designation: Raketny Kreyser (RKR — Rocket Cruiser)

Construction

Ship	Builder	Laid down	Launched	In service
Kirov	Baltiisky Yard, Leningrad	1973	Dec 1977	Sept 1980
....		Jan 1978	June 1981	

Displacement
Standard: 20,500 tons. Full load: 23,400 tons.

Dimensions
Length: 248m (814ft), overall; 230m (755ft), between perpendiculars.
Beam: 28m (92ft), upper deck; 24m (79ft), water-line.
Draught: 7.5m (25ft).

Armament
ASuW: 20 SS-N-19 launchers (20 missiles); 1–2 Ka-25 Hormone B missile targeting helicopter(s).
AAW: 12 vertical SA-N-6 launchers (96 missiles); 2 twin SA-N-4 launchers (36 Gecko missiles); 2 single 100mm (3.9in) guns; 8 30mm Gatlings.
ASW: 1 twin SS-N-14 launcher (14–16 missiles); 2–3 Ka-25 Hormone A helicopters; 1 12-barrelled RBU 6000 rocket launcher; 2 6-barrelled RBU 1000 rocket launchers; 2 quadruple banks of 533mm (21in) torpedo tubes.

Electronic equipment
Surveillance radar(s): 1 Top Pair, 1 Top Steer; 2 Palm Frond.
Fire control radar(s): ? (SS-N-19); 2 Top Dome (SA-N-6); 2 Pop Group (SA-N-4); 2 Eye Bowl (SS-N-14); 1 Kite Screech (100mm guns); 4 Bass Tilt (30mm Gatlings).
Sonar(s): 1 bow-mounted low-frequency sonar; 1 low-frequency VDS.
ECM: 8 Side Globe; 10 Bell series; 4 Rum Tub.

Machinery
2-shaft CONAS; 2 nuclear reactors, each 40,000shp, plus oil-fired superheaters; 120,000shp = 31 knots maximum.

Complement
800.

Little is known about the performance of the missile, designated SS-N-19, except that it appears to be intermediate in size and range between the SS-N-9 and the SS-N-12, and that it is, like the former, capable of underwater launch. This factor is crucial for the vertical launch mode adopted in *Kirov*, and the smaller size of the SS-N-19 as compared with the SS-N-12 deployed on *Kiev* makes the missile better suited to vertical stowage. It is unlikely, however, that such an arrangement would be possible in a smaller ship as, even in a vessel the size of *Kirov*, the missiles take up a considerable part of the hull-depth.

The great advantage of the vertical launch system is that all twenty missiles are ready for use, making saturation attacks possible against an enemy task force. Earlier Rocket Cruisers, such as the Kynda class, which carried a total of sixteen missile rounds, could launch only half that number simultaneously before commencing a complex and lengthy reloading process. The succeeding Kresta I could launch a maximum of only four missiles against an enemy task force, and even *Kiev*, with an estimated 24 missile rounds, is subject to the same limitations as the Kynda class. Vertical launch obviates the need for the bulky launchers and elevating mechanisms carried by previous cruisers; complex reloading arrangements are totally eliminated. The cost lies in the internal volume taken up by the vertical stowage system, which is probably in the region of 3000m³.

There is no visible evidence of a guidance radar for the SS-N-19 missile system. However, in the centre of the raised forecastle, there is a tall square box housing that could contain such a radar; *Kiev* has the Trap Door tracking radar for her SS-N-12 missiles similarly located.

Satellites

By the time of *Kirov*'s completion, the Soviet Ocean Surveillance System had been greatly extended by the deployment of surveillance satellites. These currently include photographic, active radar and passive ESM models. Each type of satellite has limitations if used in isolation: the intelligence provided by photographic satellites is at the mercy of cloud cover, which is a particularly important consideration in the North Atlantic and north-west Pacific areas, and a factor that a hostile enemy surface force served by good weather intelligence could use to its own advantage; active radar satellites are useful for detecting groups of ships without necessarily being able to analyse accurately the composition of such a group, and they provide little useful information about individual units; and ESM satellites can identify radar and radio transmissions but are vulnerable to deception countermeasures. It is necessary, therefore, to use a combination of these satellites in order to build up a clear picture of hostile naval activity.

Whilst there can be little doubt that Soviet satellite surveillance will prove increasingly effective in the detection and identification of NATO forces, the continuing use of Bear D reconnaissance aircraft to establish the precise identity of individual ships and groups of ships detected by satellite is an indication that land-based aircraft remain an essential component of the Soviet Ocean Surveillance System. Soviet satellites currently in service have significantly less endurance than their NATO counterparts, and, as their importance to the Soviet Command and Control structure increases, we can expect them to become a priority target for American anti-satellite systems now under development.

SA-N-6

Kirov's principal air defence system, the SA-N-6, also employs vertical launch. Forward of the armoured box housing the SS-N-19 missiles, there are twelve hatches in three rows of four; two of the rows are located to starboard and the third to port. The asymmetrical disposition of the hatches suggests, firstly, that each hatch is served by a vertical magazine ring holding between six and eight missile rounds and, secondly, that the magazine rings of the outer hatches are located on the outboard side of the hatches themselves, with those serving the inner row being located to port of their respective hatches. Curiously, the system adopted appears to negate to a large extent two of the major advantages associated with vertical launch: namely, the elimination of reloading systems — which are vulnerable to mechanical and electrical failure — and the space-saving potential of locating all the missiles in a single compact box. (The box system is not only favoured by the US Navy for future SAM installations, but is employed by *Kirov* herself for the SS-N-19 missile.)

Two clear advantages remain, however, and these are clearly the ones that counted for *Kirov*'s designers. The first is the ability to put several missiles into the air in rapid succession. The second is one that relates closely to the operating conditions of the Soviet Navy in general and of the Northern Fleet in particular: the elimination of above-decks launchers in the severe weather conditions of the Barents and the Norwegian Seas must result in significant improvements in missile-reliability.

Little is known about the performance of the SA-N-6 missile itself. It has been suggested that it may be a derivative of the land-based SA-10, although this seems unlikely given that the latter entered service after the SA-N-6 and appears to be designed to counter low-flying cruise missiles rather than high-flying aircraft. The SA-N-6 has been extensively tested over the past four years aboard the Kara-class cruiser *Azov*, and may be a purely naval development. A missile of about 6m length seems likely, with a range of perhaps 50km (27nm), although this would depend on the guidance system employed.

Two large radars designated 'Top Dome' are associated with the SA-N-6. Each comprises a bowl-shaped main antenna, together with a smaller antenna at its base which may provide a command link. Previous major Soviet air defence systems have employed command guidance, which requires a separate guidance radar for each target engaged. *Kirov* has only two such radars, and one of these is mounted on the after superstructure, thereby complicating the problem of missile acquisition. It can be safely assumed that

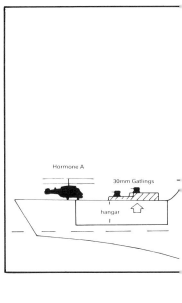

SA-N-6
In service: 1980.
Length: 6m plus (20ft).
Diameter: ?
Span: ?
Weight: 700kg? (1,540lb).
Warhead: ? kg HE.
Propulsion: Solid-propellant single stage.
Speed: Mach 5.
Range: 50km (27nm).
Guidance: TVM (track-via-missile).
Fire control: Top Dome.

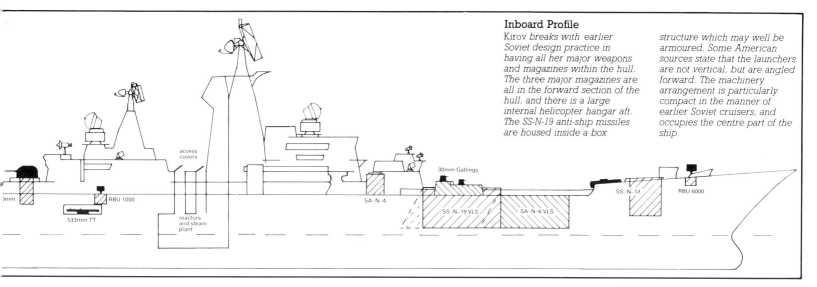

Inboard Profile

Kirov *breaks with earlier Soviet design practice in having all her major weapons and magazines within the hull. The three major magazines are all in the forward section of the hull, and there is a large internal helicopter hangar aft. The* SS-N-19 *anti-ship missiles are housed inside a box* *structure which may well be armoured. Some American sources state that the launchers are not vertical, but are angled forward. The machinery arrangement is particularly compact in the manner of earlier Soviet cruisers, and occupies the centre part of the ship.*

0mm

access covers

RBU 1000

533mm TT

reactors and steam plant

SA-N-4

30mm Gatlings

SS-N-19 VLS

SA-N-6 VLS

SS-N-14

RBU 6000

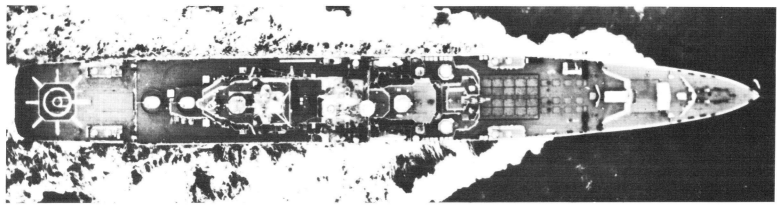

Above: *An overhead view of* Kirov. *The vertical launch systems forward of the bridge are particularly evident. Note the full waterplane typical of Soviet construction. (US Navy)*

command guidance has been abandoned, and that the SA-N-6 system installed in *Kirov* can engage a large number of targets simultaneously — a minimum requirement in an operating area such as the GIUK Gap, where a ship as important as *Kirov* might justify the attention of up to three dozen strike aircraft even from a single carrier battle group.

It has been suggested that both the SA-N-6 and the land-based SA-10 employ a track-via-missile (TVM) system. In the TVM system a phased array multi-function radar tracks and illuminates several targets in rapid succession. Each missile launched receives the radar signal reflected from its target and re-transmits it down to a computer. The computer processes the data and then transmits course corrections to the missile. Terminal homing eliminates the need for target illumination in the final phase. The ability of the tracker/illuminating radars to switch rapidly between targets enables several missiles to be kept in the air simultaneously. Although it would be surprising if the TVM system employed on *Kirov* could handle as many targets as the American Aegis — which can keep eighteen missiles in the air, in addition to those in the terminal phase — the SA-N-6 clearly represents a major advance on previous Soviet naval SAMs. It provides evidence also of increasing sophistication in the computerized tracking of multiple targets and missiles.

Other Air Defence Weapons

The SA-N-6 area defence system is backed up by the customary complement of short-range and close-in systems. SA-N-4 'bins' are fitted on either side of the tall deckhouse forward of the bridge, with their Pop Group guidance radars mounted on pedestals abreast the bridge structure itself. There are two single 100mm guns aft, with their Kite Screech fire control radar immediately above them atop the after superstructure. The single 100mm now appears to have superseded the twin 76.2mm in Soviet construction, indicating a move towards general-purpose guns with a superior anti-surface capability for use against small craft such as fast patrol boats. Paired Gatlings for close-in anti-missile defence are located fore and aft of the main superstructures on either side of the upper deck. Each pair of guns is mounted on its own deckhouse, which presumably contains the magazines, and has its own Bass Tilt fire control radar. The fire control radars for the forward guns are located on either side of the deckhouse forward of the bridge, and the radars for the after guns are fitted abreast the after radar tower.

Back-up for the radar fire control systems is provided by a new and unidentified electro-optical device fitted at the four corners of the ship. Two are located on platforms projecting from the forward end of the bridge structure, while a second pair is fitted on either side of the after radar tower. ECM provision is on a par with *Kiev*, the principal systems being eight Side Globe radomes and four Rum Tub ESM antennae, disposed on either side of the tall central 'mack'.

Surveillance Radars

The major air surveillance and tracking radars carried by *Kirov* are similar to those installed in *Kiev*. Atop the central 'mack' there is a large 3-D radar, designated 'Top Pair'. This is basically Top Sail with the addition of a long-range air search antenna mounted back-to-back in place of the counter-balancing vanes. The new antenna was at first thought to be Big Net, which it resembles in general size and configuration. A closer look, however, reveals a new aerial with a completely different lattice structure. It seems strange to Western eyes that the Soviets should deploy an advanced third-generation area defence system, such as the SA-N-6, in combination with a heavy, second-generation air surveillance aerial, such as Top Sail, with a new modification simply added on. It is, however, a development typical of Soviet design practice, which favours incremental improvements to existing systems rather than radical redesign.

The second 3-D radar is Top Steer, which is fitted atop the after radar tower. The provision of two powerful 3-D radars on a ship such as *Kirov*, which, unlike *Kiev*, does not operate large numbers of aircraft herself, suggests that these radars are important to the command and control mission. They would enable *Kirov* to monitor closely all aerial movements in her operating area, and to direct friendly aircraft against hostile ships and planes.

Command, Control and Communications

Kirov, like *Kiev*, is clearly designed to serve as a flagship; *Kiev* would operate at the centre of an anti-submarine group, *Kirov* at the centre of a surface action group. Communications and command facilities are, therefore, exceptionally complete. The high frequency direction finder mast projecting from the after radar tower is topped by two Vee Tube high frequency communications antennae. There is a mass of broad-band dipoles for long-range work at the forward end of the after superstructure, while the central 'mack' itself carries omnidirectional dipoles for VHF and UHF line-of-sight telephony. Abreast the 'mack' are two satellite communication terminals similar to those fitted in *Kiev*, and atop it are two circular tubs, designated 'Round House' — first seen on the Kara-class cruiser *Petropavlovsk* — which are thought to be for tactical air navigation (TACAN).

Anti-Submarine Systems

There is nothing startlingly new about any of the anti-submarine systems installed in *Kirov*. Her ASW outfit comprises helicopters, missiles, rocket launchers and torpedo tubes, with data provided by a large bow sonar and an independent variable depth sonar. The difference between *Kirov* and earlier cruisers, with the exception of *Moskva* and *Kiev* (which are specialist anti-submarine vessels), lies in her capacity for sustained ASW operations in areas far from Soviet bases.

Helicopters

The large helicopter hangar, which is located beneath the low quarterdeck, can accommodate about five Ka-25 helicopters (probably a mixture of the 'A' ASW version and the

Hangar Arrangement

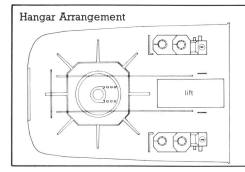
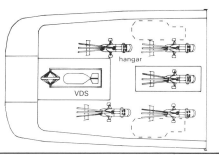

'B' missile targeting version), even allowing for the centre-line space occupied by the large variable depth sonar. One of the design features that makes this possible relates to the lift, which is located at the forward end of the quarterdeck and descends to form part of the hangar floor, the open well being closed by twin hinged doors. This arrangement enables at least three helicopters to be accommodated side by side at the forward end of the hangar, with a further helicopter on either side of the mechanism for the variable depth sonar. The helicopter is moved from the lift, which measures 15m by 5m, aft to the single helo-circle, which is covered by the customary mesh mat. The absence of the heat-resistant cladding employed on *Kiev* would appear to preclude the possibility of VTOL operations with Yak-36 Forger aircraft suggested by some commentators.

There is a small flight control cabin for helicopter operations at the after end of the superstructure, immediately above the second 100mm mounting. Palm Frond navigation radars, located on platforms projecting from either side of the central 'mack', are presumably also used for helicopter control, and there is a microwave landing radar on the star-board side of the after radar tower.

Anti-Submarine Missiles

Tucked inside the break in the forecastle is a reloadable twin-tube launcher for SS-N-14 ASW missiles, with its magazine forward of it. Since a reloadable ASW missile system, the SUW-N-1, was already in service on other major units, such as *Moskva* and *Kiev*, it is somewhat surprising that the Soviets, with their predilection for long production runs, should have developed a new reloading system specifically for *Kirov*. One possible reason may have been that the location of the SUW-N-1 magazine aft of the launcher proved unsuited to *Kirov*, given the layout of the SAM and SSM magazines at the forward end of the ship. However, a more interesting possibility is that the Soviets have consciously adopted a non-nuclear anti-submarine missile for *Kirov* in preference to the nuclear-tipped FRAS-1 associated with the SUW-N-1 launcher. The deliberate choice of a non-nuclear capability in preference to a nuclear one would have to be seen as evidence that the Soviet conception of sea-power has, over the past twenty years, been shifting slowly and subtly towards an acceptance of the possibility of naval operations in situations short of all-out (ie, nuclear) war. The installation of the SS-N-14 system in *Kirov* may be a more significant development than it might at first appear.

The abandonment of the SA-N-3 area defence system, together with its Head Lights radar, in favour of the SA-N-6, has resulted in the need for separate fire control provision for the SS-N-14 missiles, as on the Krivak class. Two small Eye Bowl guidance radars are superimposed atop the deckhouse forward of the bridge.

Rocket Launchers and Torpedoes

Close to the bow there is a single twelve-barrelled RBU 6000 rocket launcher. Six-barrelled RBU 1000 rocket launchers are located on either side of the after superstructure at upper-deck level. Just below them, quintuple tubes for the 533mm torpedoes are concealed behind sliding doors in the hull.

The bow sonar and the variable depth sonar, which is set into the stern behind a massive door bearing the ship's crest, are both high-powered low-frequency models. There is

every indication, therefore, that no expense has been spared in the effort to give *Kirov* a first-rate defensive capability against hostile submarines.

Propulsion

There was considerable initial surprise in the West when it was discovered that *Kirov* had a hybrid propulsion system. After much speculation, it now seems generally agreed that the plant is a CONAS (combined nuclear and steam) combination. During sea trials, *Kirov* was observed to maintain a speed of 24 knots without any sign of exhaust gases, thereby confirming initial assumptions about nuclear propulsion. She was also observed blowing tubes and emitting dense clouds of black smoke from the large twin uptakes angled aft from the top of the 'mack', indicating with equal certainty some form of steam propulsion system. Since unlimited endurance is the principal advantage conferred on a ship by the installation of nuclear plant it seems likely that *Kirov* uses nuclear power for a high, sustained cruising speed, and steam plant in combination with it to boost the maximum speed to a figure of 30 knots plus.

The reasons for the adoption of such an unconventional propulsion system seem to rest on the limited capacity of available proven reactors. The reactors installed in the icebreakers *Arktika* and *Sibir*, which were built at the same shipyard, have an individual power-rating estimated at 35–40,000shp. Four reactors of this type would be necessary to propel a ship the size of *Kirov* at a speed of over 30 knots, and these would make heavy demands on hull volume. In the event, the Soviets appear to have opted for a hybrid propulsion system based on only two reactors. Two large circular armoured doors are fitted between the central 'mack' and the after superstructure. These are believed to allow the removal of the reactor cores, indicating that the reactors themselves are close together on the centre-line.

Two possibilities have been suggested for the steam element of the propulsion plant. The nuclear and steam plant could power separate turbines, operating in parallel. Such a system would be perfectly feasible, especially if separate shafts were employed for each of the four power units. The position of the propeller guards, which are unusually far forward, suggests, however, that there are only two very large diameter propellers. If the steam and nuclear elements of the propulsion plant operate independently of one another, they would have to be linked by large, complex gearing. An interesting alternative put forward by some commentators is that oil-fired superheaters are used to superheat the steam generated by the nuclear reactors, thereby raising available horsepower by about 50 per cent. While the design of separately fired heaters would not be an easy matter, this is a solution worthy of close consideration. Assuming the power generated by the nuclear plant alone to be about 80,000shp, oil-fired superheating would give a total figure in the region of 120,000shp, adequate for a speed of about 30 knots.

The machinery layout adopted for *Kirov* is typically compact, and contrasts with that of much smaller US Navy cruisers in which the propulsion plant is divided into two independent units for damage control purposes. It is of interest to note, however, that the solution to the damage control problem on *Kirov* appears to be that of locating the nuclear reactors *inside* the steam plant, thereby taking advantage of the considerable beam of the ship. Longitudinal bulkheads on either side of the centre-line would enable the Soviets to isolate the operation of the nuclear plant from whatever oil-fired system is employed to provide boost, leaving the ship with more than adequate speed to extricate herself from any potentially dangerous situation.

Replenishment

Kirov continues the trend set by *Kiev* towards improved facilities for underway replenishment. Transfer stations for ASW and surface-to-air missiles are located on either side of the bow just aft the break in the forecastle. The SA-N-6 missiles are struck down via rectangular hatches inboard of the transfer stations. There is a square hatch for strike-down of the SS-N-14s on the centre-line, immediately behind the blast-shield for the launcher. On the port side, abaft the transfer stations, there is a large king-post that folds down close to the deck when not in use to avoid interference with the flight of the missiles. It seems unlikely that the large SS-N-19 missiles can be taken aboard at sea, as the silos would have to be loaded from above, and there are no heavy-lift cranes similar to those on *Kiev*.

There appear to be three stations for liquid replenishment; one is at the forward end of the superstructure to starboard with the remaining two on either side of the after structure. Amidships on the port side there is a constant-tension transfer station for dry stores. Stores and munitions can be transferred to different parts of the ship by the now-familiar 'railway track' employing wheeled trolleys. The track encircles the entire superstructure and fore-deck area, and is served amidships by a pair of light cranes for use when the ship is alongside.

The Old and the New

Kirov hovers uneasily between two distinct generations of Soviet warships. In conception — that of the oversized, all-capable cruiser at the centre of an anti-carrier surface action group — she is the product of tactical ideas prevalent in the Soviet Navy in the late 1960s and early 1970s. She should be seen as the ultimate realization of the Soviet Rocket Cruiser concept, as a unique product of the Soviet decision to circumvent the aircraft carrier and to revolutionize surface warfare by the application of post-war missile technology.

There are, however, a number of features associated with the *Kirov* design that reflect a significant shift towards Western design philosophy, a development made necessary by the transformation of the Soviet Navy from a coastal defence force into a fully-fledged ocean-going navy capable of sustained operations. The increased emphasis on internal volume, and on weapon systems with greater ship impact (that is, systems which have to be integrated closely with the overall design of the ship, and not simply slotted in or bolted on), is a feature that is also characteristic of the latest destroyers, *Sovremenny* and *Udaloy*, and which accords more closely with Western design practice than might have been expected.

On the other hand, Soviet practices as regards radar installations remain unchanged; air surveillance and tracking radars are still duplicated, and individual fire control radars are assigned to each weapon system. The result is the long, bare forecastle, contrasting with spiky superstructures bristling with radar and communications antennae. *Kirov*, in common with many other Soviet warships (and perhaps like the Soviet State itself), is a curious mixture of high technology, conservatism and improvisation.

The New Destroyers

In the late 1970s, two new classes of destroyer were laid down in the Baltic. The first unit of one class, *Sovremenny*, was laid down in 1976 at the Zhdanov Yard (Leningrad), where she followed the last of the Kresta-class cruisers onto the slipways. Further ships of this type were begun in each of the next three years. The first unit of the second class, *Udaloy*, was laid down in 1978 at Kaliningrad, but construction of this type was shared on a fifty/fifty basis with the Zhdanov Yard. The first ships of each class were duly completed within a few months of one another in 1980–81.

These two classes had been typed as 'destroyers' in the West even while building; although in terms of dimensions and displacement they were of similar size to the 'cruisers' of the Kresta class. They were not, of course, designated as such by the Soviet Navy, which classifies *Udaloy* as a Large Anti-Submarine Ship (BPK) and *Sovremenny*, presumably, as a Large Rocket Ship (BRK). The term 'destroyer' applied to both ships in the West is apt, nonetheless, as it highlights major differences in the design philosophy of these ships and that of their predecessors.

The Kresta I was designed essentially for single-ship operations and, even if accompanied by Kashin-class destroyers, would have been the capital ship of its group. Even the Kresta II anti-submarine modification would, in its time, have served at the centre of ASW hunting groups. The new ships are clearly escorts themselves, designed not as the central element of a task group, but to support and protect that central element, be it an Anti-Submarine Cruiser (PKR) of the Moskva or Kiev class, or a Large Rocket Cruiser of the Kirov class. Instead of endeavouring to perform a number of missions (ASW, air defence, anti-surface) moderately well, they are designed to specialize in one or other of the primary Soviet naval missions, to the detriment of the all-round qualities that are an essential feature of the larger cruisers.

Those two primary missions differ significantly from the two primary missions of task force escorts built for the contemporary US Navy. The Soviet missions are *anti-surface* and anti-submarine, whereas those of the US Navy's escorts are *air defence* and anti-submarine. The essential reason for this difference is that the organization of the US Navy is based on the carrier battle group, whereas that of the Soviet Navy is based on groups of surface ships that do not include large-deck carriers. The anti-surface mission of the US Navy is performed by the attack squadrons of the carrier; consequently, the escorts have the task of protecting the carrier against air and underwater attack. In the Soviet Navy, the anti-surface mission is performed by the surface ships themselves; there is no 'queen bee' that has to be protected at all costs. Anti-submarine weapons on anti-surface missile ships are for self-defence only, while those on ASW ships are for sub-hunting rather than for the protection of a single central unit. Air defence weapons are for self-defence; the larger units (such as *Moskva*, *Kiev* and *Kirov*) also have the most powerful batteries of surface-to-air missiles and do not rely, as do the American carriers, on dedicated air defence units to protect them.

The two new classes of destroyer simply confirm and reinforce earlier patterns of Soviet naval development. *Sovremenny* is optimized as an anti-surface ship with long-range cruise missiles and large-calibre guns, the latter presumably for the fire support mission; a medium-range air defence system with relatively little 'ship impact' is fitted, and anti-submarine qualities are distinctly second-rate. *Udaloy*, on the other hand, is a specialist anti-submarine vessel, carrying two helicopters in addition to the usual battery of missiles, rocket launchers and torpedoes, and fitted with first-rate underwater sensors; she carries no anti-surface weapons, and only a short-range surface-to-air missile system for self-defence.

The two types are complementary, and could find themselves operating together in all sorts of combinations and on a variety of missions; for example, ASW destroyers providing flank support for surface action groups composed of Rocket Cruisers and Large Rocket Ships, or Large Rocket Ships providing anti-surface protection for sub-hunting groups composed of Anti-Submarine Cruisers and Large Anti-Submarine Ships. Their construction and design are a logical extension of Soviet tactical thinking of the early 1970s, and owe nothing to the decision to build large-deck carriers rumoured to have taken place in about 1974. Although both types would clearly be useful as escorts for a task group centred on such a ship, both are deficient in one important respect: they lack a long-range area defence system, which would be essential to protect a unit without a major air defence capability of its own.

New Developments in Design Philosophy

The dramatic increase in size over earlier Soviet destroyer types is indicative of the adoption of volume-intensive features more commonly associated with modern Western construction. This is almost certainly a result of the Soviet Navy's experience of long-range deployments since the late 1960s. Ships built during the late 1950s and early 1960s, such as the Kynda, Kashin and Kresta classes, were heavily armed but cramped in every respect. Machinery installations and weapons systems were manpower intensive, but habitability and crew comforts received a low priority. Deck heights were lower than those of contemporary Western vessels, leaving little space for cables and other services. Electrical generating power was limited, with small safety margins available in the event of damage or mechanical failure. Both propulsion and auxiliary machinery was located as compactly as possible, with little regard for damage control and with relatively poor access for maintenance and repair.

Below-decks magazines were small, especially by US Navy standards. The relatively small size of the ships restricted the amount of space available for fuel tanks, thereby reducing endurance by comparison with their Western counterparts.

Udaloy and *Sovremenny* have approximately twice the internal volume of the Kashin class, which terminated production only in 1974. Deck heights in both new ships are about 2.6m throughout; the older Kanin class had a deck height of less than 2m. They have much smaller complements than earlier vessels of similar size: *Sovremenny*'s is estimated at 330 men and that of *Udaloy* 300 men, whereas the Kresta II has a complement estimated at 380. Since there is little increase in internal magazine stowage in either class — the anti-surface missiles of *Sovremenny* and the anti-submarine missiles of *Udaloy* are both carried above the level of the upper deck in cylindrical launchers located beneath the bridge wings — it appears likely that much more attention has been paid to the on-board maintenance of weapons and machinery, to the provision of more capable tactical data systems, and to endurance. In effect, this means larger command spaces, more stowage for spares, improved access for machinery and electronics, and greater capacity for dry and liquid stores.

Standardization

Sovremenny and *Udaloy* have almost identical overall dimensions and a similar standard displacement. It is surprising, therefore, that the two ships should have so little in common in terms of equipment and general build. The most obvious difference lies in the choice of propulsion system; *Sovremenny* has conventional steam turbines with the uptakes trunked into a single funnel; *Udaloy*, like the earlier Kashin class, is powered by four large gas-turbines with paired uptakes fore and aft.

But the lack of standardization goes deeper than this. Although the ships are built for different missions and — not unnaturally — have different major weapons systems, even where one might have expected some commonality of systems this is not always the case. This is true particularly of the air defence systems; they appear to have been developed simultaneously, yet not only are the launch systems different — *Sovremenny* has single-arm launchers with magazines beneath, while *Udaloy* has a vertical launch system — but so are the methods of guidance, the fire control radars, and the associated air search and tracking radars. The air defence system on *Sovremenny* appears to employ semi-active guidance, and uses a long-range 3-D tracker in combination with six small illuminators; that on *Udaloy* will apparently use command guidance, and will employ two large tracking and guidance radars, with initial target data being provided by two short-range back-to-back air surveillance radars.

Minor differences extend even to the smaller anti-submarine weapons; *Udaloy* has quadruple torpedo tubes and RBU 6000 rocket launchers, while *Sovremenny* has twin tubes and RBU 1000 rocket launchers. In effect, only the 30mm Gatlings and the ECM arrays are common to both classes.

Standardization of equipment has long been regarded as one of the major advantages of the Warsaw Pact in any future conflict with NATO. The new types of surface warship currently under construction for the Soviet Navy appear to break with this principle. They may, as a consequence, prove difficult to supply with spares and munitions, given that the Soviets still possess few auxiliary vessels specializing in underway replenishment.

SOVREMENNY

Although the first visual impression conveyed by *Sovremenny* is that of a completely new ship, a closer look reveals that the design is, in fact, based on the Kresta classes. This is all the more surprising because the original Kresta design dates back to the early 1960s, before the first tentative steps towards true ocean-going operations had been made by the Soviet Navy. Overall hull dimensions are virtually identical, and the similarity of internal layout is evidenced by the position of the funnel uptakes.

Two important modifications have been made to the original Kresta hull-form: the raised deckhouse that extends to the ship's sides on the Kresta's forecastle has been carried forward to the bow, resulting in a forward section that is one deck higher; and the main deck has been carried aft to the stern without a break. These modifications have had two favourable consequences: the additional height of the bow section improves sea-keeping; and there is a significant

Below left and right: *Two shots of* Sovremenny *taken in the North Atlantic in December 1981. New ECM radomes have been fitted at the base of the tower foremast and at a lower level between the bridge structure and the ship's boats. (US Navy)*

increase in internal volume, thereby correcting one of the major defects of the hull-form of the Kresta. But these changes have been made at the cost of extra topweight.

The superstructures of *Sovremenny* are considerably simplified as compared with the Kresta and Kara classes. A large block superstructure four decks high rises from the forecastle break. At its after end is a prominent tower mast carrying a Top Steer 3-D air surveillance and tracking radar. The superstructure also carries most of the fire control radars for the missiles and guns. Running forward from the superstructure is a complex of tiered deckhouses, which rise in steps towards the bridge. Running aft is a broad shelter deck carrying the ship's boats.

The after superstructure comprises a single broad funnel, which is faired into a telescopic helicopter hangar (the first such installation in the Soviet Navy), with a tall deckhouse carrying fire control radars on either side. Atop the hangar is a tall but lightly constructed lattice mast, carrying radio aerials and ESM antennae. The helicopter platform itself is two decks high, the deck below it serving as a foundation for all superstructures aft the bridge and terminating just aft the second SAM launcher. The location of the helicopter platform and hangar inboard of the after gun mountings and missile launchers recalls US Navy practice; earlier Soviet (and West European) types, including the new ASW destroyer *Udaloy*, have the platform on or above the stern, with the hangar immediately forward of it and any aft-mounted weapons systems atop the hangar (or superfiring above it in the case of the Kresta and Kara classes). The location of the hangar/platform complex at the level of the second superstructure deck in any cruiser/destroyer type is unprecedented; even in the US Navy's Spruance and Belknap classes, which have similar helicopter arrangements, the helicopter platform is at 01 and upper deck level respectively. The solution adopted by *Sovremenny* carries with it considerable topweight penalties; it does, however, provide an excellent platform for helicopter operations in all weathers.

Propulsion

It was not altogether clear when *Sovremenny* first appeared whether she was powered by steam or gas turbines. The latter seemed likely in view of previous Soviet trends evident in the Krivak and Kara classes which, like *Sovremenny*, both

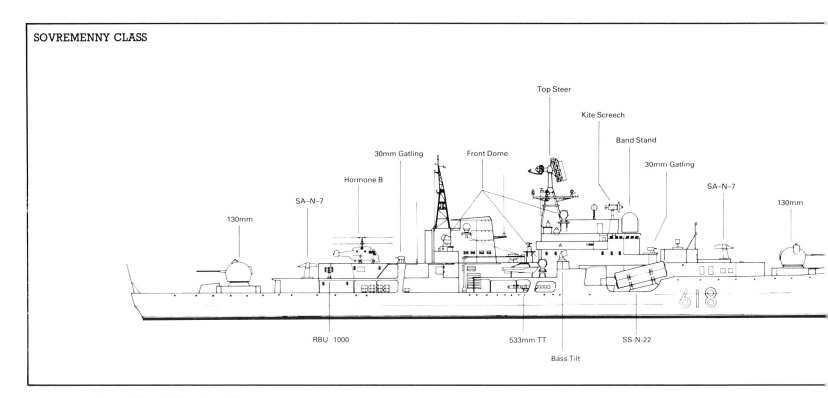

Top Steer

Kite Screech

Band Stand

30mm Gatling   Front Dome

30mm Gatling

Hormone B   SA–N–7

SA–N–7

130mm   130mm

RBU 1000   533mm TT   SS-N-22

Bass Tilt

have a single broad funnel. The size of *Sovremenny* poses few problems in this respect, as the four gas-turbines of the Kara class would be more than adequate to propel her at a maximum speed estimated at around 33 knots. Observation of *Sovremenny*'s performance on sea trials produced evidence of features generally associated with gas-turbine propulsion: the ship's engines emit a high-pitched whine, and rapid acceleration from dead in the water to 32 knots in less than two minutes was achieved.

Equally, there are a number of contrary indications. The funnel itself is somewhat smaller than that of the Kara class and does not appear to have the large air intakes at its base necessary for a four-turbine propulsion system. The location of the lattice mainmast immediately aft the funnel is also a contrary indication. Earlier Soviet ships with gas-turbine propulsion either have the funnel uptakes divided and canted outwards (for example, the Kashin class) or they have a single funnel positioned well aft of centre, with all delicate electronic apparatus forward of the hot exhaust gases (for example, the Krivak and Kara classes). West European and US Navy gas-turbine ships have adopted similar arrangements. Perhaps the most conclusive argument against gas-turbine propulsion, however, is the clear derivation of the new ships from the Kresta, which has pressure-fired, automated steam plant. It has already been noted that the position of the funnel uptakes of the two classes is identical, and the adoption of similar propulsion machinery would appear to follow naturally from the adoption of the same basic hull-form. Moreover, unlike the Udaloy class, all ships of the Sovremenny class have been laid down at the same Zhdanov Shipyard that built the Kresta II class, with the first unit of the new class following *Admiral Yumashev* (the last ship of the Kresta II class) onto the slipways in 1976.

SOVREMENNY CLASS
Soviet designation: Bol'shoy Raketny Korabl' (BRK — Large Rocket Ship)

Construction

Ship	Builder(s)	Laid down	Launched	In service
Sovremenny	Zhdanov Yard,	1976	Nov 1978	1981
Otchanny	Leningrad	1977	Aug 1980	1982
....		1978	1981	
....		1979		

Displacement
Standard: 6,200 tons. Full load: 7,800 tons.

Dimensions
Length: 159m (522ft), overall; 148m (486ft), between perpendiculars.
Beam: 17m (56ft).
Draught: 5.6m (18ft).

Armament
ASuW: 2 quadruple SS-N-22 launchers (8 missiles); 1 Ka-25 Hormone B missile targeting helicopter; 2 twin 130mm (5.1in) guns.
AAW: 2 single SA-N-7 launchers (48? missiles); 4 30mm Gatlings.
ASW: 2 6-barrelled RBU 1000 rocket launchers; 2 twin banks of 533mm (21in) torpedo tubes.

Electronic equipment
Surveillance radar(s): 1 Top Steer; 3 Palm Frond.
Fire control radar(s): 1 Band Stand (SS-N-22); 1 Kite Screech (130mm guns); 6 Front Dome (SA-N-7); 2 Bass Tilt (30mm Gatlings).
Sonar(s): 1 bow-mounted medium-frequency sonar.
ECM: 2 Bell Shroud, 2 Bell Squat, 4 new Bell.

Machinery
2-shaft geared steam turbines; 100,000shp = 33 knots maximum.

Complement
350.

Below: *Sovremenny is pictured here during her transit from the Baltic through the Mediterranean to join the Black Sea Fleet in early 1982. The full armament is now shipped, and includes twin 130mm mountings and single-arm SA-N-7 launchers fore and aft, and quadruple tubes for SS-N-22 anti-ship missiles abreast the bridge structure. (French Navy)*

Anti-Ship Missiles

Sovremenny ran sea trials with her sensor outfit virtually complete but with none of the major weapons installed. Estimations of the precise nature of the ship's armament were made possible by the Soviet practice of associating single-function fire control radars with a particular weapon system. Much of this early conjecture has been confirmed by the subsequent installation of the remaining equipment, which was fitted as it became available and was finally in place by September 1981.

In place of the SS-N-14 'boxes' of the Kresta II class, there are fixed quadruple launch tubes for anti-ship missiles. The Band Stand radome, located atop the navigation bridge, suggested initially that the missile would be the intermediate-range SS-N-9, which first appeared on the Small Rocket Ships (Maly Raketny Korabl' or MRK) of the Nanuchka class in 1969 and was subsequently installed on the Sarancha-class hydrofoil. Conceived as an over-the-horizon missile for small ships, and not as a long-range anti-carrier weapon such as the SS-N-3, the SS-N-9 is considerably smaller than the latter; a maximum range of about 165km (90nm) seems likely. It is reported that the missile carried by *Sovremenny* is a sea-skimmer, and it has duly received the NATO number SS-N-22. Nevertheless, the launch tubes themselves are identical in dimensions to those of the earlier missile, as is the radar guidance system, suggesting that the new missile is a revamped SS-N-9 rather than a completely new model.

The Ka-25 helicopter carried by *Sovremenny* is the 'B' version of the Hormone, not the more usual 'A' model, and is used for missile targeting.

A New Major Calibre Gun

One of the lessons of the Vietnam War for the US Navy was

Opposite page: In this overhead view of Sovremenny the mine-rails are clearly visible around the after 130mm mounting. They appear to be connected with the now-customary 'railway track' that encircles the ship's super-structure, and which is used for the transfer of stores and munitions during replenishment. (US Navy)

Above: *Sovremenny on sea trials in the Baltic in 1980. None of her major weapons has been installed as yet, but she carries a full outfit of surveillance and fire control radars. The Band Stand radome above the bridge provided early evidence of the intention to fit anti-ship missiles, and of the primary anti-surface mission of the class. Note the telescoping hangar, the first of its kind in the Soviet Navy. (US Navy)*

Below: *A bow view of Sovremenny, taken during her sea trials in the Baltic. The Kite Screech fire control radar is trained to starboard. The drum-shaped radars to either side of it are Front Dome illuminators, while those at a lower level are the Bass Tilt fire control radars for the 30mm Gatlings. (US Naval Institute)*

that large-calibre guns would continue to be useful — it not essential — for fire support operations against enemy positions ashore. The vessels that provided this support in the 1960s were largely war-built cruisers armed with 8in or 6in guns. In view of their age, all would decommission during the 1970s; it was imperative, therefore, that the fire-support capability they provided should be replaced. The solution envisaged was the Major Calibre Light Weight Gun (MCLWG), which was installed experimentally in the old destroyer *Hull* (DD 945) in 1975. The MCLWG was a single 8in (203mm) gun housed in a lightweight turret made of glass-reinforced plastic, capable of firing a variety of ammunition, including laser-guided projectiles. It was to have been fitted in the proposed Strike Cruiser (CSGN, see p.103) and retro-fitted in the Spruance-class destroyers from the early 1980s, but trials with the weapon appear not to have been as successful as had been hoped and the project was abandoned.

The Soviet Navy found itself in a similar position to the US Navy, except that the crisis point was reached some five to ten years later; the Soviets were still building conventional cruisers armed with 152mm (6in) guns and conventional destroyers with 130mm (5.1in) well into the 1950s, and many of these ships were still in service by the late 1970s. Indeed, the Soviet position was in some ways worse than that of the US Navy. Whereas the US Navy had at least persisted with the medium-calibre gun in the form of the single 5in (127mm) for its cruisers, destroyers and frigates of the 1960s and 1970s, no Soviet surface ship completed between 1960 and 1976 had a gun larger than 76.2mm. The single 100m, which replaced the twin 76.2mm anti-aircraft mounting on major construction in

---

SS-N-22

In service: 1981.
Length: 8.5–9m (28–30ft).
Diameter: ?
Span: ?
Weight: 3,500kg? (7,700lb).
Warhead: 500kg (1,000lb) HE or 200kt nuclear.
Propulsion: Liquid-fuel motor.
Speed: Mach 0.8.
Range: 110–170km (60–90nm).
Guidance: Radar/command; active radar/infra-red homing.
Fire control: Band Stand.

the late 1970s, was hardly an ideal weapon for fire support. In spite of this, fire support remained an important Soviet naval mission, especially in the Baltic and the Black Sea.

Although completed without her main armament, *Sovremenny* had prominent foundations for gun mountings fore and aft. The diameter of these was such that they were clearly intended for a gun mounting larger than the single 100mm fitted in *Kirov* and the Krivak II class. Within a few months of beginning her sea trials, *Sovremenny* had the new mountings installed. The guns, which revive the 130mm calibre standard on Soviet post-war destroyers, are mounted in a new twin turret of novel design. The barrels, which are exceptionally long (70cal), are set close together and presumably elevate together. The gun housing, of spherical configuration, is of lightweight construction (possibly glass reinforced plastic) and is designed for fully automatic operation, although there is the customary on-mount control position for back-up. It seems likely that the Soviets will have developed a new range of ammunition, possibly including laser-guided projectiles, for use with the gun, which is reported to have a high rate of fire.

Fire control is provided by Kite Screech, which had previously been employed only in conjunction with the single 100mm mounting. Although the gun mountings on *Sovremenny* are disposed fore and aft, there is only a single fire control radar, mounted atop the forward superstructure. This marks a departure from previous Soviet practice — witnessed in the Kashin class, for example — according to which guns covering different arcs are provided with separate fire control radars. The twin 130mm mountings installed in *Sovremenny* appear to be designed for a maximum elevation of about 85° and can, therefore, be used against aircraft, but the provision of only a single fire control radar strongly suggests a primary anti-ship and fire support mission for the new mountings.

ASW

The anti-submarine capability of *Sovremenny* is distinctly second-rate, especially if one compares the ship with specialist ASW vessels such as the Kresta II class, the Kara class and *Udaloy*. The configuration of the stem suggests a bow-mounted sonar, but the wave pattern of the ship indicates that it is relatively small. Unlike the hull sonar of other modern Soviet surface units, it is not backed up by a variable depth sonar. No anti-submarine missiles are fitted, and the helicopter is almost certainly a missile targeting version not an ASW model.

The only anti-submarine weapons are two six-barrelled RBU 1000 rocket launchers, which are fitted abreast the helicopter platform at the level of the first superstructure deck, and two twin torpedo mountings, tucked in beneath the shelter deck immediately aft of the bridge structure. This places the overall ASW capability of *Sovremenny* on a par with much smaller coastal vessels, such as the Grisha class, and serves to emphasize the low priority given 'to this area of the ship's armament.

Air Defence

The air defence missile launchers, such as the anti-ship missiles and the major-calibre guns, were not in place when *Sovremenny* was first completed and were installed only in late 1981. There is now a single-arm launcher forward, super-firing above the 130mm mounting, and a second launcher aft

130mm gun (twin)
In service: 1981.
Barrel length: 70cal.
Angle of elevation: −15/+85°.
Rate of fire: 30rpm per barrel.
Projectile weight: 27kg? (60lb).

Muzzle velocity: 1,000m/sec? (3,280ft/sec?).
Range: 28km (15nm) max.
Fire control: Kite Screech/local.

Inboard Profile

The weapon load is on a par with the Kresta design from which she is derived, but there is an increase in hull and super-structure volume to provide improved command facilities and greater endurance.

similarly disposed. Prominent blast-shields, angled out at about 45° from the after end of the helicopter deck, protect the RBU 1000 rocket launchers, which are mounted at the same level on either side.

The launchers are identical to the one installed in the trials ship *Provorny* (see p. 34) in the late 1970s, and are associated with the SA-N-7 missile. In view of the similarity between the Soviet launcher and the US Navy's Mk. 13 launcher, it seems likely that the SA-N-7 has a similar medium-range area defence role to the Tartar/Standard series. It can, therefore, be regarded as a replacement for the SA-N-1 Goa missile, which was being fitted in modernized Soviet destroyers of the Kanin class as late as 1976. The SA-N-7 missile is probably about 4.5m in length with a maximum range of about 25km (13nm) and may be a close relation of the land-based SA-11 that is now coming into service.

Air surveillance and tracking is provided, as on *Provorny*, by the large Top Steer 3-D radar, which is carried atop the tower foremast. Guidance for the missiles is provided by six small fire control radars, designated 'Front Dome', also seen for the first time on *Provorny*. On *Sovremenny* they are disposed in three pairs on the sides of the superstructures; one pair on platforms projecting from the bridge structure immediately forward of the tower mast, the second amidships on the shelter deck, and the third on the tall deckhouses that project from either side of the helicopter hangar. The 'drum' configuration of these radars, reminiscent of small Soviet gun fire control radars such as Drum Tilt and Bass Tilt, is not compatible with command guidance, which generally requires separate antennae to track the target and the missile. It seems likely that the Soviets have finally adopted the semi-active guidance method favoured in the West since the late 1960s, and that the small fire control radars on *Sovremenny*'s superstructures are charged with tracking and illuminating only the target, with the missile homing on the reflected radar beam. The tracker/illuminators are disposed in such a way that all arcs can be covered. The provision of six radars means that six targets can be engaged simultaneously — in theory at least. As the tracker/illuminators are mounted hard against the sides of the superstructure, it is questionable how much of an advantage this arrangement has over a smaller number of tracker/illuminators mounted

atop the superstructures with good all-round arcs, in the manner of the US Navy and most West European navies. The problem for the Soviet designers, as usual, is that the forward centre-line positions are already occupied or unusable; those on the forward superstructure are occupied by the fire control radars for the anti-surface weapons, while those above the hangar are unusable because of their proximity to the funnel.

The close-in anti-missile system was in place from the beginning. It comprises the usual two pairs of 30mm Gatlings, each controlled by a Bass Tilt fire control radar. An unusual feature of the installation is that the Gatlings have not been mounted close together on either side, but have been divided between the forward end of the superstructure and positions on either side of the helicopter deck. This provides more effective cover for the four corners of the ship. The Bass Tilt radars are mounted on deckhouses projecting from the sides of the forward superstructure.

ECM

Electronic countermeasures provision on *Sovremenny* is only on a par with that of the Kashin or Krivak classes. Gone are the eight Side Globe radomes that dominated the super-structures of earlier cruiser-type vessels of similar size. Only the smaller radomes of the Bell series remain, serving as a further indication that the Soviets have redrawn the line which divides the major vessels from their supporting units.

SA-N-7

In service: 1981.
Length: 4.5m? (15ft).
Diameter: 0.30m? (1ft).
Span: ?
Weight: 500kg? (1,100lb).
Warhead: ?kg HE.
Propulsion: Solid-propellant single stage.
Speed: Mach 3.
Range: 25–28km (13.5–15nm).
Ceiling: 14,000m (45,000ft).
Guidance: Semi-active radar.
Fire control: Front Dome.

Comparison of the Weapon/Sensor Fits of Sovremenny and Udaloy	Sovremenny	Udaloy
ASuW		
Anti-ship missiles	●	
Missile targeting helicopter	●	
Major-calibre gun	●	
ASW		
Anti-submarine missiles		●
Anti-submarine helicopter		●
Anti-submarine rocket launchers	●	●
Anti-submarine torpedo tubes	●	●
Low-frequency sonar		●
Medium-frequency sonar	●	
Variable depth sonar		●
AAW		
Area defence system	●	
Point defence missile system		●
Medium-calibre dual-purpose gun		●
Close-in weapon system (CIWS)	●	●
3-D tracking radar	●	
2-D air search radar		●

Note: The disparity in armament between these two ships, which appeared almost simultaneously and are of similar size and displacement, is quite remarkable. The only systems they have in common are comparatively minor ones: anti-submarine rocket launchers, torpedo tubes, and the CIWS.

UDALOY

Whereas the basic hull-form and propulsion machinery of *Sovremenny* belong to an earlier design, the new Soviet ASW destroyer *Udaloy* owes little to her predecessors. She has been designed from the keel up as a specialist anti-submarine ship. Although she bears a superficial external resemblance to earlier Soviet BPKs, in conception she marks a radical departure from the Kresta and Kara classes, in which anti-submarine qualities were almost of secondary importance by comparison with the extensive air defence provision. The anti-submarine systems in the Krestas and Karas were fitted in such a way that they would not detract from the vessels performance in the air defence role; in *Udaloy*, the anti-submarine systems take pride of place, and everything else is fitted around them. In this respect she closely resembles the US Navy's Spruance class, which carries a remarkably similar outfit of weapons on a similar displacement.

In Soviet terms, *Udaloy* can be seen as an outgrowth of the Krivak rather than as a successor to the Kresta II. She carries the same anti-submarine missile as the Krivak class, an identical outfit of torpedo tubes and rocket launchers, two short-range surface-to-air systems, and an identical gun outfit to the Krivak II. In terms of sensors, she is fitted, like the Krivak, with both bow and variable depth sonars, and only short-range air surveillance radars. The gas-turbine propulsion machinery is almost certainly a doubled-up

Krivak plant, separated into two units, as in the earlier Soviet Kashin and the US Navy's Spruance. The significant increase in size over the Krivak is due to several factors: the provision of a large double hangar for anti-submarine helicopters aft; larger and more powerful underwater sensors; improved ECM and anti-missile capabilities; and features associated with greater operational endurance, such as larger numbers of anti-submarine missiles, improved access for maintenance, increased stowage for spare parts, and larger fuel tanks.

Hull-Form and General Layout

The hull-form adopted for *Udaloy* has many of the characteristics typical of Soviet construction, but shows certain improvements on earlier vessels. *Udaloy* has the customary broad waterplane aft, and the prominent knuckle running forward from the break in the forecastle. Scuttles have been retained on the accommodation decks (suggesting that the air-conditioning plant is still small by Western standards), and the stem of the ship has the usual exaggerated overhang, with the anchors mounted well forward. The forecastle break is abaft the machinery uptakes, however, not at the forward end of the bridge as in *Sovremenny*. This gives *Udaloy* greater freeboard amidships than that of earlier types, which have a standard freeboard of about 5m compared with the 6.75m of *Udaloy*.

The other unusual feature of *Udaloy*'s hull is the reverse sheer of the bow, a characteristic of some modern West European frigates and destroyers. This type of bow was pioneered by the French in the 1960s as a means of firing the forward guns at low angles. The location of the two single 100mm mountings of *Udaloy* forward of the bridge — an unusual position in recent Soviet construction — clearly influenced its adoption for the new destroyers.

The superstructure arrangements on *Udaloy* are neat and practical, with the full beam of the ship being utilized where possible in order to maximize internal volume. The bridge structure is in the form of a large square block four decks high, with the launcher tubes for the anti-submarine missiles on either side at its forward end beneath cantilevered bridge wings. An empty circular platform and a tall pylon for fire control radars are located atop the forward part of the structure, and at its after end there is a short lattice mast. The centre part of the ship is occupied by the two pairs of funnel uptakes for the gas-turbine propulsion system. The after uptakes rise from a single superstructure deck, which extends to the side of the ship, and have a second lattice mast immediately forward of them. Abaft the second pair of uptakes the forecastle deck continues to the stern as a single superstructure deck. It is faired into the twin helicopter hangars and at the stern it forms the housing of the variable depth sonar mechanism, which serves as a base for the broad helicopter platform.

The overall appearance of *Udaloy* is that of a sleek, well-designed vessel that should prove very successful in service. Compared with earlier Soviet designs, which often appear cobbled together from different odds and ends, she is a true thoroughbred, with harmonious lines and an armament well-matched to her size and purpose.

Propulsion

In opting for COGAG propulsion machinery for *Udaloy*, the Soviets are capitalizing on extensive earlier experience with

Labels on diagram: VDS; Helix A; RBU 6000; SA–N–?; Strut Pair; Strut Pair; Kite Screech; Eye Bowl; 100mm; 533mm TT; SS–N–14; 480

UDALOY CLASS
Soviet designation: Bol'shoy Protivolodochny Korabl' (BPK — Large Anti-Submarine Ship)

Construction

Ship	Builder	Laid down	Launched	In service
Udaloy	Kaliningrad Yard	1978	1980	1981
Vitse Admiral Kulakov	Zhdanov Yard, Leningrad	1978	1980	1981
....	Kaliningrad Yard	1979		
....	Zhdanov Yard, Leningrad	1979		

Displacement
Standard: 6,200 tons. Full load: 7,900 tons.

Dimensions
Length: 162m (531ft), overall; 148m (485ft), between perpendiculars.
Beam: 19m (62ft).
Draught: 6.2m (20ft).

Armament
ASW: 2 Ka-36 Helix A helicopters; 2 quadruple SS-N-14 launchers (8 missiles); 2 12-barrelled RBU 6000 rocket launchers; 2 quadruple banks of 533mm (21in) torpedo tubes.
AAW: 8 vertical SA-N-8? launchers (48? missiles); 2 single 100mm guns (3.9in); 4 30mm Gatlings.

Electronic equipment
Surveillance radar(s): 2 Strut Pair; 3 Palm Frond.
Fire control radar(s): 2 Eye Bowl (SS-N-14); 2? (SA-N-8?); 1 Kite Screech (100mm guns); 2 Bass Tilt (30mm Gatlings).
Sonar(s): 1 bow-mounted low-frequency sonar; 1 low-frequency VDS.
ECM: 2 Bell Shroud, 2 Bell Squat, 4 new Bell.

Machinery
2-shaft COGAG; 4 gas-turbines, each 25,000bhp = 100,000bhp; 32 knots maximum.

Complement
300.

large gas-turbine-powered warships. The four turbines themselves are almost certainly the same model employed in the Krivak and Kara classes. The four turbines can be expected to yield a total horsepower identical to that of the Kara class (100–112,000bhp, twice that of the Krivak), for a top speed of around 33 knots. The Kaliningrad and Zhdanov shipyards in the Baltic have considerable expertise in the installation of gas-turbines as a result of their experience with the Krivak, and the choice of these two yards for the construction of *Udaloy* and her sisters is not without significance.

The reversion to the unit machinery arrangement of the earlier Kashin is interesting, not only because it provides yet another point of comparison with the US Navy's Spruance, but because the evidence of the Krivak and Kara classes suggested that Soviet practice was moving towards the compact machinery arrangements we associate with their steam-powered ships. The explanation appears to lie with the abandonment of the long-range air defence systems of the Kara, which occupied considerable centre-line space fore and aft and forced a variety of other weapons to the sides of the ship in the midships area. In *Udaloy*, as in the Kashin class, almost all the weapons systems are located fore and aft, allowing the propulsion machinery to be divided once more into two separate units. The provision of large lattice masts close to the funnels on the centre-line has resulted in the division of the uptakes to take the hot exhaust gases clear of the delicate electronics.

There is no evidence as yet to suggest that the selection of gas-turbines for *Udaloy* was influenced by the requirement for 'quiet' operations in the anti-submarine mission. This was a significant factor in the choice of gas-turbine propulsion for

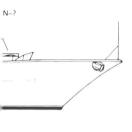

N–?

Above, top: Udaloy *in the
summer of 1981. Although not as
imposing visually as earlier
Soviet anti-submarine ships she
has a neat, business-like
appearance. The emphasis is on
sea-keeping, endurance, and a
powerful, well-coordinated suite
of ASW weapons at the expense
of the air defence capabilities of
previous designs. (Royal Navy)*
Above: *An overhead of* Udaloy,
*showing the neat, compact
layout of the superstructures
and the paired gas-turbine
uptakes. Two pairs of vertical-
launch canisters for surface-to-
air missiles are sunk into the
low deckhouse on the forecastle,
and two further pairs are
located at the after end of the
helicopter hangar. (US Navy)*

the Spruance class, which has a number of additional features designed to reduce noise emission: modular turbine installation on flexible rafts; silencing baffles in the air intakes; the use of gas-turbine generators for electrical power supplies in place of the usual diesels; and controllable-pitch propellers, which enable the blades to be feathered in trail-shaft cruise operations. It would be surprising if the Soviets had not made some progress in the direction of flexible engine mountings and silencing techniques. The absence of separate intakes for the generating plant suggests, however, that *Udaloy* still employs diesels to produce her electrical power. It is also not clear whether the Soviets have yet developed large controllable-pitch propellers. If not, the level of underwater noise must be detrimental to sonar performance in trail-shaft cruise operations.

Anti-Submarine Warfare

The anti-submarine missile carried by *Udaloy* is the SS-N-14, which is housed in quadruple box launchers on either side of the bridge structure. The quadruple box launcher has been preferred to the twin reloadable launcher recently installed in *Kirov*. The latter presumably would have taken up valuable centre-line space required by the ship's air defence systems, and the missile magazine would be too bulky to be accommodated in *Udaloy*'s smaller hull if it were to contain more than the eight rounds carried in the box launchers. Guidance for the SS-N-14 missiles is performed by two small Eye Bowl fire control radars, located side by side atop the bridge.

Quadruple 533mm torpedo tubes are fitted at main deck level immediately aft the forecastle break, and there are twelve-barrelled RBU 6000 rocket launchers above them. The large bow sonar and the variable depth sonar are thought to be the same low-frequency models installed in *Kirov*; these are the most powerful underwater sensors yet installed by the Soviets in a ship of this size.

Helicopter Arrangements

The principal innovation in terms of anti-submarine capabilities is the provision of twin helicopter hangars aft. ASW operations from destroyer-sized ships employing two helicopters are now well-established in the NATO navies. The French Tourville and Georges Leygues classes, the British Type 22 frigate, the Dutch and German Standard frigate, and the US Navy's Spruance and Oliver Hazard Perry classes are all designed to operate a wartime complement of two helicopters, even though in peacetime only one is generally carried. The West European vessels all operate the small Anglo-French Lynx, but the large double hangars of the American ships can accommodate two helicopters of a heavier type, such as the current SH-2F Seasprite or the SH-60 Seahawk now on order. The Soviets have also favoured the heavier type of helicopter for their own ASW operations. The earlier Soviet large anti-submarine ships were fitted with a single hangar and flight deck for the same Ka-25 Hormone that was flown from the larger anti-submarine cruisers.

During Exercise 'Zapad 81' held in September 1981 in the Baltic, *Udaloy* conducted trials with a new helicopter, the Ka-32 Helix. The Helix appears to be an updated version of the Hormone, slightly larger but with the same distinctive coaxial rotor arrangement. The main improvement of the Helix over the Hormone is its more capacious fuselage,

A neat, practical design,
Udaloy *has all her major*
weapons distributed fore
and aft, the centre part of
the ship being occupied by
the gas-turbine machinery.

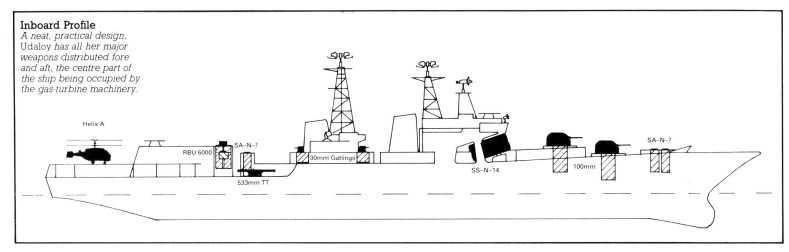

Helix A

RBU 6000

SA–N–?

533mm TT

30mm Gatlings

SS–N–14

100mm

SA–N–?

allowing more room for monitoring equipment and comunications. Beside the chin-mounted surface search radar there are boxes on either side of the fuselage which presumably contain sonobuoys. Whilst there is little startlingly new in the external configuration of the Helix, it can be safely assumed that the avionics outfit is a major advance on that of the Hormone.

Instead of adopting the broad double hangar common to all the NATO vessels, *Udaloy* has individual hangars side by side with a control cabin between them. This arrangement allows the fitting of missile tubes and fire control radars between the hangars, but there is necessarily some reduction in overall hangar space with adverse consequences regarding ease of maintenance and the stowage of spares. The hangars are on two deck-levels, as on the Kresta II and Kara classes. The helicopters are wheeled into their respective hangars on guide-rails. They are then struck down on lifts, which descend to become the hangar floor. Instead of the hinged roof employed on the Kresta and Kara, each hangar has a roof constructed in telescoping sections that slide back to enable the rotor head of the helicopter to be accommodated prior to strike-down. On the outside of the starboard hangar there is a microwave landing control radar to assist helicopter landings. Not long after completion, Round House TACAN aerials similar to those installed in *Kirov* and the Kara-class cruiser *Petropavlovsk* were fitted on the yardarms of the mainmast.

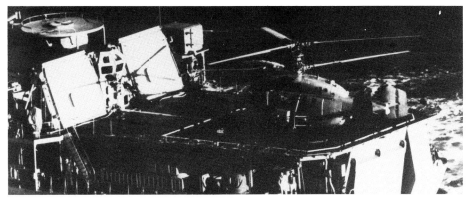

Kamov Ka-32 Helix A
In service: 1981.
Length: 11.3m (37ft), fuselage; 13.3m (44ft), overall.
Rotor diameter: 16m (52ft).
Performance details can be assumed to be similar to those of the Ka-25 Hormone, with improvements in avionics, increased combat radius, and greater weapons and sonobuoy capacity.

Air Defence
Udaloy carries anti-air systems only for her own defence. The primary air defence system is one that, at the time of writing, has received no NATO designation, although it seems likely that it will be allocated the code number SA-N-8. The system

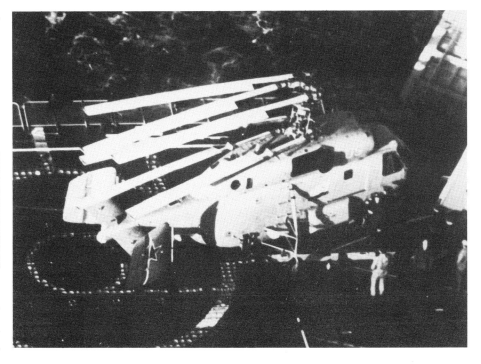

on *Udaloy* comprises eight vertical launch tubes, each of which is about 2m in diameter. Four are set into a low, flat deckhouse in the centre of the forecastle, forward of the gun mountings. The other four are disposed in pairs on the after part of the ship; one pair is set into a deckhouse located between the torpedo tubes and the other at the forward end of the twin helicopter hangars. Large circular platforms above the bridge and between the hangars will presumably carry the guidance radars for the missiles.

The absence of a long-range three-dimensional air surveillance and tracking radar makes it clear that the surface-to-air system to be installed will be of short range. It has been suggested that it may be a vertical-launch successor to the SA-N-4. The air surveillance radar carried atop the twin lattice masts of *Udaloy* is a short/medium range two-dimensional model, designated 'Strut Pair'. Developed from the Strut Curve radar, which was the standard Soviet air surveillance radar aboard Soviet small combatants in the 1960s, Strut Pair is a back-to-back version and is reported to use pulse-compression techniques. It was first installed experimentally on the Kildin-class conversion *Bedovy* in the mid-1970s. It would seem logical that command guidance will be employed for the missile and that the guidance radars, yet to be installed, will be relatively large, with separate tracking radars for the target and for the missile itself. A range of 10–12km (5–6nm) can be assumed. The system will employ a missile some 3.5mm in length.

The reloading arrangements must remain a matter for conjecture. There are only eight firing tubes, suggesting either that all the missiles carried by the ship are already in the tubes, or that the tubes are reloaded from beneath. The small size of the missile, taken together with the large diameter of the covers, makes it conceivable that all missile rounds are stowed in the tubes themselves, each tube containing some six missiles for a total of 48 rounds. Forward of the bridge, two

single 100mm dual-purpose mountings are superimposed in the manner of the Krivak II and *Kirov*. The Kite Screech fire control radar is mounted atop the tall pylon above the bridge structure, a position that affords excellent all-round arcs. The gun mountings are placed well clear of the superstructures for similar reasons. Close-in anti-missile defence is provided by the familiar 30mm Gatling. The mountings on *Udaloy* are paired on raised deckhouse/magazines abreast the after funnels, with their Bass Tilt radars above and between them.

The ECM outfit was far from complete when *Udaloy* ran her sea trials, and there remain empty platforms at the base of the mainmast. Small ECM antennae are visible at the after end of the forward superstructure, similar to the models fitted in *Sovremenny*, suggesting that at least this element of the ship's electronic equipment will be standardized. Gone are the massive Side Globe antennae associated with earlier large BPKs; their omission is yet another indication of the lower priority accorded to air defence in the design.

Replenishment
In keeping with the shift towards true ocean-going operations, *Udaloy* is provided with constant-tension transfer stations on either side, immediately aft of the torpedo tubes. Beneath the transfer stations a railway track for the movement of stores and munitions runs the length of the quarterdeck. The track doubles as a set of mine rails, and terminates in indentations at the corners of the stern. Stores and munitions destined for the forward part of the ship can be transferred from the quarterdeck by a centre-line crane located on a deckhouse immediately aft the forecastle break. A second railway track runs beneath the foundations for the Gatlings and inboard of the ship's boats, emerging close to the gunwales and encircling the forecastle.

The State of the Art
Udaloy in many ways represents the current state of Soviet progress in ship design. This progress has been achieved at considerable cost in resources, and as a result of extensive operational experience — some of it painful — in waters traditionally unfamiliar to the Soviet Navy. Comparisons with contemporary Western designs are that much more meaningful because *Udaloy* is built for the classic Western post-war destroyer mission — that of anti-submarine warfare.

In terms of the overall balance of her armament, *Udaloy* is much closer to Western anti-submarine designs than earlier Soviet BPKs. Unlike these earlier Soviet types, *Udaloy* is designed for optimum performance in her primary mission and not for marginal performance in two or three different missions. Her weapon load, expressed as a percentage of total displacement, is about 10 per cent, as compared with about 7.5 per cent for US Navy construction. Much of the difference is accounted for by the additional size and weight of Soviet shipborne weapons. The launch weight of the SS-N-14 anti-submarine missile, for example, is in the region of 2,500–3,000kg (5,500–6,500lb), whereas the US Navy's ASROC — which, admittedly, is inferior in range — weighs 450kg (1,000lb). The Soviet 'long' 533mm torpedo (1,600–1,700kg) is more than six times as heavy as the US Navy's Mk. 46 (230kg).

The propulsion machinery is heavier and noisier than that of contemporary Western vessels, and the high noise signature must necessarily result in less efficient sonar performance in sub-hunting operations. Soviet gas-turbines are

The Line of Development of the Soviet Large Anti-Submarine Ship (BPK)					
Type	Kresta II	Kara	Krivak	*Udaloy*	Spruance
In service	1970	1973	1971	1981	1975
Displacement	7,600 tons	10,000 tons	3,600 tons	7,900 tons	7,800 tons
ASW weapons					
Helicopters	1 Ka-25	1 Ka-25	— →	2 Ka-25	2 SH-2
Missiles	2×4 SS-N-14	2×4 SS-N-14	1×4 SS-N-14 →	2×4 SS-N-14	1×8 ASROC
Torpedoes	2×5 533mm	2×5 533mm	2×4 533mm	2×4 533mm	2×3 Mk. 32
Rocket launchers	2×12 RBU 6000	2×12 RBU 6000	2×12 RBU 6000	2×12 RBU 6000	—
	2×6 RBU 1000	2×6 RBU 1000			
Sonars	1 MF →	1 LF	1 MF	1 LF →	1 LF
		1 MF VDS	1 MF VDS	1 LF VDS	
AAW weapons					
Area defence missiles	2×2 SA-N-3	2×2 SA-N-3	—	—	—
Point defence missiles	— →	2×2 SA-N-4	2×2 SA-N-4	8 SA-N-?	1×8 NATO
					Sea Sparrow
Medium-calibre AA guns	2×2 57mm →	2×2 76.2mm	2×2 76.2mm	2×1 100mm	2×1 127mm
			2×1 100mm		
Close-in weapon systems (CIWS)	4×6 30mm	4×6 30mm	— →	4×6 30mm	2×6 20mm
ASuW weapons					
Anti-ship missiles	SS-N-14/SA-N-3	SS-N-14/SA-N-3	SS-N-14	SS-N-14	2×4 Harpoon

Note: The above table shows how the Kara class developed from the Kresta II design, and *Udaloy* from the Krivak. The arrows denote the areas of growth. The similarity between *Udaloy* and the US Navy's Spruance class, both in terms of size and general capabilities, is particularly striking.

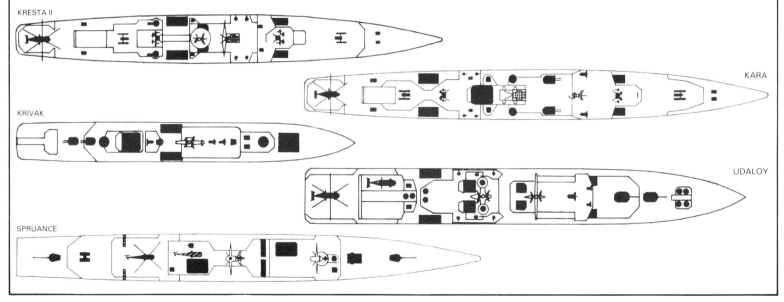

KRESTA II

KARA

KRIVAK

UDALOY

SPRUANCE

also thought to have a relatively poor specific fuel consumption (SFC) rate, which reduces overall endurance and is costly in terms of resources. Auxiliary machinery occupies considerably less space than it would in a Western vessel of equivalent size. This factor affects not only the level of services that make long deployments more acceptable to the ship's complement, but also the spare generating capacity available for weapons and sensors in the event of failure of one of the generators, and the power available to fight fires.

The advances made by the Soviets over the past twenty years are considerable nevertheless, and *Udaloy* is a thoroughly modern vessel capable of holding her own against the latest Western types. The adoption of Western 'volume-intensive' design practices amounts to recognition by the Soviets that size is a key factor in a ship's overall performance in open waters, and that the 'pocket battleship' syndrome is symptomatic of a coastal defence mentality that is no longer relevant to Soviet naval missions.

Opposite page: Udaloy *in late 1980, still without the guidance radars for her vertical launch SAM system but otherwise complete. Her build is strikingly different to that of* Sovremenny, *a reflection of the different missions for which the two ships were designed. (US Navy)*

Appendices

1: SOVIET SHIP CLASSIFICATION

Until the late 1950s the Soviet Navy persisted with the system of ship classification that it had employed throughout the previous three decades, a system which corresponded to the classical ship-types then in service or under construction. The word 'Kreyser' (Cruiser) was used to denote fleet units armed with 180mm (7.1in) and 152mm (6in) guns. Destroyers were classified as 'Eskadrenny Minonosets' (Fleet Destroyer, literally a minelayer), a term that reveals how closely the pre-war tactical thinking of the Soviet Navy was tied to operations in the Baltic and the Black Sea. Second-rate vessels designed for patrol duties inside Soviet waters continued to be designated 'Storozhevoy Korabl'' (Patrol or Guard Ship), a specifically Soviet category instituted in 1926.

The technological revolution that swept the Soviet Navy in the late 1950s demanded a new system of classification more appropriate to the new ship-types being developed. The term 'Kreyser' was retained for major warships, but, as the new cruisers would rely on missiles rather than guns to perform their anti-surface mission, it

was qualified by the word 'Raketny' (Rocket). The Eskadrenny Minonosets category was of course totally inappropriate, and it was necessary to find a new term to denote major surface warships below cruiser size. The word 'Korabl'' (Ship) was adopted. The converted destroyers of the Krupny class were therefore designated 'Raketny Korabl'', while the larger Kynda was the first Raketny Kreyser. When larger destroyer-type ships were constructed in the 1960s, an intermediate category, Bol'shoy Korabl' (Large Ship), came into being.

The first of the new large destroyers was the Kashin, which carried no anti-ship weapons, being designed instead to provide anti-air and anti-submarine protection for the new Rocket Cruisers. The completion of the early Kashins also coincided with a perceived need to upgrade anti-submarine capabilities in the Soviet Navy as a whole. The Kashin class was therefore classified 'Bol'shoy Protivolodochny Korabl' (Large Anti-Submarine Ship), a category that was to become the most important in the Soviet Navy for the next fifteen years. When major air-capable anti-submarine vessels, *Moskva* and *Leningrad* in

1967–68 and *Kiev* in 1976, were completed they were designated 'Protivolodochny Kreyser' (Anti-Submarine Cruiser). Finally, when the concept of carrier-borne aviation became more politically acceptable in the late 1970s, those Anti-Submarine Cruisers with an additional fixed-wing capability were reclassified 'Taktychesky Avionosny Kreyser' (Tactical Aircraft-Carrying Cruiser).

The following are the major warship categories currently employed by the Soviet Navy: Taktychesky Avionosny Kreyser (TAKR) — Tactical Aircraft-Carrying Cruiser; Anti-submarine warfare types, Protivolodochny Kreyser (PKR) — Anti-Submarine Cruiser, and Bol'shoy Protivolodochny Korabl' (BPK) — Large Anti-Submarine Ship; Anti-surface warfare types, Raketny Kreyser (RKR) — Rocket* Cruiser, and Bol'shoy Raketny Korabl' (BRK) — Large Rocket Ship.

*The translation 'Rocket' has been preferred to the word 'Missile' in order to avoid confusion between the Soviet ships, which have an anti-surface mission, and the Western missile cruiser (CG) and missile destroyer (DDG), which are designed for the anti-air mission.

2: NATO DESIGNATIONS FOR SOVIET EQUIPMENT

Soviet missile systems and radars are generally referred to by their NATO codenames. As a word of caution, it should be mentioned that the NATO authorities have consistently refused to confirm or deny these codenames. Nevertheless, they are the names employed by every reference work on the Soviet Navy, and they have been used throughout this book. What follows is an explanation of the derivations of these codenames.

Missile Systems

Since the Soviet Navy has never revealed the names or numbers by which it refers to its various missiles, a simple alpha-numerical system of classification originating with the US Navy is employed, giving: the function of the missile (surface-to-air, for example); the mode of deployment (naval); and a number indicating chronological sequence. The following examples will serve to illustrate how the system works: SA-N-3: the third shipborne Surface-to-Air missile system to enter service; SS-N-2: the second shipborne Surface-to-Surface missile system to enter service; and SUW-N-1: the first shipborne anti-submarine (Surface-to-UnderWater) missile system to enter service.

In addition, the missiles themselves are referred to by NATO codenames, although not all of these have been released. Surface-to-air missiles have a codename beginning with the letter 'G' (for example, Goa, Guideline, Goblet, Gecko) while anti-ship missiles have a codename beginning with 'S' (for example, Scrubber, Styx, Shaddock, Siren).

Radars

The NATO codenames allocated to Soviet radar and electronic countermeasures antennae frequently leave the average reader confused and perplexed. They are, nevertheless, based on the visual appearance of the antenna and should

therefore be far easier to comprehend and to retain than the complex alpha-numerical systems of classification employed in the West.

The NATO codenames for Soviet equipment are based on two words, each of which refers to some visual aspect of the antenna, such as its position on the ship, its construction, its size or its shape. Each word is of one syllable only, and the use of a two-word codename makes the system both simple and flexible. The word 'Net', for example, used to denote a scanner of open mesh construction, is used in combination with the words 'Head' (denoting that it is carried atop a mast), 'Big', and 'Plinth' (mounted on a prominent pedestal).

The list below does not pretend to be exhaustive, but will give some indication of the possibilities inherent in the system:

Position: Head, Top, Side, High.
Construction: Net, Strut (antenna supported by steel braces), Peel ('orange-peel' elliptical scanner), Curve (elliptical scanner), Tilt (antenna at an angle), Front (antenna on front face of housing), Plinth, Bass (on a prominent base?, or it could refer to frequency of signal), Muff (antenna supported by wrap-around trunnion yoke?).
Shape and Size: Big, Slim, Squat, (Head) Lights, Sail, Pole, Scoop, Drum, Cob, Dome, Globe, Bowl, Bell, Hat, Tee ('T'-shaped), Eye, Band Stand, Rum Tub, Palm Frond.
Multiple Antennae: Pair (two antennae back-to-back), Group (several antennae on the same housing).

Surveillance Radars

Air surveillance radars are generally located atop lattice or tower masts, and have the prefix 'Head' or 'Top'; for example, Head Net A/C, Top Sail, Top Steer and Top Pair. The exceptions are Big Net (which is generally mounted at a lower level), Strut Curve and Strut Pair (a back-to-back version of the latter). Navigation radars are generally derived from mercantile models, and have retained their 'river' names, such as Don-2 and

Don-Kay. A recent exception is Palm Frond, which may be a purely naval development.

Fire Control Radars

Guidance radars for surface-to-air missiles are generally located atop superstructures. Some have the prefix 'Top' or 'Head'; for example, Top Dome and Head Lights. Most fire control radars are, however, designated according to their configuration; for example, Peel Group (antenna comprises multiple 'orange-peel' scanners), Drum Tilt (drum-shaped antenna mounted at an angle of 20°) and Front Dome (dome-shaped antenna projecting from the face of a box housing).

Pop Group, which is associated with the SA-N-4 missile system, apparently takes its name from the 'pop-up' launcher with which it is associated.

The principal exception to this classification system is the 'Screech' series of gun fire control radars. The word 'Screech' is reported to derive from the distinctive signal emitted by the radar. The names of birds of prey are combined with it in order to differentiate between models: Hawk Screech, Owl Screech and Kite Screech.

ECM

The large ECM radomes fitted to the sides of the tower masts of many Soviet cruisers since the late 1960s are designated 'Side Globe'.

Most of the smaller radomes have the prefix 'Bell', which is certainly an allusion to their shape, and probably also to their function as noise-makers. The second half of the designation is generally a word denoting a particular noise; for example, Bell Bash, Bell Clout and Bell Slam. In more recent ECM antennae, however, the second word appears to refer to the configuration of the antenna, which is no longer a simple bell shape; for example, Bell Squat and Bell Shroud (the central 'bell' is half-concealed inside a cylindrical housing). Another series presumably denotes passive ESM receivers; for example, Guard Dog and Watch Dog.

Opposite page: Smely, *a modified Kashin.*

Select Bibliography

Baker III, A. D. 'Soviet Ship Types', *USNI Proceedings*, November/December 1980

Breyer, S. and Polmar, N. *Guide to the Soviet Navy*, Patrick Stephens, Cambridge, 1977; Naval Institute Press, Annapolis, 1970 and 1982

Couhat, J. L. (ed) *Combat Fleets of the World 1982/83*, Arms and Armour Press, London, 1982; Naval Institute Press, Annapolis, 1982

Fozard, J. W. *The Jet V/STOL Harrier*, British Aerospace, 1978

Friedman, N. *Carrier Air Power*, Conway Maritime Press, London, 1981; Rutledge Books, New York, 1981

—— *Modern Warships*, Conway Maritime Press, London, 1979; Mayflower Books, New York, 1979

—— *Naval Radar*, Conway Maritime Press, London, 1981; Naval Institute Press, Annapolis, 1981

—— *US Destroyers: An Illustrated Design History*, Arms and Armour Press, London, 1982; Naval Institute Press, Annapolis, 1982

Gorshkov, S. G. *Morskaya Moshch gosudarstva* (Sea Power of the State), Voyennoye Izdatel, 'stvo, Moscow, 1976

Kehoe, J. W. and Brower, K. S. 'US Observations on *Kiev*', *USNI Proceedings*, July 1977

—— 'One of Their New Destroyers: Sovremenny', *USNI Proceedings*, June 1981

—— 'Their New Cruiser', *USNI Proceedings*, December 1980

—— 'Another One of Their New Destroyers: Udaloy', *USNI Proceedings*, February 1981

—— 'US and Soviet Ship Design Practices', *USNI Proceedings*, May 1982

McCGwire, M. 'The Rationale for the Development of Soviet Seapower', *USNI Proceedings*, May 1980

Miles, B. *Jump Jet*, Brassey's, London, 1978

Moore, J. E. (ed) *Jane's Fighting Ships, 1981–82*, Jane's Publishing Co, London, 1981; Franklin Watts, New York, 1981

Polmar, N. and Brower, K. S. 'AEGIS: future shield for the Fleet', *Navy International*, July 1977

Pretty, R. T. (ed) *Jane's Weapon Systems, 1981–82*, Jane's Publishing Co, London, 1981; Franklin Watts, New York, 1981

Surface Warfare, 'Udaloy', US Naval Intelligence Support Center, February 1982

Taylor, J. W. R. *Jane's All the World's Aircraft, 1969–70*, Jane's Publishing Co, London, 1969; McGraw Hill, New York, 1969

Watson, B. *Red Navy at Sea: Soviet Naval Operations on the High Seas, 1956–80*, Arms and Armour Press/Royal United Services Institute for Defence Studies, London, 1982; Westview Press, Boulder, 1982

Zumwalt, E. 'High-Low', *USNI Proceedings*, April 1976

Index